economic
indicators

economic
indicators

fourth edition

Philip Mohr

UNISA PRESS
PRETORIA

© 1998 University of South Africa

First edition, first impression
Second edition 2000
Revised edition, second impression 2001
Revised edition, third impression 2002
Revised edition, fourth impression 2003
Revised edition, fifth impression 2004
Third edition 2005
Third edition, second impression 2007
Third edition, third impression 2008
Fourth edition 2011

ISBN 978-1-86888-658-6

Published by Unisa Press
University of South Africa
PO Box 392, 0003 Pretoria

Book designer: Marlé Oelofse
Editor: Lynne Southey
Project editor: Arnika Ejsmund
Typesetting: Marlé Oelofse
Printer: BusinessPrint

Telephone: 086 12 DALRO (from within South Africa); +27 (0)11 712-8000
Telefax: +27 (0)11 403-9094
Postal Address: P O Box 31627, Braamfontein, 2017, South Africa
www.dalro.co.za

Contents

Chapter 1

Introduction

Chapter 2

Total production, income and expenditure: the national accounts

Chapter 3

Chapter 4

Chapter 5

Chapter 6

Figures

Tables

Boxes

Abbreviations

Alsi	all-share index
Arima	autoregressive integrated moving average
BCI	Business Confidence Index
BER	Bureau for Economic Research
BMR	Bureau of Market Research
CPI	consumer price index
EAP	economically active population
EIU	Economist Intelligence Unit
EU	European Union
EY	earnings yield
FV	future value
fob	free on board
GDE	gross domestic expenditure
GDP	gross domestic product
GDPR	gross domestic product per region
Gear	Growth, Employment and Redistribution Strategy
GFS	Government Finance Statistics
GGP	gross geographic product
GNI	gross national income
HDI	human development index
HSRC	Human Sciences Research Council
Icor	incremental capital-output ratio
ICP	International Comparison Project
ILO	International Labour Organisation
IMD	International Institute for Management Development
IMF	International Monetary Fund
JIBAR	Johannesburg Interbank Agreed Rate
LFPR	labour force participation rate
LFS	Labour Force Survey
MFP	multifactor productivity
NIPA	national income and production accounts
OECD	Organisation for Economic Cooperation and Development
OHS	October Household Survey
Opec	Organisation of Petroleum Exporting Countries
P	price
P/E	price/earnings ratio
PPI	producer price index
PPP	purchasing power parity
PSBR	public sector borrowing requirement
PV	present value
Q	quantity
QES	Quarterly Employment Statistics
QLFS	Quarterly Labour Force Survey
RDP	Reconstruction and Development Programme
RSA	Republic of South Africa
Sacci	South African Chamber of Commerce and Industry
SADC	South African Development Community
SARB	South African Reserve Bank
SARS	South African Revenue Service
SDR	special drawing right
SNA	System of National Accounts
Stats SA	Statistics South Africa
TB	Treasury bill
UIF	Unemployment Insurance Fund
UN	United Nations

UNDP	United Nations Development Programme	**US**	United States
		USD	United States dollar
UNRISD	United Nations Research Institute for Social Development	**VAT**	value-added tax
		Y	yield

Barry Willis

Foreword

I have known Professor Mohr for many years. He is, without doubt, a "living" economist who has made an historic contribution to the study of economics in South Africa and elsewhere. He has taught many students in the discipline and also written a number of university textbooks, the most famous being on macroeconomics. His fastidiousness regarding the preciseness of economic definitions is legendary. Attention to detail is very important and if you cannot define a phenomenon in economics, I suggest that you consult his *Economics for South African students* or his *Understanding the economy (Everything you always wanted to know about the economy but thought you would not understand).*

Over the years, as a student and practitioner of economics, I have always depended on his easy to read, easy to understand books. At times, as Governor of the South African Reserve Bank, I also called upon him to assist me. An example in this regard was his evaluation of the functioning of the Monetary Policy Committee. His work led to a much improved work programme of this committee. This was much appreciated by the SARB in particular and the market and public in general. I have no hesitation at all in recommending this latest offering of his. For students and others interested in economic affairs this book is a must read and one to keep close at hand as a reference. Well done once again, Professor. Your contribution to the profession of economics will last for a long time.

By the way: what is inflation? Professor Mohr always reminds us that inflation is not the headline CPI number but the RATE of increase in the general price LEVEL. Remember this as you read his work.

TT Mboweni

Former Governor of the South African Reserve Bank (1999-2009)
February 2011

Preface

The interest in economic indicators and the importance of these indicators have grown exponentially in recent decades. A sound practical knowledge of economic indicators has therefore become essential for students in economics and related disciplines. This book provides a systematic explanation of the full range of economic indicators. It is ideally suited to modules or semester courses at universities, universities of technology, business schools and other tertiary institutions, particularly if used in conjunction with the latest edition of the *Quarterly Bulletin of the South African Reserve Bank* and/or extracts from other primary and secondary data sources.

Although aimed primarily at students of economics, most of the book should be accessible to interested lay people as well, and at the same time it will be a useful reference source for a variety of professionals, including economists, financial analysts, accountants, lawyers, industrial relations specialists, brokers, dealers, political scientists, and development specialists.

Economic indicators, like economics in general, is a dynamic subject. This edition includes all the changes and revisions introduced since the first three editions were published. It covers the most recent comprehensive revisions of the national accounts, the consumer price index, the producer price index, the various labour market surveys and government finance statistics. Each chapter contains more information than before, for example, on business cycles, money, credit and interest rates, budget deficits, foreign debt, units of measurement and various technical aspects, such as the previous-year comparison error, data revisions and the calculation of growth rates. A new section examines the impact of economic indicators on the financial markets and a number of political and politico-economic indicators have been added. A number of new boxes have also been included. All the data that are used to illustrate and explain the various indicators have been updated and, as always, a wealth of data on the South African economy are provided.

A special thank you is once again due to Elna van Rensburg, who again expertly did the word processing.

The interested reader is also referred to *Understanding the economy* (*Everything you always wanted to know about the economy but thought you would not understand*) (Pretoria: Van Schaik, 2010).

Chapter 1

Introduction

1.1   Economic indicators

Economic indicators have become part of everyday life. The latest economic indicators are covered in the press, on radio and television and are also accessible through the electronic media. This interest in economic indicators stems from a variety of reasons. Some people monitor them in an attempt to get the best return on their investments. Business people use indicators to judge if the time is right to expand their businesses or to exploit new markets. Economists and other analysts use indicators to assess the general performance of the economy, judge the effectiveness of economic policy, compare the economic performance of different countries and make economic forecasts. Speculators monitor movements in indicators to decide whether to buy or sell stocks, bonds, shares, commodities, foreign currency and other instruments or goods traded in speculative markets. Accountants, lawyers, human resource managers, trade unionists all use economic indicators for some purpose or another. The list is almost endless.

Many of the 'economic' indicators reported in the media are not economic indicators in the narrow sense of the word, but rather financial indicators, and in particular those which are of special interest to speculators and other financial investors. Nevertheless, a significant number of 'pure' economic indicators have become household terms, including the gross domestic product (GDP), the rate of economic growth, the consumer price index (CPI), the producer price index (PPI), the inflation rate, various interest rates, the money supply (or money stock), the balance of payments, exchange rates, the budget deficit and the national debt. This book explains the meaning and significance of these and other economic indicators. In each case the purpose of the indicator is emphasised, the basic concepts defined, the sources of the relevant data provided, and the manipulation and interpretation of the data explained. The emphasis is on the purpose and use of the indicators. In illustrating the application of the indicators a fair amount of information about the South African economy is provided.

To a certain extent the current interest in economic indicators is simply an extension of people's more general fascination with numbers. In all forms of sport, for example, every conceivable aspect is measured – the average driving distance of golfers, the number of greens hit in regulation and the average number of putts per round, the number of goals scored by each football player during his career, the penalty, lineout and scrum count in a rugby match, and cricketers' batting and bowling averages, to mention but a few. People like to compare and to compare numerically.

This brings us to an important point. Single numbers or bits of information are meaningless unless they are compared with something else. Economic indicators thus only indicate something if they are compared to something else. For example, a consumer price index number of 137,2 has no meaning unless the base year and the figures for the previous months or years are available. Once these other numbers are known, inflation rates can be calculated. But even an inflation rate has little meaning unless it is compared to previous inflation rates or inflation rates in other countries. This book provides guidelines or hints about linking different items of information to generate meaningful indications of the levels or trends of economic variables. In an age in which a mass of data can be accessed and manipulated electronically in myriad ways, and in a fraction of the time required a decade or two ago, it is essential to focus on the underlying significance of each manipulation. There must be method in the madness, otherwise the results of the manipulations will be meaningless and actions based on the results may prove to be ineffective, possibly even disastrous.

1.2   Assessing the performance of the economy

Different people use different criteria to judge the performance of the economy. The criteria that are selected usually depend on the primary interest of the person making the selection. For example, people involved in the financial markets probably look at interest rates first because even slight changes in interest rates could mean major financial gains or losses. Exporters and importers are mainly interested in exchange rates. Moreover, these two groups have conflicting interests in that importers generally prefer an appreciation of the rand against the currencies of our main trading partners, while exporters prefer a depreciation. Likewise, some people prefer stable interest and exchange rates which enable sound economic and business planning, while others prefer a certain amount of instability (or volatility) because it creates scope for speculation and therefore for speculative profits (and losses). Wage earners focus on wages, salaries and prices, which affect their standard of living. Different individuals and groups tend to gauge the performance of the economy in terms of their own interests.

Economists, however, are supposed to take a broader view of the performance of the economy in terms of particular goals or objectives. At the macroeconomic level the following objectives usually serve as criteria for judging the state of the economy:

- economic growth
- full employment
- price stability

- balance of payments stability
- equitable distribution of income

Much of this book is concerned with the explanation of the most important indicators that can be used to gauge the performance of the economy in terms of these objectives. By way of introduction a number of questions may be posed with regard to each objective. These questions serve as a guide to the main topics covered in this book.

Economic growth. How does one measure the performance of the economy in relation to the growth target? What measure of aggregate economic activity should be used? Is gross domestic product the appropriate yardstick or are there more suitable measures? How should inflation be handled? And population changes? What about business cycles – over which period should growth be measured? What techniques or formulas should be used to calculate growth? Are international comparisons of growth rates valid? What problems could arise in this regard?

Full employment. How is the employment performance of the economy measured? What is the difference between formal and informal employment? What constitutes unemployment? How is the unemployment rate measured? How reliable are the data? What other problems are encountered in this regard and how can they be dealt with? How reliable are international comparisons of unemployment?

Price stability. What is inflation? How is it measured? What is an index? How are index numbers calculated? What is a price index? What is the appropriate price index for measuring inflation? What are the differences between the different price indices? Over what period should the inflation rate be measured? How should it be measured? How reliable are international comparisons of inflation?

Balance of payments stability. What is the balance of payments? What is the significance of the various accounts and subaccounts of the balance of payments? How does one assess the balance of payments situation? How can balance of payments data be reconciled with other data?

An equitable distribution of income. What criteria can be used to assess the distribution of income? What techniques are available for this purpose? How can distributions be compared between countries? How reliable are these comparisons?

1.3 Sources of economic data

This section lists some of the main sources of South African economic data as well as of data required to make international comparisons. The two most important agencies which collect, publish and disseminate economic data in South Africa are Statistics South Africa (Stats SA) and the South African Reserve Bank (SARB) (see Box 1-1).

BOX 1-1: STATISTICS SOUTH AFRICA

Statistics South Africa is the central government body in South Africa that is authorised in terms of the Statistics Act to compile and publish national statistics. Originally established as the Office of the Census, this data agency became the Office of Census and Statistics in 1917, the Bureau of Census and Statistics in 1951, the Bureau of Statistics in 1963, the Department of Statistics in 1969, the Central Statistical Services in 1982, and the Central Statistical Service (without the 's') on 1 March 1986. In September 1998 the name of the agency changed yet again, this time to Statistics South Africa, abbreviated as Stats SA. Although some of the data quoted in this book were published under one or more of the earlier names, it was decided to adopt the latest name consistently. All references are thus to Statistics South Africa or Stats SA only. Stats SA data can be accessed at *www.statssa.gov.za*.

SARB Quarterly Bulletin

The *Quarterly Bulletin* of the South African Reserve Bank, abbreviated in this book as the *SARB Quarterly Bulletin*, is probably the best known and most frequently quoted of all the data sources. It is published at the end of March, June, September and December and contains economic data only. The first section of the publication, the quarterly economic review, is an extensive summary and interpretation of recent economic developments, including short-term economic policy. The greater part consists of more than 150 statistical tables, classified in eight sections which cover most aspects of the South African economy. The frequency of the time series ranges from days to years and the annual series usually contain six to eight observations. The publication is also available, along with all other publications of the South African Reserve Bank, at *www.reservebank.co.za*. All the series in the *SARB Quarterly Bulletin* are also available electronically for longer periods than those published in the *Bulletin*.

SARB Annual Report

Towards the end of August or beginning of September each year the SARB publishes an *Annual Report* for the year to 31 March, to coincide with the annual general meeting of the SARB. It incorporates the *Annual economic report*, which contains a review of economic and financial conditions during the twelve months up to 30 June. The data are usually presented as ratios or rates of change and no separate section of statistical tables is provided.

Release of Selected Monthly Data

Between publications of the *Quarterly Bulletin* the SARB updates selected monthly money and banking and other statistics by issuing a brief *Release of Selected Monthly Data*. These data are also available on the Bank's website.

South African Statistics

Statistics South Africa annually publishes *South African Statistics*, the most comprehensive collection of annual South African data. It contains detailed information on 15 different categories of data, most of which pertain to economic data. Apart from the comprehensive coverage, the individual time series are also longer than in any other regular official publication. Some of the series date back as far as 1904. However, as an annual publication of annual data, it does not contain the most recent data and therefore usually has to be updated from other sources. All series published by Stats SA, including the full *South African Statistics*, are available in electronic format at *www.statssa.gov.za*.

Bulletin of Statistics

The *Bulletin of Statistics* is the regular quarterly publication of Stats SA which can be used to update *South African Statistics*. It also covers 15 different categories of monthly, quarterly and annual data, but the individual time series are fairly short – in most cases only two or three years. It is also available electronically.

P Series of Statistical Releases

Where data regularly become available between the publication of consecutive editions of the *Bulletin of Statistics* and *South African Statistics*, Stats SA publishes these in a series of statistical releases (the *P* series). Probably the best known of these is the monthly *P0l4l Statistical release* which contains data on the consumer price index for the previous month. These data are also available on Stats SA's website.

Stats in brief

Stats SA annually publishes *Stats in brief*, a pocket guide containing data on 18 different topics, ranging from geography to government finance. This is a very handy publication which is issued free of charge.

Quarterly Labour Force Survey

From 2000 Stats SA published a *Labour Force Survey* twice a year, for March and September. However, in 2008 this was replaced by a more timely *Quarterly Labour Force Survey*, which is published approximately a month after the end of each quarter. The publication contains the results of a rotating panel household survey specifically designed to measure the dynamics of employment and unemployment in the country. It measures a variety of aspects of the labour market, including formal and informal employment, as well as unemployment.

Budget Review

The *Budget Review* is published annually by the National Treasury to coincide with the annual budget speech of the Minister of Finance. This important source of information on fiscal policy and public finance is also available at *www.treasury.gov.za*.

Secondary data sources

Apart from the primary sources of economic data, many other agencies or institutions publish official statistics in their original form or in an altered form designed to facilitate interpretation and analysis. In fact, nowadays there are certain firms who specialise in providing economic data and making them more accessible to the end-users, usually in an electronic format.

Most financial institutions publish regular monthly or quarterly reviews of the economy, while financial weeklies (eg *Financial Mail* and *Finweek*), and even the daily and weekly press, also regularly publish a selection of the latest economic indicators.

International economic data

Economists often have to obtain economic data for other countries or draw international comparisons of key economic indicators. Fortunately, it is usually not necessary to consult the original official statistics in each country for this purpose. International agencies such as the International Monetary Fund (IMF), the World Bank and the United Nations (UN) regularly collect and publish data for all countries, in printed and electronic format, while certain firms also provide a specialised service in this area.

One of the most useful sources of information in this regard is *International Financial Statistics*, a regular monthly publication of the IMF which covers all aspects of domestic and international finance. It contains data for all IMF member countries (including South Africa) on exchange rates, international liquidity, money and banking, trade and prices, as well as some national accounting data. A yearbook containing long series of annual data is also published regularly. Other useful regular publications of the IMF are *Government Finance Statistics*, *Balance of Payments Statistics* and *Direction of Trade Statistics*. The first two are published monthly and the third quarterly, along with a yearbook, and the data are also available in electronic format at *www.imf.org*, although unfortunately not free of charge.

Other useful sources of international comparisons include the *World Development Indicators*, published annually by the World Bank, and the *Human Development Report*, published annually by the United Nations Development Programme. Both these publications contain a variety of tables comparing different countries according to various criteria. The World Bank's website is at *www.worldbank.org* and that of the United Nations at *www.un.org*, or *data.un.org*.

The internationally prestigious London weekly, *The Economist*, is a handy source of information about the latest trends in the main economic indicators in a number of countries. The most recent data for a variety of countries (including South Africa) are provided on the last few pages of each issue.

Further sources of data are mentioned elsewhere in the book.

1.4   Interpreting economic data

From the previous section it should be obvious that a frequently bewildering array of economic data is available nowadays. At the same time, modern technology has enabled analysts to manipulate masses of economic data in a fraction of the time it took previously and in ways which were not even contemplated a few decades ago. But the data still have to be interpreted. This requires an understanding of the data, knowledge of which data to use in any specific case, and an awareness of the limitations of the data.

Someone once claimed that if you just torture the data long enough, they will confess. Books have also been written about how to lie with statistics. These remarks are not merely intended in jest. They also serve as a warning. Economic data can be manipulated to demonstrate almost anything and can therefore easily be abused by academics, economists, business people, politicians, students and anyone else with a vested interest in the results (see Box 1-2).

BOX 1-2: DATA MINING

In recent years there has been an explosion of data. It is estimated, for example, that the amount of digital information increases tenfold every five years. The means to utilise, mine or manipulate this information are also increasing apace. The problem, however, is that such data mining is open to abuse. Analysts may look for good statistical relationships, or relationships that are favourable to their employers or clients, without providing any justification for the relationships. Consider the following example (reported in *Business Day*, 1 September 2009:12): David Leinweber searched for a variable that would 'explain' the variation in the annual returns of the Standard & Poor's 500-stock index and found that annual butter production in Bangladesh 'explained' 75% of the variation over a 13-year period. By adding US cheese production and the total population of sheep in both Bangladesh and the US, he was able to 'explain' past US equity returns with 99% accuracy. Likewise, two British researchers, Llewellyn and Witcomb, once found a strong correlation between the incidence of dysentery (a stomach infection) in Scotland and the inflation rate in the United Kingdom a year later. Other similar examples may be cited.

While data mining may yield useful results in a number of fields (eg health), such practices should be treated with the utmost care. Analysts should avoid being accused of using statistics like a drunkard uses a lamp post – for support rather than for illumination. Incidentally, Leinweber apparently still gets inquiries from portfolio managers looking for the latest data on Bangladeshi butter production!

Economic data always have to be handled with care. The following are some of the basic requirements and hints to be kept in mind when economic data are used or interpreted:

- Always be acquainted with the **definitions** of the indicators. Some concepts (eg employment, unemployment) may seem to be quite straightforward but once they have to be measured many problems arise. The definitions of the indicators should therefore always be checked carefully (also see Box 1-3).

- Determine to which **period** the data relate. For example, an average monthly salary of R100 000 is high but a salary of R100 000 per annum is relatively low, and in government statistics there is a difference between the calendar year and the fiscal year.

- With weekly, monthly or quarterly data, always check whether the data are **seasonally adjusted**.

- Always check whether the variable in question is a **stock** or a **flow**. The difference between stocks and flows is explained in Section 1.5.

- Ascertain the **geographic coverage** of the data. This is particularly important in South Africa where a number of changes occurred as a result of constitutional developments. Until 1997 South African trade data also still included Botswana, Lesotho, Namibia and Swaziland.

- Check if the data have been **adjusted for inflation**. For example, an increase of 5% in salaries and wages (in money terms) will be rather disappointing if prices rose by 15% over the same period.

- Check **who** produced the figures. Was it a government agency or a private researcher or market research company? Also check how the data were obtained, for example, through sample surveys or other methods.

- Bear in mind that, even with official statistics, a significant proportion of the available data are not collected or estimated directly by data agencies but arise as a **by-product of some administrative process**. In these cases the definitions are usually determined by the administrative practices and procedures, rather than by statistical or economic considerations.

- Check whether the data will be **revised**, or if data for previous periods have not been revised (particularly when using two different editions of a data source). Certain data (eg in respect of the consumer price index and the producer price index) are not revised, while others (eg gross domestic product (GDP) and the value of retail sales) are often still adjusted quite some time after they were published initially.

- When examining a series of observations over time it is often useful to first **plot the data on a graph** to ascertain the trend of the variable in question and to determine whether there seem to have been structural shifts in this trend. In this way one can avoid drawing incorrect conclusions by selecting inappropriate periods for analysing the data. This is particularly important if the ultimate purpose is to project the trend.

- Ascertain the **start and end points** for calculating changes. For example, the average annual rate of change in GDP between a recession and a boom will be much more impressive than the change between a boom and a recession.

- Avoid the frequent mistake of confusing **levels** with **rates of change** (or percentages). For example, a poor country might have a high growth rate but it will still be worse off than a rich country with a low growth rate.

- Determine what **other yardsticks** will aid interpretation. For example, certain data become really significant only when expressed as a ratio of population or GDP.

- Always bear in mind that **correlation** does not imply **causation**. If two different indicators exhibit similar trends, it does not follow that one is the cause of the other. One might simply be part of the other or they might both be influenced by a set of other factors.

- Always be extremely careful when **international comparisons** are attempted or interpreted. Definitions may differ between countries, while valuation in different domestic currencies also creates a number of problems.

- Remember that some of the most serious errors in using economic data result from the failure to make elementary checks (eg on the comparability of the statistics).

Most of these hints and warnings will be dealt with or illustrated further elsewhere in this book.

The government are very keen on amassing statistics.
They collect them, add them, raise them to the nth power, take the cube root and prepare wonderful diagrams. But you must never forget that every one of these figures comes in the first instance from the village watchman, who just puts down what he damn well pleases.

Anonymous

BOX 1-3: UNITS OF MEASUREMENT

All time series are expressed in terms of a unit of measurement (eg money, mass, volume, rate, index number). The first thing to do when analysing economic data is to establish which units of measurement are being used, thus avoiding being tempted to compare metric tons of chalk and long tons of cheese.

In essence, measurement of a physical quantity entails comparing it with an agreed and clearly defined standard. The result is expressed in terms of a unit and is thus a ratio of the unit concerned. South Africa adopted the metric system in 1972 and all official statistics are expressed in terms of units of the International Metric System (Système International d'Unités or SI).

LIST OF PREFERRED SI PREFIXES FOR MULTIPLES AND SUB-MULTIPLES				
Factor		Factor in words	SI prefix	SI symbol
1 000 000 000 000	10^{12}	billion	tera-	T
1 000 000 000	10^{9}	milliard	giga-	G
1 000 000	10^{6}	million	mega-	M
1 000	10^{3}	thousand	kilo-	k
0,001	10^{-3}	thousandth	milli-	m
0,000 001	10^{-6}	millionth	micro	μ
0,000 000 001	10^{-9}	milliardth	nano-	n
0,000 000 000 001	10^{-12}	billionth	pico-	p

Symbols

- Symbols are written in lower case except for monetary units (eg R for rand), when the symbol is derived from a person's name (eg W for watt) and when multiples of a million or more are used (eg MW for megawatt).
- Symbols have no plural (eg 1 m and 2 m or R1 and R10).
- Symbols are not abbreviations and are therefore not followed by a fullstop unless they occur at the end of a sentence.
- The product of two or more symbols is indicated by a point or space (eg t.km or t km for ton kilometre).
- A negative power or forward slash is used to indicate division of symbols (eg R kg^{-1} and R/kg for rand per kilogram).
- The measurement of area is indicated by the symbol being raised by the power of two (eg km^{2} for square kilometre) except where the unit itself is already a unit of area (eg hectare).
- Volume is indicated by the symbol being raised by the power of three (eg m^{3} for cubic metre) except where the unit is already one of capacity (eg litre).

Units written in full

- When written out in full, the name of a unit is in lower case only, even if it is derived from the name of a person.
- The plural form is used in English but not in Afrikaans (eg two metres but *twee meter*). The plural of rand, however, is rand and not rands.
- Multiplication of units is indicated by a space (eg ton kilometre) but in Afrikaans a hyphen is used (eg *ton-kilometer*).
- Division is indicated by the word per in both English and Afrikaans (eg kilometres per hour and *kilometer per uur*).

Numbers

- The comma is used as the decimal indicator (eg R2,25).
- A zero must precede the comma if the number is less than one (eg R0,75).
- Thousands or thousandths must be separated by spaces (eg R1 000 000).

Millions, billions and trillions

There is some confusion regarding the nomenclature of high numbers because of differing usage in various countries. For example, a US trillion is equal to a classic British billion. However, even the British Treasury has been officially using the '1 000 million' billion since December 1974. In financial statistics a billion is normally 10^9. Milliard is a French term which is permissible in English but is almost as rarely used as milliardth.

Mass

- It is important not to confuse metric ton (sometimes spelt tonne, 1 t = 1 000 kg), Imperial or British ton (1 long ton = 2 240 lb = 1 016,047 kg) and US ton (1 short ton = 2 000 lb = 907,185 kg). Also note that a ton in shipping is a measure of volume and not mass.
- The use of the term carat can lead to confusion because, when applied to precious stones, it is a unit of mass (1 carat = 200 mg), but when applied to gold, it is a measure of purity (equal to a 1/24th part of pure gold in an alloy) and should more properly be spelt karat.
- Gold is measured in troy ounces (1 oz t = 480 grains = 31,10348 g) which should not be confused with the avoirdupois ounce (1 oz = 28,350 g). Also note that there are 12 troy ounces in a troy pound but 16 ounces in a pound.

Volume

The US barrel is the unit of measurement in the oil trade (1 barrel = 42 US gal = 158,987 litre). Note that American and British gallons are different (1 UK gal = 1,2 US gal = 4,546 litre or 1 US gal = 0,833 UK gal = 3,785 litre).

1.5   Some basic concepts and techniques

Volume, price and value

Many economic indicators are expressed in monetary or value terms (ie in rand and cents). Value is obtained by multiplying volume (or quantity) by price. Thus

value (PQ) = price (P) × volume or quantity (Q)

or

volume (Q) = value (PQ) ÷ price (P)

Real and nominal values

Many economic indicators are originally available only in monetary (value) terms, but analysts are often primarily interested in volumes rather than values. Changes in values therefore have to be adjusted to eliminate the effect of price changes (ie inflation). The indicators are then expressed at constant prices or in real terms. The unadjusted original values are expressed at current prices or in nominal terms. The current price (or nominal) data are then deflated by a price index to obtain constant price or real data, which reflect volume changes only. The difference between nominal and real data and the techniques for deflating nominal data are explained and illustrated in Chapters 2, 6 and 8.

In symbols:

nominal value = PQ
real value = $Q = PQ/P$

Percentages

The percentage difference or change between two numbers is calculated by expressing the absolute difference between the two numbers as a ratio of the original number and multiplying the result by 100. Alternatively, the new number can first be expressed as a ratio of the original number. The percentage change can then be calculated by subtracting 1 from this ratio and multiplying the result by 100.

Consider the following example. If the price of a certain good increases from R20 to R25, the percentage increase is

$$\frac{25-20}{20} \times 100 = \frac{5}{20} \times 100 = 25\%$$

or

$$(\frac{25}{20} - 1) \times 100 = (1{,}25 - 1) \times 100$$
$$= 0{,}25 \times 100$$
$$= 25\%$$

Note, however, that a decline from 25 to 20 does not yield the same percentage as an increase from 20 to 25. The direction of the change is thus important. If the price falls from R25 to R20, the percentage change is

$$\frac{20-25}{25} \times 100 = \frac{-5}{25} \times 100 = -20\%$$

or

$$(\frac{20}{25} - 1) \times 100 = (0,8-1) \times 100$$
$$= -0,2 \times 100$$
$$= -20\%$$

This difference is important, for example, when changes in the exchange rate between two currencies (eg the rand and the US dollar) are calculated. The percentage change in the value of the rand expressed in dollar terms will differ from the percentage change in the value of the dollar expressed in rand terms.

Percentages, percentage points and basis points

When the value of an economic indicator increases from 10% to 11% it is often reported as a 1% increase. This is incorrect. The correct way of describing such an increase is to refer to an increase of one percentage point. An increase from 10 to 11 is actually a 10% increase:

$$(\frac{11}{10} - 1) \times 100 = (1,1-1) \times 100 = 0,1 \times 100 = 10\%$$

Likewise, an increase in (say) the inflation rate from 5% to 7% is an increase of two percentage points, not 2%. The percentage increase in this case is 40%:

$$(\frac{7}{5} - 1) \times 100 = (1,4-1) \times 100 = 0,4 \times 100 = 40\%.$$

In the financial markets each percentage point consists of 100 basis points. An increase in interest rates of one percentage point is thus referred to as an increase of 100 basis points, an increase of half a percentage point as an increase of 50 basis points, and so on. Likewise, if the interest rate on one type of financial asset is 8% per annum and that on another asset is 6,25%, the difference between the interest rates is 175 basis points.

Levels and rates of change

Probably the single most important source of error in using or interpreting economic indicators is the tendency to confuse levels with rates of change. A high level should not be confused with a high rate of change, nor should low levels be confused with low rates of change. This tendency, which was also mentioned in the previous section, is dealt with and illustrated at various points in this book. China, for example, has experienced high rates of economic growth, but average living standards (levels) are still relatively low. Sloppy reporting often adds to the confusion in this regard. As explained in Chapter 6, the consumer price index (CPI) indicates the level of the cost of a representative basket of consumer goods and services, but when the latest figures are released, the CPI is often reported as a rate (a percentage change), rather than as a level. In other words, the level of the cost of living is confused with the inflation rate (ie the rate at which it is changing) (see Chapter 6).

Stocks, flows and ratios

Another frequent source of confusion in respect of economic indicators is the failure to distinguish between stocks and flows. A stock has no time dimension and is measured at a particular point in time while a flow is measured over a period (irrespective of how short that period might be). The difference between stocks and flows is usually explained by using the example of a dam. The volume or level of the water in the dam is measured at a particular point in time and is therefore a stock. The reason is that the level is constantly changing over time due to the inflow and outflow, evaporation, rain and so on. The inflow or outflow, on the other hand, is measured over a period; for example, so many cubic metres per second, minute, hour, day or week, and is therefore a **flow**. Stocks (or stock variables) in economics include the capital stock, the money stock, the balance on a savings account and the wealth of an individual. Flows, on the other hand, include production, spending, income, investment, consumption and saving.

Some indicators are neither stocks nor flows, but **ratios.** Ratios can be calculated between two stocks, two flows, or a stock and a flow (or vice versa). Ratios between two stocks or between two flows have no time dimension, but a ratio between a stock and a flow or between a flow and a stock has a time dimension. For example, production per worker is a ratio between a flow (production) and a stock (the number of workers) and has a time dimension since the period during which the production occurred has to be specified.

When ratios are calculated, the data should always be comparable. Both the numerator and the denominator should, for example, apply to the same time period or moment, either be adjusted for (say) inflation or seasonal influences or not adjusted, be measured in the same way, and apply to the same geographic area. Ratios are frequently used in economic analysis but they should always be interpreted and handled with care.

Averages

It is often useful to describe a given set of data by using a single number which expresses the central or representative value of the data set. Such a measure is called a measure of central tendency. The most commonly used measure of central tendency is the **average** or **mean**. The **simple average** or **arithmetic mean** of a data set is simply the sum of the values of the different observations divided by the number of observations. Other averages often used in economics are weighted averages and moving averages (both weighted and unweighted).

Weighted averages are calculated when the different observations are not equally important, with the result that their values should not simply be added and their sum divided by the number of observations. Suppose, for example, a consumer purchases two goods only, namely food, which costs R10 per unit, and clothing, which costs R100 per unit. Suppose further that 90% of the consumer's income is spent on food and 10% on clothing. To determine the average price paid by the consumer per unit of goods purchased it would be wrong to simply add the unit price of food to the unit price of clothing and divide the answer by two. The correct procedure is to weight each price by the portion of the consumer's income spent on the goods in question. The weighted average price is thus obtained as R $[(10 \times 0{,}90) + (100 \times 0{,}1)] = $ R $(9 + 10) = $ R19. If the two prices had simply been added and divided by two, an incorrect answer of R55 would have been obtained. Weighting is important, for example, when price indices and other indices are compiled (see Chapter 6).

Moving averages are used to smooth erratic movements in time series to obtain a general trend. The moving average for a specific period is the average of previous, current and future values, with the current value as the centre of the number of values used to calculate the average. For example, suppose the values for 2006, 2007, 2008, 2009 and 2010 are 20, 15, 25, 20 and 45 respectively. The three-year moving average for 2007 will thus be the average of the values for 2006, 2007 and 2008, that is $(20 + 15 + 25) \div 3 = 60 \div 3 = 20$. Likewise, the three-year moving averages for 2008 and 2009 will be 20 and 30 respectively. The five-year moving average with 2008 as the current (or central) value will be 25, that is $(20 + 15 + 25 + 20 + 45) \div 5 = 125 \div 5 = 25$. Moving averages can also be **weighted** by assigning weights to the different observations. As mentioned earlier, moving averages smooth out random fluctuations and make long-term trends clearer. However, one disadvantage is that they tend to lag behind movements in the economy. Moving averages are slow to respond when there is a genuine change in the economy's direction.

The **median** is another measure of central tendency. The median is the value of the middle item (or the average of the two middle items) **when the items are arranged in an increasing or decreasing order of magnitude**. If the number of observations in a population or sample is odd, there will always be a middle value which will be the median. For example, if the observations are 1, 2, 4, 8, 12, 32 and 112, then 8 is the median. If the number of observations is even, there will never be a middle item. In this case the median is given by the average of the two middle items. For example, if the observations are 1, 2, 4, 8, 12 and 32, then the median is the average of 4 and 8, that is, 6.

1.6   Plan of the book

The material in the rest of the book is organised around eleven broad topics. Chapter 2 deals with the basic national accounting concepts, which are essential tools of the practising economist's trade. This is followed, in Chapter 3, by an examination of the measurement of economic growth. Growth does not occur smoothly, however, but is characterised by recurrent fluctuations. Booms are followed by recessions and vice versa. Chapter 4 deals with this phenomenon, commonly known as the business cycle. Chapter 5 is concerned with the measurement of employment and unemployment, employment creation or the minimisation of unemployment being one of the most important macroeconomic objectives. This is followed, in Chapter 6, by an examination of the measurement of inflation. This is a long chapter, since index numbers and the construction of price indices have to be explained before the actual measurement of inflation can be dealt with. Chapter 7 deals with foreign transactions and is also a long chapter since it incorporates important indicators such as the balance of payments and exchange rates. In the highly integrated international economy, indicators relating to transactions with the rest of the world are very important, particularly in a relatively small, open economy like the South African economy. Chapter 8 deals with a variety of topics, including wages, productivity, unit labour cost and income distribution. This is followed, in Chapter 9, by an examination of some financial indicators, including the impact of economic indicators on financial markets. Chapter 10 deals with a variety of fiscal indicators. As government's share in economic activity increased in the wake of the recent global financial and economic crisis, a variety of fiscal problems reappeared or intensified, with the result that fiscal indicators are often in the news today. Chapter 11 contains a brief discussion of some social indicators which are frequently used to supplement economic indicators (in the narrow sense), particularly by development economists. Some broad political indicators are also touched on. The final chapter, Chapter 12, deals with some of the problems experienced in international comparisons of economic indicators. International comparisons are referred to in earlier chapters, but they are important enough to warrant a separate chapter as well.

The most difficult period to forecast is the immediate past.

Bernie de Jager

Not everything that can be counted counts,
and not everything that counts can be counted.

Albert Einstein

Chapter 2

Total production, income and expenditure: the national accounts

The gross domestic product (GDP) is often in the news. The release of the latest data is covered prominently in the media and everyone knows that GDP data are important. Unfortunately, however, few people know what the concept means and how it is estimated. In this chapter GDP is explained in some detail, along with other important national accounting concepts.

2.1 The national accounts

The national accounts constitute the most important source of information about the condition and performance of the economy, in the same way as the operating and financial accounts of an individual firm convey information about the condition and performance of that firm.

The task of preparing a detailed set of accounts is anything but simple or straightforward, at both the corporate and national level. That is why it is entrusted to trained people. In South Africa the national accounts are compiled jointly by Statistics South Africa (Stats SA) and the South African Reserve Bank (SARB). The compilers of the national accounts at Stats SA and the SARB may therefore be regarded as 'super' or 'macro' accountants who have to draw up the accounts for the economy as a whole.

The parallel with an individual firm can be taken further. Like the accountant who prepares the operating and financial statements of a company, the compilers of the national accounts have to contend with all kinds of conceptual and data problems when they draw up these accounts. The only real difference is that the problems associated with the national accounts are much greater than those presented by the accounting systems of individual firms. To cope with these problems a variety of conventions are used to classify, measure or exclude various items. These conventions have to be taken into consideration when the national accounts are interpreted.

The national accounts are prepared in accordance with the System of National Accounts (SNA), a framework devised by the United Nations, in conjunction with the Organisation for Economic Cooperation and Development (OECD), Eurostat (the Statistical Office of the European Commission), the International Monetary Fund (IMF) and the World Bank. The SNA consists of a coherent and integrated set of accounts, balance sheets and tables based on a set of internationally agreed concepts, definitions, classifications and accounting rules. The most recent edition of the SNA was published in two volumes in 2008 and 2009 and South Africa's national accounts are revised from time to time to conform with the SNA. Comprehensive revisions were undertaken in 1999, 2004 and 2009.[1]

The full set of national accounts includes a variety of types of account, including input-output tables, flow-of-funds accounts, national balance sheets and the foreign account. In this book, however, we follow the conventional practice of using the term national accounts to refer to the national income and production accounts (NIPA) only.

Although private estimates of national product, income and spending in certain countries date back to at least the seventeenth century, official national accounts are a fairly recent phenomenon. The first official national accounts were published in the United States in 1942. South Africa was not far behind. In 1946/47 the then Bureau of Statistics (now Statistics South Africa) was instructed to estimate the domestic product and the national product, and since 1951 South African national accounting data have been published regularly in the *SARB Quarterly Bulletin*.

All national accounting equalities are identities (or definitions) and should not be confused with theories or behavioural equations (see Box 2-1). Many national accounting concepts have counterparts in economic theory – in fact our present national accounting system and the concepts used were originally derived from Keynesian macroeconomic theory – but there is a radical difference between national accounts and macroeconomic theory. The accounts are compiled to estimate the historic performance of the economy, while the purpose of macroeconomic theory is to understand, explain and predict that performance.

---

1.   For full details of the most recent revisions, see *South Africa's national accounts 1946-2004: an overview of sources and methods*. Supplement to the *SARB Quarterly Bulletin*, June 2005 and *South Africa's national accounts 1946-2009: an overview of sources and methods*. Supplement to the *SARB Quarterly Bulletin*, March 2010. See also Section 2.7.

BOX 2-1: IDENTITIES AND EQUATIONS

There are two types of equality: an identical equality (or identity) and a conditional equality (or equation). The difference between an identity and an equation is that any value(s) of the unknown variable(s) will satisfy an identity, while an equation is satisfied by a unique value or set of values. Consider the following example: $a^2 = a \times a$ is an identity, while $a^2 = 4$ is an equation. Any value of a will satisfy the first equality, but the second equality will only hold for $a = 2$ or -2.

An identity is a statement that is derived directly from definitions or arithmetical ratios and is therefore always true. Where they are incorporated in economic models or theories, identities (or definitions) do not reflect aspects of economic behaviour, but they are frequently an indispensable means of ordering or organising our thinking. To distinguish them from equations, identities are often indicated by the $\equiv$ sign, instead of the = sign used for equations.

The distinction between identities and equations may appear to be hair splitting, but confusion between the two often results in faulty reasoning and incorrect conclusions. All the accounting relationships in the national accounts are identities and one should therefore always guard against the tendency to read more into these relationships than is justified.

2.2   Total production, income and expenditure

The most important identity in the national accounts is the equality of total production, income and expenditure in the economy during a particular period. Production gives rise to income, which is spent on production. For the economy at large the value of the total product always equals the value of total income. The factors of production (land, labour, capital, entrepreneurship) generate production and income (rent, wages, interest and profit) which implies that the value of income will always be equal to the value of production. Total (or aggregate) production and total (or aggregate) income in the economy can therefore be regarded as two sides of the same coin (ie synonyms).

Income is spent to purchase the product. Will total expenditure on production always equal the total value of the product and the total value of income in the economy? In the national accounts the answer is always yes, because any difference between total production and total expenditure results in a change in inventories which is added back to expenditure as part of total investment spending. This accounting convention or trick ensures that the following identity always holds in the national accounts:

product $\equiv$ income $\equiv$ expenditure on product

Suppose the value of total production in South Africa for a particular year is R2 500 billion. This means that the value of total income for that year is also R2 500 billion. Suppose, too, that goods and services to the value of only R2 400 billion were sold during the same period. This implies an increase in inventories of R100 billion (ie the difference between production and sales). The increase in inventories is then added to the total value of sales (R100 billion + R2 400 billion) to obtain the total expenditure on the product (R2 500 billion), which in turn equals the total value of production and total income. In the national accounts the accumulation of inventories is therefore effectively treated as expenditure by producers and traders on their own inventories.

Similarly, if production and income equal R2 500 billion while expenditure equals R2 550 billion, inventories will decline by R50 billion. This decline is then subtracted from total expenditure and as a result we again have production = income = expenditure = R2 500 billion.

The main implication of the identity between total production, income and expenditure in the national accounts is that there are always three approaches to measuring the total value of economic activity in a particular period: the *production method*, the *income method* and the *expenditure method*. These methods are explained in Section 2.4 below.

Note, however, that the equality of total product, total income and total expenditure only holds if all three variables pertain to the same period and the same geographic area and if all three are valued at the same set of prices.

2.3   Gross domestic product (GDP)

The central concept in the national accounts is the gross domestic product (GDP). The **gross domestic product** is defined as **the total value of all final goods and services produced within the geographic boundaries of a country in a particular period (usually one year).** GDP is one of the most important indicators of the performance of the economy. To explain how the national accountants succeed in adding up the value of all the different types of economic activity during a particular period, we have to examine the various elements of the definition of GDP.

- The first important element is **value**. By using the prices of goods and services the national accountants can obtain the value of production. In this way it becomes possible to add together various goods and services such as apples, pears, shirts, dresses, medical services, education and computers to arrive at a meaningful figure representing the total value of all goods and services produced in the economy. In other words, once the production of each good or service is expressed in rand and cents, the total value of production can be determined by adding the different values together. The same applies to income and expenditure.

- The second important element of the definition of GDP is the word **final**. To avoid **double counting**, only final goods and services are taken into account. Final goods are goods that are used or consumed by individuals, households and firms and not processed further or resold. There are two broad classes of final goods: consumer goods and capital goods. Consumer goods are those goods that are consumed by households and the government sector, while capital goods are those man-made goods that are used by firms or the government to produce other goods. Examples of the latter include machinery, equipment, buildings, dams, roads and bridges. Goods that are purchased to be resold or used as inputs in producing other goods are called **intermediate goods**. For example, flour purchased by a household is a final good, since the household will consume the flour in some form or another, but the flour purchased by a baker is an intermediate good. The baker does not consume the flour but processes it into bread, cake or something else which is then sold to consumers, the latter then being final (consumer) goods. To avoid double counting, the value of intermediate goods and services has to be ignored. In other words, only final goods and services have to be taken into account. The avoidance of double counting is explained further in Section 2.4.

• The third important element of the definition of GDP is the term 'within the geographic boundaries of the country'. In some definitions this term is replaced by 'in the economy'. The important point is that GDP is a geographic concept which includes all production within the geographic area of a country. This is what is signified by the term **domestic** in gross domestic product. We return to this aspect in Section 2.8. See also the discussion of gross geographic product in Box 2-2.

BOX 2-2: GROSS GEOGRAPHIC PRODUCT

GDP is a geographic concept which refers to the total production of final goods and services in a certain geographic area (the total area of the country concerned) during a particular period. It is also possible to estimate the total value of production in other geographic areas such as the different provinces. In such cases the term **gross geographic product** (GGP) is used to distinguish it from GDP. Thus, when the term GGP is used, it usually indicates that the figures apply to a region within a country.

Although GGP is similar to GDP in principle, a number of additional complications are encountered when GGP is estimated. For example, when the GGP of a particular province, say Mpumalanga, is estimated, all transactions involving residents of other provinces should be treated as exports or imports.

However, since no records are kept of transactions across provincial boundaries, it is quite difficult to estimate the GGP of a particular province. Another complication is that a firm may have its head office in one province, but most of the actual production may occur in other provinces. For example, much of the economic activity in Mpumalanga is owned or controlled by companies based in Gauteng. GDP data for the different provinces, also called **GDPR data (gross domestic product per region)**, are published from time to time by Stats SA. See also Section 3.5 in Chapter 3.

- The fourth important element to note is that only goods and services produced **during a particular period** are included in GDP. GDP concerns the production of new goods and services (also called **current production**) during a specific period. The value of goods produced during earlier periods and sold during the period under consideration is not included in GDP for the latter period. The resale of existing goods such as houses or motorcars is not part of GDP either. GDP only reflects production which occurred during the period in question.

- Fifthly and finally, the word **gross** in the title indicates that no provision has been made for consumption of fixed capital (or depreciation, as it is generally known), which refers to that part of a country's capital equipment (buildings, roads, machinery, tools, etc) which is 'used up' in the production process. Subtracting consumption of fixed capital from a gross aggregate (eg GDP) will yield a net aggregate. However, net aggregates are no longer published in South Africa's national accounts and are seldom used in economic analysis, one of the reasons being that data on consumption of fixed capital at constant prices (see Section 2.6) are not available.

2.4   Three approaches to the measurement of GDP

The three different approaches to estimating GDP can be explained with the aid of a simple example. Suppose a farmer produces 100 bags of wheat, using only his own labour, seed and fertiliser on a smallholding which he rents. He sells the wheat to a miller for R1 000 and pays R500 rent to the owner of the land. His net income or profit is therefore R500.

The miller buys the wheat and produces 200 kg of flour which he sells to a baker for R3 000. His production costs are R1 000 for labour (wages) and R500 for overheads (interest and rental), which leaves a profit of R500.

The baker produces 1 000 loaves of bread with the flour, which he sells direct to the final consumers for R5 000. His labour costs are R750 and his overheads amount to R400, which means that his profit is R850.

What was the total contribution to GDP in the example, that is to say, how will it be reflected in the national accounts?

Production method

Is the value of total production equal to R9 000, that is, R1 000 (the farmer's production) + R3 000 (the miller's production) + R5 000 (the baker's production)? **NO!** Why not? Because such a calculation involves double counting. The appropriate procedure is to compute only the **value added** during each round, and to total these figures. Thus we find that the farmer's production did in fact run to R1 000, but that the miller added only R2 000 (ie R3 000 less R1 000) to this value. What do we call the original R1 000 now? In the miller's case it represents **intermediate** goods. In turn the value added by the activity of the baker was another R2 000 (R5 000 less R3 000). The total value added, or the total production calculated according to the production method, therefore, is R1 000 + R2 000 + R2 000 = R5 000. Thus, from the production side double counting is avoided by working only with value added (which, incidentally, also serves as the basis for value-added tax (VAT)).

Income method

The income method focuses on the income earned in the form of rent, interest, wages and profits in the production process. The total is calculated as follows: rent earned by the landowner (R500) + the farmer's profit (R500) + wages of the miller's workers (R1 000) + rent and interest paid by the miller (and received by other people) (R500) + the miller's profit (R500) + the wages of the baker's workers (R750) + rent and interest paid by the baker (R400) + the baker's profit (R850), which gives a total of R5 000. The subtotals are: rent and interest R1 400, wages R1 750 and profit R1 850. The total income must by definition be equal to the total value of the production.

Expenditure method

What is the total expenditure in this case? Is it R1 000 + R3 000 + R5 000? **NO!** To avoid double counting, the expenditure on intermediate goods (the wheat and the flour) should be ignored and only the expenditure on **final** goods and services (the bread) should be considered. In this case the total expenditure on final goods and services (the 1 000 loaves of bread) is R5 000, which is the same as the total production and income.

In the national accounts the transactions included in this example would be recorded as follows according to the three different methods:

Production (value added)		Income		Expenditure on final goods and services	
Farmer	R1 000	Rent and interest	R1 400	Bread	R5 000
Miller	R2 000	Wages	R1 750		
Baker	R2 000	Profit	R1 850		
Total	**R5 000**	**Total**	**R5 000**	**Total**	**R5 000**

In South Africa, Stats SA is responsible for estimating the gross domestic product according to the production and income approaches, while the SARB is responsible for compiling the expenditure side of the national accounts. Stats SA releases the first estimate of quarterly GDP (from the production side) approximately six weeks after the end of the quarter, while the SARB publishes the data from the expenditure side in its *Quarterly Bulletin* approximately three months after the end of each quarter. In compiling the national accounts there is close cooperation between Stats SA and the SARB.

In the *SARB Quarterly Bulletin* the data collected according to the three methods are presented in three tables:

- National income and production accounts of South Africa (Account 1)
- Gross value added by kind of economic activity (Account 2)
- Expenditure on gross domestic product (Account 3)

The first few items in Account 1 represent the **income** of the factors of production. However, instead of distinguishing between wages, rent, interest and profit, the only distinction is between the **compensation of employees** (ie wages and salaries) and the **net operating surplus** (which includes rent, interest and profit). Together with the consumption of fixed capital these items yield gross value added at factor cost, which is equivalent to GDP at factor cost (see Section 2.5).

The breakdown from the **production** side in Account 2 is more comprehensive. Nine kinds of economic activity are distinguished and they are grouped into the three broad sectors of the economy: the primary sector, the secondary sector, and the tertiary sector. The valuation is at basic prices (see Section 2.5) and the data are provided at constant prices as well as at current prices (see Section 2.6). Table 2-1 illustrates the breakdown for 2009 (at current prices). Note that gross value added at basic prices is equivalent to GDP at basic prices.

Table 2-1: Gross value added by kind of economic activity at current prices, 2009

	R millions	%
Primary sector		
Agriculture, forestry and fishing	66 049	3,0
Mining and quarrying	212 469	9,7
Secondary sector		
Manufacturing	329 166	15,1
Electricity, gas and water	53 133	2,5
Construction (contractors)	84 450	3,9
Tertiary sector		
Wholesale and retail trade, catering and accommodation	290 957	13,3
Transport, storage and communication	206 271	9,5
Financial intermediation, insurance, real-estate and business services	474 111	21,7
Community, social and personal services	464 632	21,3
Gross value added at basic prices	**2 181 238**	**100,0**

Source: SARB Quarterly Bulletin, March 2010.

The breakdown which is probably used most is the one from the **expenditure** side, published under the heading **Expenditure on GDP** (Account 3). As one would expect, valuation is at market prices (see Section 2.5). Once again the data are presented at both current and constant prices (see Section 2.6). This account contains data on the main components of expenditure, as illustrated in Table 2-2. A further twenty or so tables in the *SARB Quarterly Bulletin* provide detailed breakdowns of most of these components, particularly final consumption expenditure by households and capital formation (ie investment).

Table 2-2: Expenditure on gross domestic product at current prices, 2009

	R millions
Final consumption expenditure by households	1 472 824
Final consumption expenditure by general government	504 169
Gross fixed capital formation	543 392
Change in inventories	–75 514
Residual item	–921
Gross domestic expenditure	**2 443 950**
Exports of goods and services	657 113
minus Imports of goods and services	–677 740
Expenditure on gross domestic product (at market prices)	**2 423 323**

Source: SARB Quarterly Bulletin, March 2010.

The basic distinction in the table is between **final consumption expenditure** and **gross capital formation**. The former is split into final consumption expenditure by households and general government respectively, while gross capital formation is split into gross fixed capital formation and the change in inventories.

Final consumption expenditure by households is the largest single element of total expenditure in the economy. In the national accounts this is divided into four categories and a number of items. The categories are durable goods, semi-durable goods, non-durable goods and services. In 2009 spending on services represented 44,2% of private consumption expenditure in South Africa. The shares of the other components were as follows: non-durable goods 39,5%, semi-durable goods 9,1% and durable goods 7,2%. The SARB also publishes a table in which final consumption expenditure by households is classified according to purpose.

Final consumption expenditure by general government consists of current expenditure on salaries and wages and on goods and other services of a non-capital nature by the service departments (not business enterprises) of general government. General government includes central government, provincial governments and local governments. Note that final consumption expenditure by general government does not represent total spending by government, since capital formation (ie investment spending) is included elsewhere.

Two types of final consumption expenditure by general government are distinguished in the national accounts: **individual** consumption expenditure and **collective** consumption expenditure. The former pertains to government expenditure on individual consumption goods and services such as education, health and welfare, while the latter pertains to government expenditure on collective consumption expenditure such as defence, law and order and public administration. Final consumption expenditure by general government is discussed again in Section 10.3.

As mentioned earlier, **gross capital formation** (or gross investment) is divided into **gross fixed capital formation** and the **change in inventories**. **Capital formation** (or investment) refers to additions to the country's capital stock (ie the purchase of capital goods). Gross capital formation means that no provision has been made for consumption of fixed capital (ie depreciation). **Fixed** capital formation (ie fixed investment) refers to the purchase of capital goods such as buildings, machinery and equipment, while **changes in inventories** reflect goods produced during the period that have not been sold, or goods produced in an earlier period but only sold during the current period. Changes in inventories can be positive or negative, but they are usually small in relation to the size of fixed capital formation. Note, however, that the **change** in inventories is subject to large **variations** from year to year, which often account for a significant portion of the overall **change** in GDP.

Detailed information is provided in the national accounts on gross fixed capital formation according to kind of economic activity, type of organisation and type of asset. Data on the change in inventories are also provided by kind of economic activity and by type of organisation.

The **residual item** is a statistical discrepancy which arises because different approaches are used to estimate GDP. Although the production, income and expenditure methods should in principle yield the same result in any particular period, the margin of error in estimating GDP is such that it would be a miracle if the three totals tallied. A residual error is therefore inevitable. The value of GDP (or gross value added) estimated according to the production and income methods is assumed to be correct and the residual item is therefore included in the estimate according to the expenditure method. The residual item is usually small relative to the **level** of GDP but both the **size** of the residual item and **changes** therein can be large relative to **changes** in GDP (see Section 3.4). A further problem with the residual item is that there is no direct or systematic relationship between its value at current prices and its value at constant prices (see Section 2.6).

The first five items in Table 2-2 constitute **gross domestic expenditure** (GDE), which is explained in Section 2.9. By adding exports and subtracting imports, GDP (or expenditure on GDP) at market prices is obtained. Note that both exports and imports pertain to goods and services.

2.5   Valuation at market prices, basic prices and factor cost

The different methods of calculating GDP will only yield the same result if all the values are determined using the same set of prices. Three sets of prices are used in the national accounts: **basic prices**, **factor cost** (or **factor income**) and **market prices**.

The differences between basic prices, factor cost and market prices are due to the impact of **indirect taxes** and **subsidies**. When there are indirect taxes (ie taxes on production and products) or subsidies, the amount paid for a good or service differs from both the cost of production and the income earned by the relevant factors of production. For example, the amount paid by a consumer for a packet of cigarettes is much higher than the combined income earned by the merchant, the manufacturer, the workers, the tobacco farmer and everyone else involved in the process of producing and selling the packet of cigarettes. The difference is the result of excise duty and VAT, which together constitute almost 50% of the market price of a packet of cigarettes in South Africa. **Indirect taxes** (ie taxes on production and products) thus have the effect of making the market prices of goods and services **higher** than their **basic prices** or **factor cost**, where the latter is equal to **factor income** (ie the income earned by the relevant factors of production).

In some instances, however, the market price is lower than the basic price or factor cost. This happens, for example, when a subsidy is paid to the relevant producers for the very purpose of keeping the market price artificially low. In earlier years the South African government subsidised the price of bread in this way. **Subsidies** thus have the effect of making the **market prices** of goods and services **lower** than their **basic prices** or **factor cost**.

In the national accounts, **production** is valued at basic prices, **income** at factor cost (or factor income) and **expenditure** at market prices. As mentioned earlier, the differences between basic prices, factor cost and market prices can be ascribed to the existence of various taxes and subsidies on production and products. The national accountants nowadays distinguish between taxes on products and other taxes on production. Likewise, they distinguish between subsidies on products and other subsidies on production.

Taxes on products refer to taxes which are payable per unit of some good or service. Examples include VAT, customs and excise duties, and taxes on financial and capital transactions.

Other taxes on production refer to taxes on production which are not linked to specific goods or services. They consist of taxes on labour employed or on the ownership of land, buildings or other assets used in production. Examples include payroll taxes, recurring taxes on land, buildings or other structures, business and professional licenses, taxes on the use of fixed assets, stamp taxes and taxes on pollution.

Subsidies on products include direct subsidies payable per unit exported to encourage exports and product-linked subsidies on products used domestically.

Other subsidies on production refer to subsidies that are not linked to specific goods or services. Examples include subsidies on employment or the payroll and subsidies to reduce pollution.

Factor cost represents the amount received by the various factors of production. The **basic price** is the amount receivable by the producer from the purchaser for a unit of a good or service produced as output (ie the **market price**) minus any tax payable plus any subsidy receivable on that unit as a consequence of its production or sale. In other words, basic prices indicate what the producers actually receive.

The formal relationships between factor cost, basic prices and market prices are as follows:

market prices = factor cost *plus* all taxes on products and production *minus* all subsidies on products and production

market prices = basic prices plus taxes on products *minus* subsidies on products

basic prices = factor cost *plus* other taxes on production *minus* other subsidies on production

basic prices = market prices *minus* taxes on products *plus* subsidies on products

factor cost = market prices *minus* all taxes on products and production *plus* all subsidies on products and production

factor cost = basic prices *minus* other taxes on production *plus* other subsidies on production

The following identities thus apply:

Gross value added (or GDP) at factor cost
+ other taxes on production
− other subsidies on production
= Gross value added (or GDP) at basic prices

Gross value added (or GDP) at basic prices
+ taxes on products
− subsidies on products
= GDP at market prices

When using national accounting data, one should always check at which prices the aggregates are valued. The amounts may differ considerably. In 2009, for example, South African GDP at market prices was 11,1% greater than gross value added (or GDP) at basic prices (mainly as a result of VAT). If no valuation is specified, it can usually be assumed that valuation is at market prices.

2.6   Valuation at current prices and at constant prices: nominal and real GDP

Another important aspect of the valuation of national accounting statistics is the distinction between current and constant prices. Initially all national accounting data are measured at **current** prices (ie in **nominal** terms). For example, when calculating GDP for 2009, the national accountants had to use the prices paid for the various goods and services in 2009. In this way **GDP at current prices** or **nominal GDP** for 2009 was obtained. Economists, however, are not interested only in the size of GDP during a particular period. They want to know how GDP changed from one period to the next, but in a world of inflation (ie a world in which prices tend to increase from one period to the next) it makes little sense to compare GDP at current prices or nominal GDP between different years. For example, in 2009 the South African GDP at current market prices was 6,1% higher than in 2008. But this did not mean that 6,1% more goods and services were produced in South Africa in 2009 than in 2008. This increase simply reflected the fact that most prices were higher in 2009 than in 2008.

To solve this problem, the national accountants at Stats SA and the SARB convert GDP at current prices to **GDP at constant prices** or **real GDP**. This is done by valuing all the goods and services produced each year using the prices ruling in a certain year, called the base year. Since December 2009, the base year in the South African national accounts has been 2005. Each year's GDP is therefore also expressed at 2005 prices. In this way the impact of price increases is eliminated, thus allowing for comparisons in real or volume terms only. For example, once the adjustment had been made, it was found that the South African real GDP was actually 1,8% lower in 2009 than in 2008. The real growth rate (or the growth in GDP at constant prices) was thus −1,8%. The difference between this real rate and the nominal growth rate of 6,1% was the result of price increases (ie inflation).

Note that the conversion from GDP at current prices (nominal GDP) to GDP at constant prices (real GDP) also yields an estimate of the inflation rate for the economy as a whole. The ratio between nominal GDP and real GDP is called the GDP deflator. The use of the GDP deflator and other similar implicit price deflators to arrive at inflation rates is explained in Section 6.7.

The South African nominal GDP and real GDP (both at market prices) and the nominal and real growth rates for the period 2001 to 2009 are shown in Table 2-3.

The transformation of GDP at current prices to GDP at constant prices is a complicated process. Nominal GDP is broken down into its different components and each of these is then converted to values measured at the prices ruling in the base period. The values of the different components at constant prices are then added together to obtain real GDP. Details of these processes fall beyond the scope of this book. The difference between valuation at current prices and valuation at constant prices (ie between nominal and real values) is crucially important, however, when national accounting data are analysed or interpreted.

Table 2-3: Nominal and real GDP and nominal and real growth rates, 2001 to 2009

Year	GDP at current market prices (nominal GDP) (R millions)	GDP at constant 2005 prices (real GDP) (R millions)	Growth rates (% change since previous year)	
			Nominal	Real
2001	1 020 007	1 337 382	–	–
2002	1 171 086	1 386 435	14,8	3,7
2003	1 272 537	1 427 332	8,7	2,9
2004	1 415 273	1 492 330	11,2	4,6
2005	1 571 082	1 571 082	11,0	5,3
2006	1 767 422	1 659 121	12,5	5,6
2007	2 017 102	1 750 139	14,1	5,5
2008	2 283 823	1 814 521	13,2	3,7
2009	2 423 323	1 782 061	6,1	–1,8

Source: SARB Quarterly Bulletin, March 2010.

2.7   Some problems associated with GDP

Although GDP is the best available measure of aggregate activity in the domestic economy, it is not a perfect measure. As a result GDP is sometimes jokingly referred to as the 'grossly deceptive product' or the 'grossly distorted picture'. Users of national accounting data should always remember that the estimation of total production, income and expenditure in the economy is an enormous task. Various conceptual and measurement problems are encountered, it is often difficult to define precisely what should be measured, and the information is also often inadequate. As a result, the compilation of the national accounts involves liberal use of estimation and guesstimation, interpolation and extrapolation, and approximation and adjustment. Moreover, because the agencies concerned (Stats SA and the SARB) have to produce timely estimates, there is often a trade-off as far as accuracy is concerned. National accounting figures should therefore always be treated as the best available estimates rather than completely accurate figures. Some of the problems of GDP measurement are outlined below.

Non-market production

It is difficult to measure or estimate the value of goods and services that are not sold in a market. A case in point is the production of goods and services by the government. Since most of these goods and services are not sold in a market, they have to be valued at cost. It is assumed, for example, that the value of the services provided by a civil servant is equal to his or her salary, irrespective of the volume or usefulness of the services actually provided. Other examples of non-market production are farmers' consumption of their own produce, do-it-yourself work and volunteer work. Certain services, such as those provided by housewives or the gardening or home repairs done by members of the family, are not taken into account. Thus, when a domestic servant or gardener is hired to perform duties previously undertaken by members of the household, measured GDP rises. Likewise, recorded national income falls every time a man or woman marries his or her housekeeper!

Unrecorded activity

A related problem is that many transactions or activities in the economy, including many that go through the market, are never recorded officially. These unrecorded activities range from illegal activities such as smuggling, drug-trafficking and prostitution to legal activities such as hawking, flea-market trading and backyard repair work. For example, anyone who pays cash for a handyman's services may be participating in a transaction that is not recorded in the national accounts. Such transactions or activities are described by terms such as the unrecorded economy, the unobserved economy, the shadow economy, the underground economy or the **informal sector**. See also Section 5.3.

The existence of unrecorded activities implies that the actual **level** of GDP is not particularly significant. However, as long as the relative importance of unrecorded activity stays the same, this is not a serious problem since **changes** in the level of measured GDP will still reflect changes in the aggregate level of economic activity. The problems arise when the relative importance of unrecorded activity changes, and this has unquestionably happened during the past decade or two. For example, as tax rates increased it became more tempting not to declare sales or income. At the same time, the growing lack of sufficient job opportunities in the formal sector of the economy forced an increasing number of people to turn to the informal sector as a means of survival. Note, however, that in the case of informal traders who purchase their supplies in the formal sector only, the mark-ups of the informal traders are not recorded in the national accounts, since the original purchases ought to be picked up in the accounting system.

As a result of the growing importance of the informal sector, Statistics South Africa started to publish official estimates of the size of the informal sector in 1990. In 1994 an important further step was taken by including estimates of the value of informal sector activity in the official South African GDP figures. This resulted in an upward adjustment of 5,6% in nominal GDP. The inclusion of estimates of the value of informal sector activity implied, among other things, that the ratios between other variables (eg the budget deficit) and the GDP all declined.

Until 2009 only legal informal sector activities were included in the GDP estimates, but from the third quarter of 2009 illegal activities (eg dagga production, perlemoen smuggling, prostitution, drug-trafficking, illegal mining, illegal alcohol and medicine production, pirate copying, illegal imports of clothes and trade therein and illegal trade in vehicles and firearms) were also included. Stats SA do not reveal the extent of such illegal activity, but it constitutes only a small fraction of GDP. At the time of writing, the total informal sector still contributed only about 6% of GDP.

While on the topic of crime, it should be noted that theft as such does not add to GDP since it merely involves the transfer of an asset from one owner to another. The replacement of stolen items is captured along with other consumer spending. All spending on security is also part of GDP.

Data revisions

Another problem for the compilers of the national accounts (and a source of frustration for the users of these accounts) is the unavoidable revision of certain data after they were originally published. The publication of data invariably involves a trade-off between timeliness and accuracy. To assess the current state of the economy, fresh data are required. For this reason, preliminary estimates of GDP and other national accounting data are released as early as possible. Most data, however, are subject to successive revisions as additional and better information become available and as data collecting methods and techniques improve. Definitions and the geographic coverage of data may also change. There are basically two types of revision of national accounting data: routine annual revisions and benchmark or comprehensive revisions (see Box 2-3). In South Africa the national accounts are revised comprehensively every five years, the most recent revisions being those in 1994, 1999, 2004 and 2009. In 1994, for example, GDP data were revised to include the former independent states and the informal sector. Some particulars of the 2009 revision are provided in Box 2-3.

As indicated in Box 3-2 in Chapter 3, data revisions can be quite large. A few years ago, Van Walbeek examined the magnitudes and implications of official revisions of the South African national accounting data.[2] His findings clearly indicate that initial data releases should always be treated with great caution. He also emphasised that the magnitude of relationships (eg between imports and gross domestic expenditure) is strongly affected by data revisions.

Thus, although the original data are invariably reported in the media as gospel truth, preliminary estimates should always be treated with caution and special care is required if different sources or different editions of the same source are used to compile a data series covering a number of years.

---

2.   C van Walbeek, 2006, Official revisions to South African national accounts data: magnitudes and implications, *South African Journal of Economics* 74(4), December:745-765.

BOX 2-3: ANNUAL AND COMPREHENSIVE REVISIONS OF NATIONAL ACCOUNTING DATA

Annual revisions are necessary to

- correct possible inaccuracies in the original data
- replace judgemental projections with source data
- replace preliminary source data with more comprehensive source data that became available after the original estimates had been made

Benchmark or comprehensive revisions incorporate

- changes in definition and classification
- changes in estimating procedures and methods
- changes of the base year and all associated modifications
- changes in the seasonal adjustment factors
- new data sources and revised source data

Apart from the annual revisions, the South African national accounts are revised comprehensively every five years, the most recent being those in 1994, 1999, 2004 and 2009.

The benchmark revision of 2009, for example, included the following changes:

- The value added by the finance subsector was expanded to include estimates of output by brokers active in the bond and derivatives markets.
- The value added by the banking sector was revised to incorporate newly available data (as a result of more comprehensive reporting by banks).
- Final expenditure by households per product group was expanded (eg to show expenditure on privately owned computers and security services).
- New price indices were used to deflate nominal values from 2002 onwards and the base year was changed to 2005.
- Capital expenditure on computers and related equipment was shown separately.
- More informal sector activities were included.
- Internationally recommended classifications were adopted.

GDP as a measure of wellbeing or welfare

GDP and the other national accounting concepts are indispensable indicators of economic performance but they are not necessarily good indicators of economic wellbeing or welfare. A larger physical flow of goods and services does not necessarily increase the wellbeing of the residents of a country. The first problem is that unwanted byproducts (or externalities) such as environmental pollution, congestion, noise and psychological stress are not measured. These negative externalities are sometimes called 'bads', as opposed to 'goods'. A related problem is that no allowance is made for the depletion or exhaustion of natural resources (eg scarce mineral resources). A third problem is that the data say nothing about the purpose of production or expenditure. For example, R100 million spent on military equipment is treated in the same way as R100 million spent on health or education. Another problem is that it is difficult to account for changes in the quality of goods and services. There may, for example, be technological improvements (eg in electronic goods) or a deterioration in the quality of services provided by artisans which are very difficult to account for. Likewise, no allowance is made for the value of increased (or reduced) leisure.

In 2008 the French president, Nicolas Sarkozy, appointed a commission comprising 25 prominent social scientists (including five with Nobel prizes in economics) to investigate alternative measures of wellbeing. The commission's report, published in September 2009, and available at *www.stiglitz-sen-fitoussi.fr*, listed all the criticisms of GDP and examined possible measures of the 'quality of life'. However, as yet no generally accepted alternative to GDP has been found.

Distribution of income

A related problem which deserves separate mention is that national accounting data say nothing about the distribution of total income within the country. The residents of a country with a high GDP are not necessarily better off than the residents of a country with a low GDP. At the very least, an adjustment has to be made for the size of the population. In other words, GDP has to be expressed on a per capita basis before comparisons can be made (see Box 3-3 in Chapter 3). But even per capita data may be misleading because the distribution of income differs from country to country and can also change over time. Even when GDP growth is sluggish, some sections of the economy and society might be booming. For example, on 3 August 1996 *The Economist* reported sharp increases in the sales of luxury goods and services in Britain at a time when annual GDP growth was estimated at a mere 1,8%. Among these goods and services were luxury motorcars, expensive country houses, exotic holidays, chauffeur services, pedigree dogs and cosmetic surgery. At that stage there thus appears to have been a significant redistribution of income and wealth in Britain in favour of those at the top end of the income scale. The measurement of the distribution of income is discussed in Section 8.6.

2.8   Gross national income

As explained earlier, GDP is a geographic concept – the adjective domestic indicates that the production occurred within the geographic boundaries of the country. It does not matter who produces the goods or who owns the factors of production. It could be a British, Japanese or any other firm. Nor does it matter to whom the goods are sold. They could be sold locally or exported to another country. As long as the production takes place on South African soil it forms part of South African GDP.

But economists also want to know what happens to the income of all South African citizens or permanent residents of the country. To answer this question, all income earned by foreign-owned factors of production in South Africa (ie all primary income to the rest of the world) has to be subtracted from GDP. In this way the South African element of GDP can be ascertained. In addition, all income earned by South African factors of production in the rest of the world (ie all primary income from the rest of the world) has to be taken into account. Once these adjustments have been made, we have an indication of the national income, that is, the income of all permanent residents of the country. This is called the **gross national income (GNI)**, which is equivalent to the gross national product (GNP).

To derive GNI (or GNP) from GDP the following must therefore be done:

Subtract from GDP all primary income to the rest of the world, for example:

- all profits, interest and other income from domestic investment which accrue to residents of other countries (eg the profits earned in South Africa by foreign owners of companies such as Lever Brothers, Colgate-Palmolive or BMW, interest paid by South Africans to foreign lenders and the dividends paid to foreign shareholders in South African companies)
- all wages and salaries of foreign workers engaged in domestic production (eg the wages earned by residents of Lesotho, Mozambique and Malawi on the South African gold mines)

Add to GDP all primary income from the rest of the world, for example:

- all profits, interest and other income from investments abroad which accrue to permanent residents (eg the profits earned by a South African construction company that builds roads in the rest of Africa and the dividends earned by South African shareholders in foreign companies)
- all wages and salaries earned outside South Africa by permanent residents (eg the income earned by South Africans working in Britain)

In the case of South Africa, foreign involvement in the domestic economy has always been larger than involvement by South African factors of production in the rest of the world. In other words, primary income to the rest of the world (ie the remuneration of foreign-owned factors of production in our economy) exceeds primary income from the rest of the world (ie the remuneration earned by South African factors of production in the rest of the world). South Africa's GNI (or GNP) has therefore always been smaller than its GDP. For example, in 2009 South African GNI was R2 347 377 million while the GDP was R2 423 323 million. Note, however, that the difference is not particularly large (in 2009 it was only 3,1% of GDP).

Formally:

GNI (or GNP)   = GDP + primary income from the rest of the world
                                        – primary income to the rest of the world
                       or   (since payments are larger)

GNI   = GDP – net primary income to the rest of the world
where net primary income = primary income to the rest of the world
                                          – primary income from the rest of the world

In some countries GNI (or GNP) is larger than GDP. Take Lesotho, for example. Lesotho is a small, landlocked, mountainous country. Production in Lesotho is limited. Many citizens of Lesotho work in South Africa, particularly on the mines. Lesotho's GNP is thus greater than its GDP. In highly developed industrial countries whose citizens and firms invest heavily abroad, such as the United States, the United Kingdom and Germany, GNP is also usually larger than GDP.

Economists use both GDP and GNI when measuring or analysing the state of the economy. GDP is the best measure of the level of economic activity in the country and of the potential for creating jobs for the country's residents. Economic growth is therefore usually measured by calculating the percentage change in real GDP from one year to the next. GNI, however, is a better measure of the income or standard of living of the residents of a country. If we want to know how South Africans as a group are faring, we therefore examine the level and rate of change in real GNI. More details about the calculation and significance of real GDP and real GNI are provided in Section 3.2.

2.9   Expenditure on GDP versus GDE

In Section 2.4 it was explained that there are three approaches to calculating GDP: the **production approach** (which measures the value added by all the participants in the economy), the **income approach** (which measures the income received by the different factors of production) and the **expenditure approach** (which measures the spending on final goods and services by the different participants).

In terms of the expenditure approach, national accountants add together the final consumption expenditure and capital formation by households, firms, government and the foreign sector. The components of expenditure on GDP can be expressed as follows:

- final consumption expenditure by households (C)
- capital formation (or investment spending) (I)
- final consumption expenditure by general government (G)
- expenditure on exports (X) minus expenditure on imports (Z)

In symbols we can write:

$$\begin{aligned}\text{GDP} &= \text{expenditure on GDP}\\ &= C + I + G + X - Z\end{aligned}$$

The composition of expenditure on GDP in South Africa in 2009 was shown in Table 2-2. Expenditure on GDP is always valued at market prices.

A substantial portion of the expenditure on South African GDP originates in the rest of the world. This spending on South African **exports** of goods and services has to be **added** to the other components of spending on GDP. However, C, I, G and X all include spending on goods and services not produced in South Africa. Such **imports** of goods and services therefore have to be **subtracted** to obtain the total expenditure on South African produced goods and services. **Expenditure on GDP does not include imports**, since **imports are produced in the rest of the world**. Expenditure on GDP includes spending on South African produced goods and services only.

Expenditure on GDP is always equal to GDP at market prices. It indicates the total value of spending on goods and services produced in the country. However, it does not indicate the total value of spending within the borders of the country. As indicated above, part of the expenditure on South African GDP occurs in the rest of the world, while part of the spending by domestic households, firms and the government in the country is on goods and services produced in the rest of the world.

The three central domestic expenditure items (C, I and G) do not distinguish between goods and services produced locally and those produced in the rest of the world (such as French wine, Italian shoes, Japanese CD players and German machinery). These three items constitute gross domestic expenditure (GDE). Economists are particularly interested in GDE, which indicates the total value of spending originating within the borders of the country. It includes imports of goods and services, but excludes exports of goods and services, since spending on exports originates in the rest of the world.

The relationship between GDP (or expenditure on GDP) and GDE is very important and needs to be emphasised. In symbols we have

$$\begin{aligned}\text{GDE} &= C + I + G\\ \text{GDP} &= C + I + G + (X - Z)\end{aligned}$$

GDE includes imports (Z) and excludes exports (X), while GDP includes exports (X) and excludes imports (Z). See also Table 2-2 in Section 2.4.

The difference between GDE and GDP is therefore reflected in the difference between exports and imports of goods and services $(X - Z)$. This can be seen clearly by examining the equations for GDE and GDP given above. Incidentally, $(X - Z)$ is often called **net exports** (NX).

If GDP is greater than GDE, it follows that exports are greater than imports. This is quite logical. If the value of production in the domestic economy exceeds the value of spending within the country, it follows that the value of exports is greater than the value of imports. Thus if GDP > GDE, it follows that $X > Z$.

Similarly, if the value of spending within the country exceeds the value of production within the country, it follows that the value of imports is greater than the value of exports. Thus if GDE > GDP, it follows that $Z > X$.

Box 2-4 provides some further perspective on GDE and GDP by giving examples of how specific transactions would be treated in the South African national accounts.

2.10   The national income and production accounts

The various components and aggregates introduced in this chapter are summarised in the *SARB Quarterly Bulletin* in an account titled *National income and production accounts of South Africa*. Table 2-4 provides an outline of the main elements of this account, using the data for 2009. Note the relationships between the various components of the table.

Table 2-4: National income and production accounts of South Africa, 2009

	R millions (current prices)
Compensation of employees	1 086 907
Net operating surplus	728 426
Consumption of fixed capital	332 824
Gross value added at factor cost	**2 148 157**
Plus: Other taxes on production	38 173
Less: Other subsidies on production	–5 092
Gross value added at basic prices	**2 181 238**
Plus: Taxes on products	245 198
Less: Subsidies on products	–3 113
Gross domestic product at market prices	**2 423 323**
Final consumption expenditure by households *(C)*	1 472 824
Final consumption expenditure by government *(G)*	504 169
Gross capital formation *(I)*	467 878
Residual item	–921
Gross domestic expenditure (GDE)	**2 443 950**
Plus: Exports of goods and services *(X)*	657 113
Less: Imports of goods and services *(Z)*	–677 740

Expenditure on gross domestic product (GDP at market prices)	**2 423 323**
Plus: Primary income from the rest of the world	34 075
Less: Primary income to the rest of the world	–87 593
Gross national income at market prices (GNI)	**2 369 805**
Plus: Current transfers from the rest of the world	10 334
Less: Current transfers to the rest of the world	–32 762
Gross national disposable income at market prices	**2 347 377**

Source: SARB Quarterly Bulletin, March 2010.

BOX 2-4: SOME HYPOTHETICAL EXAMPLES OF HOW TRANSACTIONS ARE RECORDED IN THE NATIONAL ACCOUNTS

National accounting is a complex subject. The complete system of national accounts involves an intricate application of double-entry accounting which falls beyond the scope of this book. The system is also modified substantially from time to time in an attempt to deal with unresolved issues and to accommodate changes in the domestic and international economy.

Without going into all the details, this box sheds further light on the national accounts by providing some examples of how certain hypothetical transactions would be recorded in the South African national accounts. The focus is on the expenditure approach, which is the one used most often in economic analysis and by practising economists. Since the expenditure approach is adopted, all the values are expressed at market prices and therefore include VAT and other taxes on products and production (ie indirect taxes).

Sophie Smith of Stellenryk purchases goods to the value of R483,12 from the local branch of Shoprite. This is an example of final consumption expenditure by households which forms part of GDE. GDE includes spending on imported goods but to obtain GDP (or expenditure on GDP) the total value of all imports of goods and services has to be subtracted from GDE. The full amount therefore will not necessarily form part of South African GDP. GDP includes only goods manufactured in South Africa.

Francina Mahlangu of Benoni purchases a set of books by mail order from the United States and pays for it in US dollars. This is also an example of final consumption expenditure by households which forms part of GDE. At the same time, however, the total amount is spent on imports, which have to be subtracted from GDE to arrive at GDP (or expenditure on GDP). Thus we know that this transaction will not affect the size of GDP.

Maans Wiese, a farmer in the Moorreesburg district, purchases a new tractor from a dealer in Cape Town. This forms part of gross fixed capital formation (since the tractor is a capital good) and is thus included in GDE. If the dealer had imported the tractor, the value of the imported tractor would have been recorded as part of total imports of goods and services and would therefore be deducted when GDP (or expenditure on GDP) is calculated.

James Malatsi of Giyani purchases a second-hand tractor from his neighbour, Hendrick Mathebula. This does not form part of capital formation (ie investment spending), GDE or GDP since no new goods are involved. It is simply an example of a change of ownership of an existing capital good.

Peter Mavundla of Nelspruit purchases a new German tractor from a dealer in Maputo to use on his farm in the Barberton district. This item will be recorded as gross fixed capital formation which forms part of GDE but it will not affect the size of GDP, since all imports (of which this is an example) are deducted from GDE to arrive at GDP. Remember, GDE includes all spending on goods and services by residents, while GDP (or expenditure on GDP) includes only the value of goods and services actually produced in the country.

Apex Pty Ltd from Kimberley imports a machine from Germany. The full amount is recorded both as capital formation (ie investment spending) and as imports. It is thus recorded as part of GDE but does not affect the size of GDP. In other words, the transaction is treated similarly to the one immediately above.

South African Breweries sells Castle Lager to the value of R1 million (brewed at its plant in Rosslyn near Pretoria) to a liquor wholesaler in Zimbabwe. The full amount is recorded as exports and thus forms part of South African GDP. However, it does not form part of South African GDE since the expenditure occurs in Zimbabwe.

A group of Japanese tourists spend R1 million while touring through South Africa. This is a slightly complicated one, since all spending by foreign tourists in South Africa is regarded as exports (of tourist services) (see Section 7.1). The spending therefore does not form part of South African GDE even though it occurred within the borders of the country. The spending originated outside the country and is therefore classified as exports and included as such in GDP (or expenditure on GDP).

The Schoeman family from Pretoria North spend R85 000 while touring through Britain. The full spending is recorded as imports in the South African national accounts. Although the spending occurred in Britain, it originated in South Africa and therefore forms part of South African GDE. However, it does not form part of South African GDP (or expenditure on GDP).

The South African National Treasury purchases stationery to the value of R20 million from Waltons, a major South African stationery company. This is an example of final consumption expenditure by general government and is included in South African GDE and GDP.

Hans Meyer, an employee at Statistics South Africa, receives his monthly pay cheque. This is also an example of final consumption expenditure by general government, included in both GDE and GDP. The major portion of final consumption expenditure by general government consists of the compensation of employees.

The Department of Water Affairs spends R100 million on a new dam in the Harrismith district. This is recorded as gross fixed capital formation and forms part of GDE and GDP. Note that gross fixed capital formation includes capital formation (or investment spending) by government as well as by the private sector. The value of any machinery imported to construct the dam will, of course, be recorded as imports and will therefore be subtracted from GDE when GDP is calculated.

2.11   Saving

Saving is defined as the difference between income and expenditure. **Gross saving** for the economy as a whole consists of saving by households, corporate saving, saving of general government and consumption of fixed capital (or provision for depreciation). Data on gross saving and its components are summarised in the *SARB Quarterly Bulletin* in the account entitled *Financing of gross capital formation* (see Table 2-5). Data on saving are available at current prices only and therefore the saving performance of the economy or a sector is usually expressed as a ratio, called the **saving rate**. For the economy as a whole it is the total saving rate which is important. This is obtained by expressing gross saving as a ratio or percentage of GDP.

Net saving is equal to gross saving minus consumption of fixed capital. The first three items in Table 2-5 thus represent net saving. By adding the consumption of fixed capital gross saving is obtained, as in the table. Saving data for the different sectors of the economy are included in the production, distribution and accumulation accounts (see Box 2-5).

BOX 2-5: THE PRODUCTION, DISTRIBUTION AND ACCUMULATION ACCOUNTS

Nowadays the SARB publishes a set of six production, distribution and accumulation accounts for South Africa. They are for:

- financial corporations
- non-financial corporations
- general government
- households and non-profit organisations serving households
- the total domestic economy
- the rest of the world

These accounts contain a wealth of information and form the basis of the system of national accounts. Although some of the details of the accounts differ (on account of the different nature of the various sectors), the following outline of the account for the total domestic economy provides a good indication of the type of information they contain.

PRODUCTION, DISTRIBUTION AND ACCUMULATION ACCOUNTS: TOTAL DOMESTIC ECONOMY

Output at basic prices
Less: Intermediate consumption

Gross value added at basic prices
Plus: Taxes on products
Less: Subsidies on products

Gross domestic product at market prices
Less: Compensation of employees
Less: Taxes on production and imports
Plus: Subsidies

Gross operating surplus
Plus: Compensation of employees
Plus: Taxes on production and imports
Less: Subsidies
Plus: Property income received (interest, dividends, rent)
Less: Property income paid (interest, dividends, rent)

Gross national income
Plus: Other current transfers received
Less: Other current transfers paid

Gross disposable income
Less: Final consumption expenditure (individual and collective)
Less: Residual (explained earlier)

Gross saving
Less: Consumption of fixed capital

Net saving

Apart from the information in this consolidated outline, the accounts provide useful data for the component sectors, for example, the taxes on income and wealth paid by the financial corporations, non-financial corporations and households (and received by government).

Source: SARB Quarterly Bulletin.

Saving by households (sometimes called personal saving) is equal to the difference between the disposable income of households and final consumption expenditure by households. The household (or personal) saving rate is obtained by expressing saving by households as a ratio or percentage of the disposable income of households.

Corporate saving (net) is the difference between the total current income and expenditure of incorporated business enterprises.

Total **private saving** is equal to saving by households plus corporate saving. In other words, it is the sum of saving by households and companies.

Government saving (net) is equal to current income of general government less current expenditure.

Consumption of fixed capital (or **provision for depreciation**) is the amount set aside to replace capital equipment which is 'used up' in the production process. Data on the consumption of fixed capital by general government, public corporations and private business enterprises are provided in the *SARB Quarterly Bulletin* in the account entitled *Gross and net capital formation by type of organisation*. Net capital formation is obtained by deducting consumption of fixed capital from gross capital formation. By the same token, net saving is obtained by deducting consumption of fixed capital from gross saving.

At the practical level it is important to realise that saving by households, which is often the subject of intense debate, is calculated as a **residual** in the national accounts. The level of saving by households is derived from the accounting relationship between gross capital formation and gross saving, as summarised in Table 2-5.

Table 2-5: Financing of gross capital formation, selected years (R millions)

	2000	2005	2009
Saving by households	6 097	1 142	−6 030
Corporate saving	37 827	44 519	74 085
Saving of general government	−20 585	−5 816	−29 574
Consumption of fixed capital	120 221	187 790	332 824
Gross saving	**143 560**	**227 635**	**371 305**
Net capital inflow from the rest of the world	4 636	91 336	110 886
Change in gold and other foreign reserves[1]	−3 444	−36 841	−14 313
Gross capital formation	144 752	282 130	467 878
Total saving rate[2] (%)	15,6	14,5	15,3
Household saving rate[3] (%)	1,0	0,1	−0,4

1 Increase −; decrease +
2 Gross saving as percentage of GDP at market prices.
3 Saving by households as percentage of disposable income of households.
Source: SARB Quarterly Bulletin, March 2010.

A first point to note is that in an accounting sense gross capital formation can be financed by any or a combination of gross saving, a net capital inflow and a decrease in gold and other foreign reserves. As explained earlier, gross saving consists of saving by households, corporate saving, saving of general government and consumption of fixed capital. The balancing item in this account (Table 2-5) is saving by households, which is therefore subject to a considerable margin of error. A second point is that final consumption expenditure by households is not financed only by current income. It can also be financed out of past savings (ie by dissaving) or through credit. Thus even if the household saving figure in the national accounts is correct, it is actually a 'net' figure, obtained by subtracting all credit granted to finance final consumption expenditure by households from total saving by households (in the sense of funds actually flowing into savings institutions) during a given period. Hence, while certain households are saving (eg through life assurance premiums or contributions to pension or provident funds) others are in effect dissaving by using credit to finance consumption expenditure. In fact, even a single household can simultaneously save and dissave. In this regard it is useful to distinguish between contractual saving and discretionary saving. **Contractual saving** refers to the act of saving against agreed contracts (eg life assurance premiums, contributions to pension funds or retirement annuities). **Discretionary saving** is all current disposable income that is not spent or saved contractually. It includes, for example, deposits in savings accounts and fixed deposits. In South Africa contractual saving is quite substantial, but discretionary saving has been negative in recent years, since final consumption expenditure by households (financed in part by credit) plus contractual saving have regularly exceeded the disposable income of households.

A third point to be noted is that not all countries treat items such as spending on consumer durables, pension and life insurance contributions, social security, household interest payments, capital transfers and consumption of fixed capital in the same way. It has been found, for example, that adjusting for these factors significantly reduces the gap between saving rates in Japan and the United States.

Finally the basic lesson, therefore, is that data on saving should be interpreted with the utmost care, particularly when international comparisons are made. Moreover, the focus in macroeconomic analyses should be on total saving rather than on household saving only. As indicated in Table 2-5, the household saving rate in South Africa is very low and declined between 2000 and 2009. Part of this decline was counteracted by an increase in corporate saving (including consumption of fixed capital) but the total saving rate was still lower in 2009 than in 2000. At the same time it is obvious that government **dissaving** was still a serious problem in South Africa in the new millennium, although government did save in 2006, 2007 and 2008 (for the first time since 1981).

True, the statistics are not as good as we want them to be,
but what would we do without them?

Oskar Morgenstern

When figures are first published they grab headlines, put markets in a flutter, and give power to strange people … governments usually call an election to coincide with nicely improving economic statistics, …

The culprits are not imperfect statisticians but their gullible customers – economists, market-makers and journalists with an insatiable appetite for numbers and an eagerness to accuse governments of deception if figures are delayed …

There is clearly excess demand for statistics, so governments should flood the world with figures. They should daily put on to open computer access all of the many figures that become available daily. If there were daily trade balances and weekly inflation rates, the price of any single statistic (that is the value its interpreters attach to it) would healthily plummet. Students switching back from the classics could then tell economists that the words 'figure' and 'fictitious' come from the same Latin root.

The Economist, 19 September 1987

Statistics can be made to dance to any tune you want to play.

William Davis

Figures can't lie but liars can figure.

Anonymous

Chapter 3

Economic growth

Economists, business people and other observers are usually interested in the growth in total production or income rather than in the level of these variables. In other words, they are interested primarily in the rate of economic growth. The measurement of economic growth is no easy task, however. As one economist once put it, it is subject to the deficiencies of data (the shortcomings of GDP etc), the vagaries of valuation (the difficulties experienced in valuing various items), the aberrations of averages (the fact that a single average growth rate often conceals important underlying trends and structural changes) and the treacheries of timing (eg the impact of the business cycle (see Chapter 4)).

The growth performance of the economy is usually measured in terms of the growth in real gross domestic product (real GDP) or real GDP per capita. Nominal (or current-price) GDP cannot be used, since changes in nominal GDP reflect changes in prices (ie inflation) as well as changes in the volume of economic activity. Nominal GDP therefore has to be adjusted to obtain real GDP (or GDP at constant prices) before economic growth can be measured. In principle real GDP should also be expressed on a per capita basis by dividing it by the size of the population. In practice, however, economic growth is usually measured as the rate of change in real GDP rather than the rate of change in real GDP per capita. Other possible measures of economic growth will also be discussed in this chapter. First, the calculation of growth rates (or rates of change) requires some attention.

3.1   Calculating annual rates of change

Since economic growth is usually expressed as an annual rate, the calculation of annual rates (or the **annualisation** of rates) over different periods is explained in this section. An annual growth rate calculated over a period of less than a year indicates what will happen if that pace were sustained for a full 12 months.

The figures in Table 3-1 show quarterly and annual South African real GDP data for 2006 to 2009.

Table 3-1: Growth in South African GDP, 2006 to 2009

Year and quarter*	GDP at constant 2005 prices (Rm)	% change in real GDP at annual rate	
		Current period on previous period at annual rate (a)	Current period compared with same period of previous year (b)
2006 I	395 449	–	–
II	410 298	15,89	–
III	420 695	10,53	–
IV	432 679	11,89	–
Total	**1 659 121**	–	–
2007 I	421 249	–10,16	6,52
II	432 724	11,35	5,47
III	442 104	8,96	5,09
IV	454 062	11,27	4,94
Total	**1 750 139**	**5,49**	**5,49**
2008 I	438 553	–12,98	4,11
II	454 641	15,50	5,06
III	458 757	3,67	3,77
IV	462 570	3,37	1,87
Total	**1 814 521**	**3,68**	**3,68**
2009 I	435 389	–21,51	–0,72
II	442 169	6,38	–2,74
III	448 606	5,95	–2,21
IV	455 897	6,66	–1,44
Total	**1 782 061**	**–1,79**	**–1,79**

*   The quarterly figures are not seasonally adjusted. Strictly speaking, the rates for quarters in column (a) therefore cannot be compared to the rates in column (b). The primary aim, however, is to explain the methods used to calculate growth rates rather than to make inferences about the performance of the South African economy. At the same time the rates in column (a) clearly indicate the need for seasonal adjustment, which is discussed in the next chapter (see Box 4-1).

Source of basic data: SARB Quarterly Bulletin, March 2010.

The growth rate between any two successive periods, expressed as an annual rate, can be calculated with the aid of the following basic formula:

$$\% \text{ change between } t - 1 \text{ and } t = [(\frac{I_t}{I_{t-1}})^f - 1] \times 100$$

where I = variable in question (eg real GDP)
t – 1 = initial period (eg 2009 I)
t = current period (eg 2009 II)
f = frequency of time series (12 for monthly, 4 for quarterly and 1 for annual data)

For **quarterly data** the formula is thus:

$$[(\frac{I_t}{I_{t-1}})^4 - 1] \times 100 \dots\dots\dots(1)$$

and for **annual data** the formula is:

$$(\frac{I_t}{I_{t-1}} - 1) \times 100 \dots\dots\dots(2)$$

For example, the annual rate of growth in real GDP between the first and second quarters of 2009 is calculated as follows (using Formula (1)):

$$[(\frac{\text{Real GDP 2009 II}}{\text{Real GDP 2009 I}})^4 - 1] \times 100$$
$$= [(\frac{442\ 169}{435\ 389})4 - 1] \times 100 = (1,015574 - 1) \times 100$$
$$= (1,0638 - 1) \times 100$$
$$= 0,0638 \times 100$$
$$= 6,38\%$$

Likewise, the annual rate of growth in real GDP between the fourth quarter of 2008 and the first quarter of 2009 is calculated as follows:

$$= [(\frac{435\ 389}{462\ 570})^4 - 1] \times 100 = (0,94124 - 1) \times 100$$
$$= (0,7849 - 1) \times 100$$
$$= -0,2151 \times 100$$
$$= -21,51\%$$

You can use this formula to verify the other rates of growth between successive quarters provided in column (a) of Table 3-1. *Note that it is incorrect to simply multiply the rate of change between two successive quarters by four to obtain an annual rate.*

The growth rate in real GDP between successive annual totals is calculated with the aid of Formula (2). For example, the rate of change between the annual real GDP for 2009 and that for 2008 is calculated as follows:

$$[(\frac{I_t}{I_{t-1}})-1] \times 100 = (\frac{1\ 782\ 061}{1\ 814\ 521} - 1) \times 100$$
$$= (0,9821 - 1) \times 100$$
$$= -0,0179 \times 100$$
$$= -1,79\%$$

Likewise, the growth in real GDP between 2007 and 2008 was:

$$(\frac{1\ 814\ 521}{1\ 750\ 139} - 1) \times 100 = (1,0368 - 1) \times 100$$
$$= 0,0368 \times 100$$
$$= 3,68\%$$

Another way of obtaining an annual growth rate is to compare the figure for a period (say quarter or year) with the figure for the corresponding period in a previous year. In this case, the same basic formula as for annual data is used. For example, the rate of growth in real GDP between the first quarter of 2008 and the first quarter of 2009 is calculated as follows:

$$(\frac{\text{Real GDP 2009 I}}{\text{Real GDP 2008 I}} - 1) \times 100 = (\frac{435\ 389}{438\ 553} - 1) \times 100$$
$$= (0,9928 - 1) \times 100$$
$$= -0,0072 \times 100$$
$$= -0,72\%$$

Similarly, the annual rate of growth in real GDP between the last quarter of 2007 and the last quarter of 2008 can be calculated as follows:

$$(\frac{462\ 570}{454\ 062} - 1) \times 100 = (1,0187 - 1) \times 100$$
$$= 0,0187 \times 100$$
$$= 1,87\%$$

Use this formula to verify some of the other figures in column (b) of Table 3-1.

A similar type of formula can be used to calculate the **average annual growth rate in annual data over periods spanning more than one year**. Economists and decision makers often wish to calculate or compare average annual rates of growth over longer periods. The general formula is as follows:

$$[(\frac{I_t}{I_{t-k}})^{\frac{1}{k}} - 1] \times 100 \dots\dots\dots\dots\dots\dots\dots\dots\dots\dots\dots\dots\dots\dots\dots\dots\dots\dots\dots\dots\dots (3)$$

where t = final period (year)
   t − k = initial period (year)
      k = number of years over which the rate is calculated

For example, in South Africa real GDP was R1 659 121 million in 2006 and R1 782 061 million in 2009. The average annual growth in real GDP between 2006 and 2009 can be calculated as follows, using Formula (3):

$$[(\frac{\text{Real GDP 2009}}{\text{Real GDP 2006}})^{1/3} - 1] \times 100 = [(\frac{1\ 782\ 061}{1\ 659\ 121})^{1/3} - 1] \times 100$$
$$= [(1,07410)^{1/3} - 1)] \times 100$$
$$= (1,0241 - 1) \times 100$$
$$= 0,0241 \times 100$$
$$= 2,41\%$$

Note that this is an **unweighted** annual growth rate (for a period of three years), since only the data for the initial and final periods are taken into account. In the above example the figures for 2007 and 2008 are ignored. A more sophisticated method is to estimate a **weighted annual growth rate** by fitting a mathematical function to all the observations. In this way all the annual variations in growth rates are taken into account. Such calculations can be performed relatively easily with the aid of computing packages but a detailed explanation of the formulae and techniques falls beyond the scope of this book. This type of calculation is only required if one or both of the observations used for the calculation of the growth rate differ significantly from the long-run growth path. If there are no major deviations in the growth trend, Formula (3) will generally yield satisfactory results. Note, however, that *one cannot obtain an average annual growth rate by simply calculating the percentage change between the initial and final values and dividing the answer by the period (number of years) in question.* Neither can one calculate the growth rate for each year, add the growth rates and divide the result by the number of years.

Consider the following example:

Year	1	2	3	4	5	6	7
Value	100	110	110	125	130	150	160
Growth rate (%)	–	10,0	0,0	13,6	4,0	15,4	6,7

Over the period of six years from Year 1 to Year 7 the value grew from 100 to 160, that is, by 60%. The correct average annual growth rate, calculated according to Formula (3), is 8,1%. Dividing 60% by 6 yields an incorrect 10%. By adding the 6 growth rates and dividing by 6 we get 49,7/6 = 8,3%, which is closer to 8,1% but still incorrect. The data also show that one cannot add annual growth rates (49,7%) to obtain the cumulative growth over time (60%).

Box 3-1 indicates another possible pitfall when working with data on economic growth, while Box 3-2 reminds us of the possible impact of data revisions.

BOX 3-1: QUARTERLY ECONOMIC GROWTH AT A SEASONALLY ADJUSTED ANNUAL RATE: HANDLE WITH CARE

Economic growth is fundamentally a long-term phenomenon and should therefore in principle always be measured over a relatively long period. However, since GDP data become available quarterly and since there is enormous interest in short-term economic growth trends, growth rates for the latest quarter invariably receive a lot of publicity. But as was indicated in Table 3-1, annualised quarterly economic growth can be very erratic. Before such growth rates can be calculated, the original GDP data should be seasonally adjusted to eliminate possible seasonal influences such as the Christmas and Easter holidays (see Box 4-1).

The data in Table 3-1 were not seasonally adjusted, but even if they had been, a significant degree of variation would have remained and one should therefore be careful when calculating and interpreting economic growth over short periods.

Consider the following example: when Stats SA published the GDP estimate for the first quarter of 2010, the media reported an economic growth rate of 4,6%. This rate was obtained by comparing the seasonally adjusted figure for the first quarter of 2010 with the seasonally adjusted figure for the last quarter of 2009 and annualising the rate, using Formula (1). Although an annual rate, the 4,6% pertained to one quarter's growth only, and indicated what would happen if the growth in that quarter were to be sustained for a full year. If one compared the seasonally adjusted level of GDP in the first quarter of 2010 with the corresponding figure for the first quarter of 2009, using Formula (2), then a growth rate of 1,6% would have been obtained. The latter figure provides a better indication of the economic growth that had occurred, just as the figures in the last column of Table 3-1 are much more meaningful than those in the second-last column. Data pertaining to quarterly economic growth at a seasonally adjusted annual rate should be handled with extreme care.

BOX 3-2: THE IMPACT OF DATA REVISIONS

As explained in Chapter 2, agencies that supply data are usually under tremendous pressure to get the data out as quickly as possible. As a result, accuracy and completeness are inevitably sacrificed in order to produce timely data.

Annual and comprehensive (or benchmark) revisions may result in significant changes to the published data and therefore also to the growth rates based on these data. For example, Van Walbeek (whose study was cited in Box 2-3) found that the annual growth in real GDE for the first quarter of 1993, was originally estimated as 8,2% in the *SARB Quarterly Bulletin* of June 1993 but by March 1994 it had been revised to 3,9%. Likewise, the original growth rate for the second quarter of 1993 was revised from –11,5% in September 1993 to –3,0% by December 1994. The growth rate for the third quarter of 1993 was originally published as 15,7% in December 1993, but by December 1994 it had been revised to 9,7%. Numerous similar examples can be cited, particularly when the various components of GDP are examined separately. The moral of the story is that growth rates based on original estimates should always be treated as provisional estimates.

Having dealt with some technical aspects of calculating or estimating economic growth, we now turn to some other issues relating to the measurement of economic growth.

3.2   The appropriate basis for calculating economic growth

Which aggregate should be used to calculate economic growth? A nominal aggregate (expressed at current prices) is obviously inappropriate, but should real GDP, real GDP per capita, real GNI, real GNI per capita or any other measure of real aggregate economic activity be used to calculate economic growth?

The basic choice is between real GDP and real GNI. Recall, from Chapter 2, that GDP is a geographic concept which measures the total value of economic activity within the geographic boundaries of a country, while GNI measures the total production or income of the residents of a country on a worldwide basis (ie irrespective of where it occurs). The difference between the two is the net primary income to the rest of the world.

The choice seems relatively simple. If, on the one hand, one is interested in the volume of production within the boundaries of the country, real GDP should be used. If, on the other hand, one is interested in the economic welfare of the residents of a country, real GNI is more appropriate. There is, however, a technical complication which has to be borne in mind when the growth rates of real GDP and real GNI are calculated or interpreted.

The problem stems from the fact that GDP includes exports and excludes imports. When real GDP is estimated, changes in export prices are therefore taken into account but changes in import prices are effectively ignored (since imports do not form part of GDP). For example, when the price of gold increases, the value of gold production is adjusted for the price increase when real GDP is calculated. In other words, if the price of gold increases but the volume of gold production remains unchanged, nominal GDP will increase but real GDP will remain unchanged, *ceteris paribus* (ie other things being equal). But as long as import prices remain unchanged, the higher nominal value of gold exports will enable the country to afford a greater volume of imports than before, implying an increase in the volume of goods available for domestic consumption.

However, if the price of an important category of imported goods (eg oil) increases, real GDP will also be unaffected as long as the volume of oil imports remains unchanged, but such a price increase will mean that the country will, *ceteris paribus*, be able to afford a smaller volume of imports with the same volume of exports as before the price increase. Relative movements in export prices and import prices are therefore important. These relative movements are captured in the **terms of trade**, which are calculated as the ratio between export prices and import prices. The terms of trade are explained in Section 7.4. When export prices increase at a faster rate than import prices (ie when the terms of trade improve) the country can purchase a greater volume of imports with an unchanged volume of exports. Exactly the opposite occurs when import prices increase at a faster rate than export prices (ie when the terms of trade deteriorate). The country is then able to afford a smaller volume of imports for a fixed volume of exports (ie the volume of goods available for domestic consumption decreases).

These effects are not captured when real GDP is estimated. A massive increase in the gold price will leave real GDP unaffected, *ceteris paribus*, while a sharp rise in the oil price will also have no effect on real GDP, *ceteris paribus*. When export prices are rising rapidly relative to import prices, real GDP data tend to underestimate economic growth (and to overestimate inflation – see the discussion of implicit price deflators in Section 6.7). Likewise, when import prices are increasing rapidly relative to export prices, real GDP data tend to overestimate growth (and underestimate inflation).

In principle, the same problem should apply to real GNI, which also includes exports and excludes imports. In practice, however, national accountants make an adjustment for changes in the terms of trade when real GNI is estimated. This accounting convention is applied to arrive at better estimates of changes in the welfare of the nation (ie the residents of the country) – remember that the N in GNI refers to 'national'. Real GNI data thus indicate the volume of goods available for domestic consumption, while real GDP data indicate the volume of domestic output.

When export prices and import prices are increasing at roughly similar rates (ie when the terms of trade remain steady) real GDP data and real GNI data should yield approximately the same real growth rates (and inflation rates), since net factor payments (ie the difference between GNI and GDP) are relatively small and fairly stable. However, when the terms of trade are subject to large swings (as has often been the case in South Africa since the early 1970s) real GDP data and real GNI data can yield significantly different growth rates, as illustrated clearly in Table 3-2.

The above argument might seem quite complicated, but the important point to note is that the difference between real GDP and real GNI is not only the net primary income to the rest of the world. In estimating real GNI, the national accountants also make an adjustment for changes in terms of trade. When the terms of trade fluctuate significantly, real GNI is a better basis for calculating economic growth (or changes in national economic welfare) than real GDP.

Economists agree that changes in real GNI are a better measure of changes in **economic welfare** than changes in real GDP. The latter, however, remain the best indicator of changes in the level of domestic **economic activity** and therefore of changes in employment (and unemployment). In practice, real GDP is still the most popular basis for measuring economic growth, irrespective of the problems mentioned above, as well as those outlined in Section 2.7. Even the United States, Germany and Japan, which all traditionally favoured the use of GNI, switched their focus to GDP in the 1990s.

Table 3-2: Economic growth and changes in the terms of trade in South Africa, selected years

Years	Annual growth in		Change in terms of trade (%)
	Real GDP (%)	Real GNI (%)	
1973	4,6	13,0	18,8
1974	6,1	10,1	9,3
1975	1,7	−2,2	−8,6
1979	3,8	6,0	5,0
1980	6,6	10,6	12,0
1981	5,4	0,8	−12,7
1982	−0,4	−3,6	−11,6
1983	−1,8	−1,8	0,5
1984	5,1	6,8	5,6
1998	0,5	0,3	−2,5
1999	2,4	1,2	−3,7
2000	4,2	3,7	−2,5
2004	4,6	5,8	2,0

Source: SARB Quarterly Bulletin, various issues.

Although real GDP or GNI can serve as a yardstick for estimating economic growth, neither the rate of change in real GDP nor the rate of change in real GNI reflects the impact of economic growth on the average member of society. This problem can be eliminated by first expressing real GDP or GNI on a **per capita** basis. Per capita (or, more correctly, *per caput*) means per head or per person. Per capita data are thus ratios which express values in terms of averages per head of the population. The population can pertain to an area, country, sector or other category such as gender or level of education.

In principle it is very simple to calculate per capita data. The relevant economic variable is simply divided by the appropriate population figure. When comparing annual flows (eg real GDP) to the population, it is preferable to use mid-year population estimates (rather than the estimates of the population at the beginning or end of the year). When comparing a stock (eg the number of houses, hospital beds or television receivers) to the population, both figures should pertain to the same date.

Per capita data are only as reliable as their components (ie the numerator and the denominator). As far as real GDP per capita is concerned, some of the problems associated with real GDP (the numerator) have already been discussed in this chapter and the previous one. Even population data (the denominator) can be subject to a large margin of error, as was illustrated by the 1996 population census in South Africa (see Section 5.1). In the case of economic growth, however, the **rate of change** in the population is more important than its absolute **level**. For example, in South Africa the rate of population growth is approximately 1%. This implies that real GDP or GNI has to increase by more than 1% before an increase in real GDP or GNI per capita is recorded. According to the SARB real GDP per capita in South Africa fell in 10 of the 17 years from 1982 to 1998. Incidentally, the SARB estimated that the level of South African real GDP per capita was at about the same level in 2004 as in 1974.

Table 3-3 shows the growth in real GDP per capita and real GNI per capita in selected periods, along with the corresponding growth in real GDP and real GNI. See also Box 3-3.

Table 3-3: Growth in real GDP per capita, real GNI per capita,
**   real GDP and real GNI, selected periods***

Period	Annual percentage growth in			
	Real GDP per capita	Real GNI per capita	Real GDP	Real GNI
1966-1970	2,3	2,8	5,1	5,6
1971-1975	1,0	3,8	3,6	6,6
1976-1980	0,5	1,4	3,1	4,0
1981-1985	−1,2	−2,3	1,4	0,2
1986-1990	−0,7	−0,8	1,7	1,6
1991-1995	−1,3	−1,2	0,8	1,2
1996-2000	0,7	0,2	2,7	2,2
2001-2005	2,2	2,7	3,8	4,4
2006-2009	2,0	2,8	3,2	4,0

*   Growth rates are average annual rates for the periods.

Source: *SARB Quarterly Bulletin,* June 1994, March 2000, 2005 and 2010.

BOX 3-3: FURTHER COMMENTS ON PER CAPITA DATA

Per capita data are **averages** per head of the population and therefore provide no information on the **distribution** of the variable(s) in question. For example, real GDP per capita only reflects real production or income per person. The distribution of income may be very unequal, in which event per capita data may convey a totally incorrect picture of the level of or changes in the average standard of living of the population. Kuwait, for example, has one of the highest levels of per capita real income in the world, but it does not follow that the average citizen in Kuwait is better off than the average citizens in countries with a lower per capita real income. Most of the income in Kuwait could accrue to a limited number of people. By the same token, a year-on-year increase in real GDP per capita does not imply that the material living standards of all citizens have improved. (A fall in real GDP per capita, however, does indicate that at least some of the population are worse off than before.)

As mentioned in the text, the absolute **level** of a per capita figure is only as meaningful or reliable as the numerator and the denominator of the ratio. For example, depending on the extent of unrecorded economic activity, per capita GDP may be a serious underestimation of the actual average income per head. This drawback is particularly important in international comparisons because of the variation in the relative size of the unrecorded sector between countries and differences in the treatment of this sector in the national accounts. Further problems in respect of international comparisons are discussed in Chapter 12.

Another problem which made it difficult to estimate per capita values in South Africa between 1976 and 1994 is that South African population figures during this period did not cover the independent national states (Transkei, Bophuthatswana, Venda and Ciskei), while the national accounting data included these areas. The numerator or the denominator thus had to be adjusted before meaningful ratios could be calculated, thereby introducing a further source of error.

A further aspect which requires some attention when growth rates are calculated is the **period** for which the calculation is carried out. Economic growth (or decline) does not occur smoothly. Instead it usually follows a cyclical pattern of upswings and downswings, called the **business cycle** (see Chapter 4). If growth is measured from the trough of one cycle to the peak of a next cycle, the result is an overestimation of the long-run trend. However, if the growth is measured from the peak of one cycle to the trough of a later cycle, the result is an underestimation of the long-run trend. It is always difficult to separate the cyclical and long-run influences, particularly with recent data. Nevertheless, it is in principle always advisable to measure economic growth over fairly long periods, using the technique for calculating growth rates over periods of longer than one year explained in the previous section, and to avoid using starting and end years that represent different phases of the business cycle.

A related problem is the issue of **structural breaks** in growth trends. When selecting an appropriate period over which a long-run growth rate is to be estimated, one should first attempt to establish whether there has been a structural change in the long-run trend. The existence of structural changes can be investigated by plotting the basic data on a semi-logarithmic scale, which is explained in the next section.

Some further technical issues pertaining to growth rates are dealt with in Box 3-4.

BOX 3-4: FURTHER TECHNICAL ISSUES RELATED TO GROWTH RATES

During inflationary periods the rate of growth in nominal GDP (the nominal growth rate) is significantly higher than the rate of growth in real GDP (the real growth rate). The real growth rate is often approximated as the difference between the nominal growth rate and the inflation rate. Although this is a useful rule of thumb, it is not fully accurate. Consider the following example.

Suppose the nominal growth rate is 10% and the inflation rate is 6%. The real growth rate is then approximately equal to the nominal growth rate (10%) minus the inflation rate (6%). The resulting real growth rate of 4% is only approximately correct. It can be shown that the correct rate is obtained as follows:

Real growth rate = [(1 + nominal growth rate)/(1 + inflation rate) – 1] x 100
                   = [(1,10/1,06) – 1] x 100
                   = (1,0377 – 1) x 100
                   = 0,0377 x 100
                   = 3,8%

Growth is an **exponential phenomenon** which occurs off an ever-changing base. If consumer spending increases by 1% per month, the total increase over a full year will be 12,7%, not 12%. Each month spending is 1% greater than the previous month and each percentage increase is calculated (compounded) from a higher base. A rate of 12,7% a year is thus the same as 1% a month annualised. An **annualised change** is the change which would occur if the change in any period shorter than 12 months were to continue for exactly 12 months. Note that the same principle applies to the difference between compound interest and simple interest (see Section 9.2).

The exponential nature of growth can also be illustrated by considering longer periods. For example, at an annual growth rate of 1,5% a variable will double in about 46 years. At 3% it will double in about 23 years. Before World War II no country could sustain an average annual growth rate of more than 2,3% in real per capita income, but after World War II some countries achieved per capita growth rates of more than 8,0% per annum. The difference between 2,3% growth and 8,0% growth can be illustrated by pointing out that, at 2,3% growth per capita, real income approximately doubles every 30 years (ie every generation). At such a growth rate children will therefore become twice as rich as their parents, but at 8% annual real per capita growth children will become ten times as rich as their parents (ie per capita real income will increase tenfold over a period of 30 years).

There is a convenient way of figuring out approximately how long it takes for any quantity or value to double if a particular exponential growth rate is applied to that quantity or value. It is to divide the number 70 by the percentage growth rate. Thus if the population is growing at 2,0% per annum, it will double in approximately 35 years (= 70/2). If the growth rate rises to 3%, the doubling time drops to 23+ years (70/3). This is often referred to as the 'rule of 70' or, more precisely, the 'rule of 72'.[1]

The following table provides some examples of precisely how long it takes for a variable increasing at a constant rate to double. Note that the rule of thumb supplied in the previous paragraph yields remarkably good results compared to the precise figures. The first column shows the rate at which the variable is increasing, while the second column shows the corresponding doubling time. For example, if the rate of increase is 2% per annum, the doubling time is 35 years. Likewise, if the rate of increase is 2% per month, the doubling time is 35 months.

The third and fourth columns show the annualised rates if the rate in the first column is a quarterly and a monthly rate respectively. For example, a variable increasing at a rate of 2% per quarter is increasing at an annual (or annualised) rate of 8,2%. Likewise, a variable increasing at a rate of 2% per month is increasing at an annualised rate of 26,8%.

Observed rate (%)	Doubling time	Annualised rate (%) if the observed rate is	
		Quarterly	Monthly
0,1	693,5	0,4	1,2
0,5	139,0	2,0	6,2
1,0	69,7	4,1	12,7
1,5	46,6	6,1	19,6
2,0	35,0	8,2	26,7
2,5	28,1	10,4	34,5
3,0	23,4	12,6	42,6
3,5	20,1	14,8	51,1
4,0	17,7	17,0	60,1
4,5	15,7	19,3	69,6
5,0	14,2	21,6	79,6
6,0	11,9	26,2	101,2
7,0	10,2	31,1	125,2
8,0	9,0	36,0	151,8
9,0	8,0	41,2	181,3
10,0	7,3	46,4	213,8
15,0	5,0	74,9	435,0
20,0	3,8	107,4	791,6

Source: *The Economist, 1994, Guide to economic indicators.* London: Hamish Hamilton: 20.

The previous-year comparison error

Percentage changes can be calculated from one period or date to the next or between the present period and the same period of the previous year. The data below, which show the index of the physical value of manufacturing production (2005 = 100), illustrate how these two types of change (respectively called current rates and previous-year comparisons) can yield completely different results.

Volume of manufacturing production (2005=100)		
Quarter	2008	2009
I	112,2	96,5
II	115,0	94,5
III	111,5	96,3
IV	103,6	99,6

For the third and fourth quarters of 2009 the following growth rates can be calculated:

Year and quarter	Percentage change	
	Quarter on same quarter of previous year	Quarter on previous quarter at an annual rate
2009 III	−13,6	7,8
2009 IV	−3,9	14,4

The previous-year comparisons in the third and fourth quarters of 2009 indicate declines (negative signs) although there had been an upswing from the third quarter of 2009. By contrast, current rates immediately register positive rates of change. In the case of downturns a similar tendency is evident (in the opposite direction). Current comparisons, however, may be quite unstable if the variable that is measured is quite volatile.

Stepped rates of change

When calculating current rates of change for a time series with a frequency of less than a year, one must be aware of the possibility of stepped changes (increases/ decreases) in the time series. This situation occurs, for example, when all the components of the time series are not measured regularly for every period. Some components may be collected or changed less frequently than others (see the discussion on the consumer price index in Chapter 6). This can significantly distort current-period comparisons. In fact, even previous-year comparisons may be affected, since a few large changes in monthly data may be recorded, instead of smaller, more regular ones. The previous-year rate of change will not be affected as much as the annualised current rate of change but the effect will last longer. The same applies in the case of any other outlier value in a time series.[2]

1. The basis for this rule of thumb is as follows: let y_o be the initial value of a variable, y_t the value of the variable in period t, and g the growth rate per period (expressed as a fraction, not a percentage), then

$$y_t = y_o e^{gt}$$
where e is the base of the natural logarithm (e ≈ 2,71828)
The time it takes for y_o to double to $2y_o$ is given by t* so that $2y_o = y_o e^{gt}$
The value of t* which solves this equation is t* = log2/g ≈ 0,7/g, since log 2 ≈ 0,7.

Thus, for a growth rate of 2% or 0,02 the doubling time is 0,7/0,02 = 35. Multiplying the denominator and the numerator by 100 yields 70/2 which is again 35.

2. See PJ Mohr, C van der Merwe, ZC Botha and EJ Inggs, 1995, *The practical guide to South African economic indicators* (second edition), Johannesburg: Lexicon:112-114.

3.3   Graphic representation of economic growth

When examining time-series data it is always useful to plot the data on a graph. To obtain a visual impression of the **growth** in a variable, it is preferable to plot the data in a chart with the vertical axis (y-axis) measured in terms of logarithms (ie on a logarithmic or ratio scale) instead of the more customary arithmetic scale. **Arithmetic scales** have the same distance (eg in centimetres) between two points when the absolute difference between one set of numbers is the same as the difference between another set of numbers, irrespective of the absolute value of the numbers. For example, the difference between 10 and 100 is the same as the distance between 100 and 190, or between 190 and 280. In each case the absolute difference is 90. On a **logarithmic (or ratio) scale**, however, equal intervals represent equal differences in the logarithms of the numbers (or in the ratios between them). On a logarithmic scale, therefore, the distance between 10 and 100 is the same as the distance between 100 and 1 000 since the ratio of the two numbers is ten to one in both cases. Thus, whereas arithmetic scales are used to illustrate absolute changes, logarithmic (log) or ratio scales are used to illustrate relative changes. The advantage of a log scale is that it enables the user to read both the absolute numbers (plotted on the y-axis) and the rates of change simultaneously. A graph which contains a logarithmic vertical scale is called a **semi-logarithmic (or semi-log) graph**.

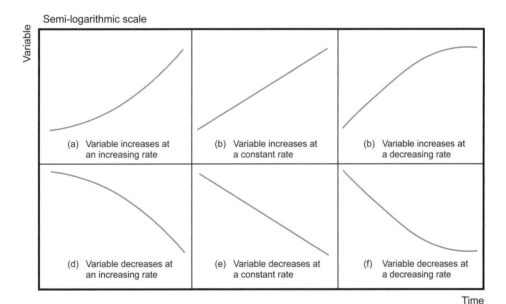

Figure 3-1: Typical patterns of semi-logarithmic graphs

On a semi-logarithmic graph a straight line represents a **constant percentage change** over the period, whereas a straight line on an ordinary arithmetic graph represents a constant absolute change. The steeper the line, the greater the percentage change. The six typical patterns of semi-logarithmic graphs are illustrated in Figure 3-1 above. Note, in particular, that an increase at a decreasing rate (as illustrated in (c)) still amounts to an increase in absolute terms (ie the numbers are still increasing). In fact, the **absolute** change may even increase from one period to the next, but because the base figure on which the rate of change is based changes each time, the **percentage** change falls. This is yet another aspect of the crucial distinction between **levels** and **rates of change** which is emphasised in various places in this book.

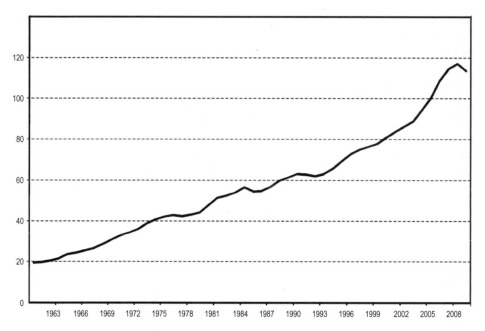

Figure 3-2: Index of annual real private consumption expenditure, 1960-2009 (2005 = 100), arithmetic scale

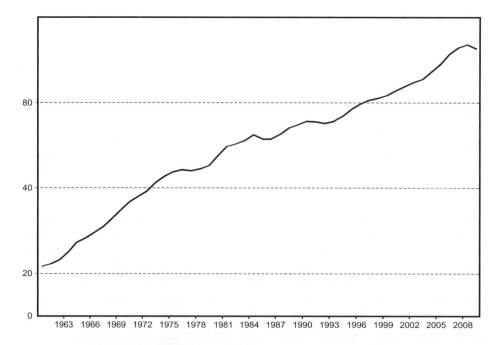

Figure 3-3: Index of annual real private consumption expenditure, 1960-2009 (2005 = 100), logarithmic scale

The difference between an ordinary arithmetic graph and a semi-logarithmic graph is illustrated in Figures 3-2 and 3-3. Figure 3-2 shows the index of real private consumption expenditure in South Africa for the period 1960-2009 (2005 = 100) on an ordinary graph, while Figure 3-3 shows the same information plotted on a semi-logarithmic graph. Note how the logarithmic scale telescopes along the y-axis. A doubling of the value on the y-axis is always represented by the same distance (eg 20 to 40 = 40 to 80) as shown in Figure 3-3. Figure 3-2 shows that the level of real private consumption expenditure increased fairly steadily between 1960 and 2009. Figure 3-3, on the other hand, shows that the rate of increase in this variable did not change much.

Semi-logarithmic graphs also help to avoid the illusion of increased **variablility** (or **volatility**) in a time series and to identify possible **structural breaks** in a growth trend. On an ordinary scale a variable with a positive long-run trend might appear to be exhibiting increased volatility since the **absolute changes** increase over time. A semi-logarithmic graph, however, keeps the variability (expressed as the ratio of the actual numbers to the long-run trend) visually in proportion because it relates the absolute changes to the level of the variable. Possible breaks in trends can therefore be identified by examining the series graphically using a semi-log scale.

3.4   Analysing economic growth from the expenditure side

As mentioned in the previous chapter, real GDP is estimated and published from both the expenditure side and the production side. The data published in the relevant tables in the *SARB Quarterly Bulletin* can therefore be used to obtain an indication of the contribution of each component of aggregate spending (expenditure side) or of each sector or kind of economic activity (production side) to economic growth.

Table 3-4: Annual growth in expenditure on gross domestic product
at constant 2005 prices, 2006-2009

Component/aggregate	Annual percentage change			
	2006	2007	2008	2009
Final consumption expenditure by households	8,3	5,5	2,4	–3,1
Final consumption expenditure by general government	4,9	4,7	4,9	4,7
Gross capital formation	12,9	12,2	3,4	–5,7
Gross fixed capital formation	12,1	14,2	11,7	2,3
Gross domestic expenditure	**8,6**	**6,4**	**3,3**	**–1,8**
Exports of goods and services	7,5	5,9	2,4	–19,5
Imports of goods and services	18,3	9,0	1,4	–17,4
Expenditure on gross domestic product	**5,6**	**5,5**	**3,7**	**–1,8**

Source: SARB Quarterly Bulletin, March 2010.

Table 3-4 shows the annual real growth in the main components of final demand. The elements of the table are basically the same as those of Table 2-2, except that the emphasis is now on **rates of change** rather than on the levels of the variables. Another difference is that the data on which Table 3-4 is based are at constant 2005 prices (ie in **real** terms), whereas the data in Table 2-2 are at current prices (ie in **nominal** terms). Gross fixed capital formation and the change in inventories have been combined to obtain gross capital formation, but gross fixed capital formation is also shown separately. The annual change in the **residual item** has been omitted since it makes no real sense to calculate growth rates in respect of this item. It should be noted, however, that although the **level** of the residual item is relatively insignificant, **changes** in the real values of the residual item may make a significant 'contribution' to the overall growth in real GDE and real GDP. For example, in 2009 the real value of the residual item was R10 874 million, compared to R4 177 million in 2008, that is, an increase of R6 697 million. Had it remained unchanged, the decline in real GDE would have been 2,2% (instead of the 1,8% actually recorded), while the decline in real GDP would also have been 2,2% (instead of the 1,8% actually recorded). Although this is technically not the correct way of looking at it (recall that the residual item accounts for any discrepancies in the estimation of GDP using the production and expenditure methods), the example illustrates the point that changes in the real value of the residual item can have a significant statistical impact. It is therefore not surprising that analysts sometimes disparagingly remark that 'a change in the residual item has been the main cause of the growth or decline in real GDP'. The annual change in the change in inventories can have a similar impact to the change in the residual item and therefore needs to be scrutinised closely when economic growth is analysed. For example, if the level of inventories had remained unchanged in 2009, both GDE growth and GDP growth would have been positive instead of negative (in real terms).

Note from Table 3-4 that the growth in capital formation and exports and imports can be quite volatile. Also note that high rates of growth in fixed capital formation are accompanied by high rates of growth in imports. This is a significant feature of the South African economy. Whenever the rate of capital formation increases, imports also accelerate, since a large proportion of South African imports consist of capital goods (see Section 7.2). This link between capital formation (or investment spending) and import spending is a key element of the balance of payments constraint which has often constrained economic activity and economic policy in South Africa.

3.5   Analysing economic growth from the production side

Table 3-5 provides an example of the examination of economic growth from the production side. It shows the annual real growth in the output of the different kinds of economic activity. Note, for example, the large fluctuations in the real growth of agriculture, forestry and fishing (agriculture for short). When interpreting figures such as these, the **rates of change** always have to be interpreted along with the levels of the different components. The percentage contributions of the different kinds of economic activity in 2009 (at current prices) are indicated in Table 2-1. Although the real output of agriculture is subject to sharp fluctuations, the contribution of this kind of economic activity to real GDP (ie at constant prices) is relatively small (2,5% in 2009). The impact of the swings in real agricultural production (eg the change from a decline of 5,5% in 2006 to a growth of 3,5% in 2007, or from a growth of 10,9% in 2008 to a decline of 3,2% in 2009) is thus smaller than the magnitude of the swings would seem to indicate at first glance. Nevertheless, the impact can still be significant. For example, if real agricultural production had remained at the same level in 2008 as in 2007 (instead of increasing by 10,9%), the growth in real GDP at basic prices in 2008 would, *ceteris paribus*, have been 3,6% instead of the 3,8% actually recorded. The real growth in manufacturing production usually tends to be more stable than the real growth in agricultural production (except in 2009!), but a small change in the growth in manufacturing has a relatively large impact on the overall growth rate since manufacturing comprises about a sixth of real GDP at basic prices.

Table 3-5: Rates of change in real contributions of different kinds of economic activity to gross value added (or GDP) at constant 2005 prices, 2006-2009

Kind of economic activity	Annual percentage change			
	2006	**2007**	**2008**	**2009**
Agriculture, forestry and fishing	–5,5	3,5	10,9	–3,2
Mining and quarrying	–0,6	0,0	–5,4	–7,2
Manufacturing	6,4	5,0	2,7	–10,7
Electricity, gas and water	3,4	3,4	1,0	–0,5
Construction (contractors)	10,4	14,3	0,3	7,8
Wholesale and retail trade, catering and accommodation	6,0	5,3	1,1	–2,9
Transport, storage and communication	5,1	6,3	3,9	0,5
Financial intermediation, insurance, real estate and business services	9,6	7,9	7,9	1,3
Community, social and personal services	3,7	4,5	4,0	3,8
Gross value added at basic prices	**5,5**	**5,5**	**3,8**	**–1,5**

Source: SARB Quarterly Bulletin, March 2010.

Data from the production side are also required to examine long-run structural changes in the economy. Table 3-6 shows how the contributions of the various sectors and subsectors to South African GDP changed from 1950 to 2009. Note, in particular, the persistent decline in the contribution of agriculture, forestry and fishing, the volatility of the contribution of the mining sector, the fairly steady contribution of manufacturing and the sharp growth in the share of the services sector, particularly financial and government services. Similar trends have been recorded in other countries during their process of economic development.

Table 3-6: Percentage contribution by kind of economic activity to total gross value added at basic prices

Sector and subsectors	1950	1960	1970	1980	1990	2000	2009
Primary sector	28,8	23,6	15,9	26,8	13,8	10,8	12,8
Agriculture, forestry and fishing	16,0	11,2	7,2	6,2	4,6	3,3	3,0
Mining and quarrying	12,7	12,4	8,8	20,6	9,2	7,6	9,7
Secondary sector	23,0	25,5	29,4	27,8	30,9	24,2	21,4
Manufacturing	18,2	20,1	22,8	21,6	23,6	19,0	15,1
Electricity, gas and water	1,7	2,4	2,5	3,0	4,0	2,7	2,4
Construction	3,1	3,0	4,1	3,2	3,3	2,5	3,9
Tertiary sector	48,3	50,9	54,7	45,4	55,3	64,9	65,8
Wholesale, retail and motor trade, catering and accommodation	14,5	13,9	14,4	11,6	14,3	14,6	13,3
Transport, storage and communication	9,1	9,9	9,4	8,5	8,3	9,6	9,5
Finance, insurance, real-estate and business services	9,3	10,6	14,3	10,9	13,7	18,6	21,7
Community, social and personal services	15,4	16,5	16,6	14,4	19,1	22,0	21,3
Gross value added at basic prices	100	100	100	100	100	100	100

Source: SARB Quarterly Bulletin, March 2010 (Supplement).

Regional economic growth

As mentioned in Box 2-2, Stats SA also publishes annual estimates of GDP by province, albeit with a significant lag. The GGP or GDPR of each province is sometimes included in *Statistical release P0441* which contains quarterly GDP data. At the time of writing, the most recent available data were those for 2007, published on 24 February 2009, along with GDP data for the fourth quarter of 2008. Table 3-7 contains the estimated real growth rates for the nine provinces for 2007 and for the period from 1997 to 2007, along with the absolute levels of nominal GDP for each province and the percentage contributions of each to total GDP in 2007. These data provide an indication of both the size (*level*) of GDP in the various provinces as well as their respective growth *rates*. Note the large contributions of Gauteng, KwaZulu-Natal and the Western Cape, along with their relatively high growth rates.

Along with the aggregate figures, Stats SA also publishes breakdowns of the GDP of each province by kind of economic activity, at both current and constant prices.

Table 3-7: Levels and growth of GDP (or GGP) per province, selected periods

Province	Growth in real GDP (% per annum)		Level of GDP at current prices, 2007	
	2007	1997-2007	R millions	% of total GDP
Western Cape	5,7	4,1	290 607	14,5
Eastern Cape	4,7	3,0	155 520	7,8
Northern Cape	3,3	2,5	44 159	2,2
Free State	4,1	2,3	108 892	5,4
KwaZulu-Natal	5,2	3,6	324 216	16,2
North West	3,7	2,3	120 972	6,5
Gauteng	5,7	4,1	668 926	33,5
Mpumalanga	4,2	3,1	138 732	6,9
Limpopo	4,4	3,9	138 163	6,9

Source: *Statistics South Africa, Statistical release P0441, 24 February 2009.*

Any figure that looks interesting is probably wrong.

Motto of the British Central Statistical Office

To measure is to know.

Lord Kelvin

If you can't measure it, measure it anyway.

Milton Friedman

Chapter 4

Business cycles

The first question people usually ask about the economy is: 'What is happening to the economy?' or 'How is the economy performing?' This is usually followed by 'What is going to happen?' 'What are the country's economic prospects?' 'Are we going to experience a recession?' All these questions relate to a phenomenon called the business cycle. In this chapter various aspects of the business cycle are discussed, including possible ways of forecasting economic activity.

4.1 Definitions

Economic growth (or decline) does not occur smoothly. Periods of rapid growth or expansion are invariably followed by periods of lower growth or decline. The **business cycle** refers to the fluctuations in the overall level or pace of economic activity. Sometimes also called the **trade cycle**, it can be defined as the pattern of expansion (recovery) and contraction (recession) in economic activity relative to its long-term trend. One complete cycle, which usually lasts a number of years, consists of four elements: a **trough**, an **upswing** or **expansion** (often called a **boom**), a **peak**, and a **downswing** or **contraction** (often called a **recession**). The different elements of the business cycle are illustrated in Figure 4-1.

A full cycle in aggregate economic activity is called a **reference cycle**. Thus, when people want to know whether the economy is in an expansionary phase or in a recession, they are inquiring into the position of the economy in terms of the reference cycle. Apart from the aggregate movement in economic activity, each individual time series (eg the physical value of agricultural production, the number of new motorcars sold, real merchandise imports) exhibits a cyclical pattern. In contrast to the reference cycle, a **specific cycle** is a full cycle exhibited by such an individual time series. As will become clear later, the reference cycle is actually an 'average' of a large number of specific cycles.

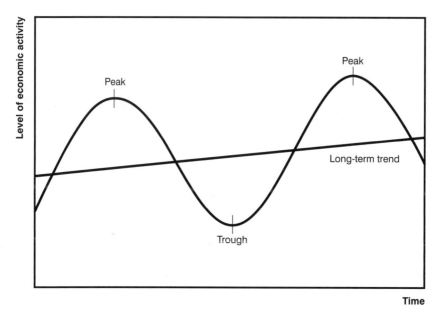

Figure 4-1: Idealised business cycle

4.2 Determining the turning points of the reference cycle

At first glance identification of the peaks and troughs of the reference cycle (ie the turning points of the fluctuations in aggregate economic activity) appears to be a relatively simple task. Surely all that is required is an examination of the movements in real GDP which is, after all, the measure of the level of aggregate economic activity. But the matter is not so simple. As will be explained shortly, the isolation of the cyclical component of any time series (including real GDP) requires that the series first be decomposed into its different components. Even when this has been done, changes in a broad-based aggregate such as real GDP do not necessarily capture the changes in the different sectors of the economy. For example, changes in real GDP are strongly influenced by large changes in agricultural production, which could create a distorted picture of the general trend in economic activity. Another drawback is that the first preliminary estimates of real GDP only become available after a significant time lag. Historic movements in real GDP also do not provide a sound basis for forecasting possible future changes. To analyse business cycles and to predict movements in aggregate economic activity, different techniques and more recent data are required. Of course, movements in real GDP have to be taken into account but such movements do not provide sufficient information to date the turning points of the cycle and to predict where the economy is heading.

Determining the dates of the troughs and peaks of the reference cycle is quite a complicated task. In South Africa this task is undertaken by the SARB. The turning points of the post-war South African business cycle, as estimated by the SARB, are provided in Table 4-1.

In this section we provide a brief summary of some of the methods which can be used to determine these turning points. But before this can be done, some observations about the components of a time series are called for.

A **time series** is a set of observations of a phenomenon taken at different points in time or over different periods, usually at fixed intervals (eg weekly, monthly, quarterly, annually). Time-series data are distinguished from **cross-section data**. Whereas a time series is ordered according to time, cross-section data are for a particular moment or period and are ordered according to criteria other than time (eg age, gender, geographic location, education level).

There is also a third type of data, called **panel data**, which has become increasingly popular in recent years. A **panel** is a cross section or group of people, firms, countries, etc that are observed or surveyed periodically. Panel data, also called longitudinal data or cross-sectional time-series data, are thus a combination of time-series data and cross-section data obtained by 'pooling' the two types of data.

A time series can exhibit four types of variation: **trend, cycles** (or **cyclical variations**), **seasonal variations** and **random variations.**

- **Trend** (T) is the long-term pattern or movement of a time series. In economic time series the long run is a period which spans at least one complete business cycle.

- **Cyclical variations or cycles** (C) are non-periodic recurring fluctuations around the long-run trend which are usually associated with business cycles.

- **Seasonal variations** (S) occur within a year and are variations in the level of the variable which recur from year to year. The term does not necessarily refer to the climatic seasons of the year. It may refer, for example, to holidays, pay practices and tax deadlines, as well as to weather conditions. Retail sales, for example, tend to exhibit sharp increases during the Christmas and Easter periods (see Box 4-1).

- **Random or irregular variations** (I) are the erratic and unpredictable variations in time-series data as a result of a myriad of unpredictable disturbances (eg strikes, natural disasters, political developments). They are specific to a certain point in time or period and include any variation in a time series that is not described by the first three components.

BOX 4-1: SEASONALITY AND SEASONAL ADJUSTMENT

There is considerable seasonal fluctuation in economic activity during the course of the year as a result of factors such as weather changes, holidays, model changes, tax deadlines and pay practices (eg payment of bonuses). These fluctuations affect different industries or sectors at different times of the year and at differing rates.

For example, consumer spending tends to increase during the Christmas and Easter holidays, but at the same time the rate of manufacturing production tends to decline, since factories either close down for the holidays or work reduced shifts. The seasonal variations in agricultural production require no explanation.

The existence of seasonal fluctuations means that all indicators which are measured for periods shorter than one year (eg daily, weekly, monthly and quarterly) have to be adjusted for seasonal movements before meaningful comparisons can be made (for periods shorter than a year). Failure to do so may result in seasonal lows and highs during the year being interpreted as basic changes in the economy. In the case of annual data this problem is not encountered, since the seasonal factor averages out over a period of twelve months.

The elimination of the seasonal variation in a time series is called seasonal adjustment. Probably the most popular technique for seasonal adjustment is the X – 11 Variant of the Census Method II Seasonal Adjustment Program, developed by the Bureau of Census of the United States Department of Commerce. An explanation of this surprisingly ad hoc method falls beyond the scope of this book. The important point is that one should always check whether data with a frequency of less than a year have been seasonally adjusted. See Box 3-1 and the discussion in Section 6.4 on the use of the consumer price index to calculate an inflation rate.

The four components $(T, C, S$ and $I)$ combine in two basic ways to generate a time series. Using the symbol Y_t to indicate a time series observation (with the subscript t denoting the time variable), the two basic time series models can be written as follows:

Multiplicative model: $\quad Y_t = T_t\,C_t\,S_t\,I_t$
Additive model: $\qquad\quad Y_t = T_t + C_t + S_t + I_t$

The multiplicative model is generally used for economic time series because these series usually exhibit exponential trends and because the various influences are usually interrelated rather than independent of each other. To isolate the cyclical variation (C_t) in such a time series, all the other components $(T_t, S_t$ and $I_t)$ have to be estimated and eliminated by division. This leaves the cyclical variation:

$$\frac{Y_t}{T_t S_t I_t} = \frac{T_t C_t S_t I_t}{T_t S_t I_t} = C_t$$

The techniques for estimating and eliminating the various components of a time series fall beyond the scope of this book.[1]

As mentioned earlier, the measurement of the business cycle (ie the estimation of the turning points of the reference cycle) is not a simple task. Measuring the direction and changes in aggregate economic activity is difficult because the different elements of total

---

1.   The interested reader is referred to P J Mohr, *et al*, 1995. *The practical guide to South African economic indicators*, Johannesburg: Lexicon.

economic activity do not move in concert or change at the same rate. In any given period, for example, some sectors grow while others stagnate, and some change faster than others.

One possible method of estimating the turning points of the reference cycle is to examine a national accounting aggregate such as GDP and to identify its cyclical component. This is called the **composite series method**. However, as pointed out earlier, GDP figures are of limited value as an aid to analysing business cycles.

A more satisfactory and more useful approach is to analyse as many individual time series as possible. The cyclical component of each time series is isolated and this information is then combined to form a picture of the general business cycle. This approach is used by researchers at the South African Reserve Bank to determine the turning points of the South African reference cycle. These turning points are called **reference turning points** or **reference dates**. The reference turning points of the post-war South African business cycles are listed in Table 4-1. Note, again, that the reference cycle is an 'average' of all the specific cycles analysed.

Table 4-1: Post-war business cycles in South Africa

Lower turning point (trough)	Length of expansion (months)	Upper turning point (peak)	Length of contraction (months)	Length of cycle: trough to trough (months)
Jul 1945	12	Jul 1946	9	21
Apr 1947	19	Nov 1948	15	34
Feb 1950	22	Dec 1951	15	37
Mar 1953	25	Apr 1955	17	42
Sep 1956	16	Jan 1958	14	30
Mar 1959	13	Apr 1960	16	29
Aug 1961	44	Apr 1965	8	52
Dec 1965	17	May 1967	7	24
Dec 1967	36	Dec 1970	20	56
Aug 1972	24	Aug 1974	40	64
Dec 1977	44	Aug 1981	19	63
Mar 1983	15	Jun 1984	21	36
Mar 1986	35	Feb 1989	51	86
May 1993	42	Nov 1996	33	75
Aug 1999	99	Nov 2007	–*	–*

*   – means that the next trough was not yet finalised at that stage.

Source: *SARB Quarterly Bulletin,* March 2010.

Reference turning points are determined more or less as follows:

- All available time series are collected. At the time of writing the SARB used almost 200 individual time series, ranging from real GDP to the physical volume of cement production and the average monthly wages and salaries paid by certain large employers.

- If necessary, some of the series are first adjusted for such factors as price changes and the number of working days in each month or quarter.

- Each individual series is then analysed to isolate the cyclical component and determine the turning points. These turning points are called **specific turning points** (or the turning points of **specific cycles**).

- The information on specific turning points now has to be assembled to determine the **reference turning points** (ie the turning points of the **reference cycle**). Two broad techniques are usually used for this purpose: the cluster of turning points and diffusion indices.

- The **cluster of turning points** involves using a sufficiently large number of specific turning points of time series to represent all the various economic sectors. Concentrations of peaks and troughs at particular points in time are then taken as indications of reference turning points.

- A **diffusion index** is a measure of the distribution of changes in a number of time series occurring within a particular period. The value of the index for a particular month is obtained, for example, by expressing the number of time series which exhibited an increase as a percentage of the total number of time series investigated. For each series that remained unchanged ½ is added to the number exhibiting an increase. A variation of this method is to subtract the percentage of series exhibiting a decrease from the percentage which showed an increase during the period concerned. Diffusion indices can also be weighted to allow for the relative importance of the various time series.

- As a rule two diffusion indices are calculated: a **historic** and a **current** diffusion index. The historic index is determined by first dating the specific turning points. In each period from a trough to the next peak the series is then deemed to rise, while in each period from a peak to the next trough the series is deemed to decline. The calculation of the historic index thus merely requires a set of specific turning points for each time series. The current index, however, is calculated without first determining specific turning points. Instead, the calculation is based on the actual change in an individual time series after its long-run trend and seasonal component have been eliminated.

The SARB uses the growth cycle definition of business cycles to determine the reference turning points. The long-run trend is not eliminated from the seasonally adjusted data. Business cycles are therefore defined as the fluctuations around the long-run growth trend of aggregate economic activity. The upward phases indicate that the pace of growth in total economic activity was greater than its long-run growth rate, while the downward phases indicate that aggregate economic activity either contracted or increased at a slower rate than its long-term growth trend.

The SARB uses a combination of methods to determine whether or not a reference turning point has occurred. To start with, three composite business cycle indicators (see Section 4.3 below) are monitored on a continuous basis. If these indicators indicate that a turning point may have occurred, two comprehensive diffusion indices (a current one and a historical one) are then calculated to identify and date a possible reference turning point.

Both the current and the historical diffusion index are based on 186 seasonally adjusted time series and, in both instances, sectoral contributions are weighted according to each sector's contribution to gross value added. The deviation of the current diffusion index from its long-term trend traces a business cycle pattern and provides a proxy for the cyclical movement in aggregate economic activity. The historical diffusion index, however, shows the number of time series that are increasing relative to each one's long-term trend as a percentage of the total number of time series considered. An index value greater than 50 thus indicates that most time series are increasing and that the economy is thus in an upward phase. Likewise, an index value of less than 50 indicates a downward phase of the business cycle.

The identification and dating of reference turning points is, however, not merely a purely statistical exercise. The results of the statistical methods are analysed along with other macroeconomic data and information to arrive at a decision about a reference turning point.

The reference dates (or reference turning points) listed in Table 4-1 are frequently used in quantitative economic analyses as well as in graphic representations of time series (by shading the upswings or the downswings). Such graphic representations enable observers to gauge how certain variables behave relative to the business cycle.

The reference turning points, however, are historic data and the estimation of these dates is a time-consuming process. Moreover, the turning points provide no information about the intensity or amplitude of the upswings and downswings in economic activity. They are thus of limited use to economists who have to analyse current and expected economic conditions.

Reference turning points do, however, have one important further application. They are used to identify various leading, coincident and lagging indicators, which can then be used to analyse current and expected economic conditions, as well as to identify possible reference turning points.

4.3 Business cycle indicators

Business cycle indicators are identified by comparing the turning points of the cyclical components of individual time series with the reference turning points. If the specific turning points of an individual time series tend to always precede the reference turning points, the relevant variable is identified as a **leading indicator**. If the specific turning points tend to coincide with the reference turning points, the relevant variable is deemed to be a **coincident indicator**. If the specific turning points tend to occur after the reference turning points, the relevant variable is designated a **lagging indicator**. A business cycle indicator should:

- represent an important economic variable or process
- bear a consistent relationship over time with business cycle movements and turning points
- not be dominated by irregular and other non-cyclical movements
- be promptly and frequently reported

Some of the main leading, coincident and lagging indicators used in South Africa are listed in Table 4-2.

TABLE 4-2: Some leading, coincident and lagging business cycle indicators in South Africa

Leading indicators	Coincident indicators	Lagging indicators
BER Business confidence index	Gross value added at constant prices, excluding agriculture, forestry and fishing	Value of non-residential buildings completed (at constant prices)
Index of prices of all classes of shares traded on the JSE	Total formal non-agricultural employment	Cement sales in tons
Number of residential building plans passed	Industrial production index	Ratio of households' use of instalment sale credit to their disposable income
Job advertisement space in the *Sunday Times*: percentage change over 12 months	Value of wholesale, retail and new vehicle sales at constant prices	Predominant prime overdraft rate of banks

These indicators can be used to analyse current and expected economic conditions. For example, if all or most of the leading indicators are improving, an upswing can be expected. Likewise, if the coincident indicators are worsening, this may be regarded as an indication that general economic conditions are deteriorating. In practice, most economists who have to analyse and predict economic conditions tend to focus on a selection of indicators when making their predictions.

As a next step, the cyclical components of the indicators in each group can be combined to obtain a set of weighted **composite business cycle indices**. The components of such indices should represent as broad an array of activities and sectors as possible. The South African Reserve Bank regularly compiles and publishes composite indices of leading, coincident and lagging indicators. The composite leading indicator consists of 12 economic indicators that have historically preceded turning points in the aggregate business cycle (ie the reference cycle). The composite coincident indicator consists of five economic indicators that have historically coincided with the business cycle and the composite lagging indicator consists of seven economic indicators that have historically followed the aggregate business cycle. Note, however, that these composite indices record only the **direction of change** in economic activity and not the level of economic activity.

Figure 4-2 shows the movements in the composite coincident indicator of the South African business cycle for the period 1971 to 2009 with 2000 as the base year. Note that this graph is much more irregular and erratic than the idealised business cycle illustrated in Figure 4-1.

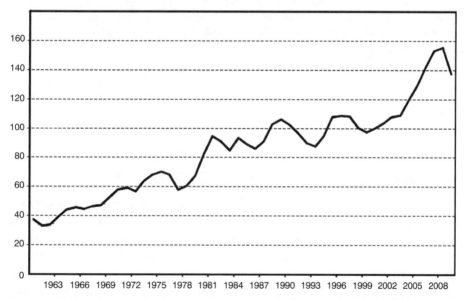

Figure 4-2: Composite coincident business cycle indicator, 1971-2009 (2000 = 100)

Most economists have their own particular views on the salient features of the different phases of the business cycle and on the individual indicators which they monitor to forecast the direction of economic activity. See also Box 4-2.

BOX 4-2: SOME POPULAR INDIVIDUAL TIME SERIES

Apart from the composite business cycle indicators discussed above, analysts use various individual time series in their attempts to gauge the current and prospective state of the economy. These include most of the individual indicators used by the SARB to construct the composite indicators, as well as the indicators mentioned in Section 4.4.

One of the most popular indicators of cyclical movements in the economy is the monthly volume (or real value) of retail sales. To serve as a meaningful indicator, the raw data on nominal retail sales have to be adjusted for seasonal influences and inflation. However, even the seasonally adjusted retail sales at constant prices have to be interpreted with caution. The problem is that there is no specific price index that can be used to deflate retail sales. The consumer price index for goods (see Chapter 6) is used to obtain the inflation-adjusted (real) data, but the problem is that not all consumer goods are included in the retail sales figures. The most important exception is petrol. The result is that movements in the petrol price affect the price index that is used to obtain the real value of retail sales, even though the value of petrol sales is not included. Thus if the petrol price is reduced, the real value of retail sales tends to be overstated (because the deflator (see Chapter 6) is too low). Likewise, if the petrol price is raised significantly the real value of retail sales will tend to be understated.

Some of the other popular cyclical indicators, such as the number of vehicles sold, the number of building plans passed, employment/unemployment figures and the results of anticipation surveys are all volume data and do not have to be adjusted for inflation.

4.4   Other approaches to forecasting economic activity

Economists often differ as to the nature and causes of economic fluctuations, but they generally agree that the host of factors which can affect the future course of economic activity makes economic forecasting a hazardous exercise. Many economists would therefore gladly refrain from venturing quantitative projections of the future course of economic activity. There is, however, a definite demand for such forecasts in both the public sector and the private sector, which has to be met in one way or another. As variables such as interest rates and exchange rates became more volatile, this demand increased. In this section we briefly discuss some further approaches to economic forecasting (ie apart from the business cycle indicators outlined in the previous section).

Single variable extrapolation techniques

One possibility is to simply extrapolate the past values or behaviour of a time series. If the economy grew or declined steadily, forecasts could be made by simply extrapolating along the trend line. Similarly, if the economy were characterised by a regular cycle, forecasts could simply be made by extrapolating along the trend path. Unfortunately, the growth path of the South African economy is decidedly irregular, with the result that simple extrapolation techniques are inappropriate. To deal with the problem, a number of sophisticated extrapolative methods have been developed, including the Box-Jenkins method, the autoregressive integrated moving average (ARIMA) method and spectral analysis. These methods, which are similar to the so-called technical analysis employed by analysts who forecast movements in share prices, are not based on economic theory, nor do they link the variable in question to any other variable(s). They are all based on the premise that the causal relationships which affect the course of a variable are too complicated, perhaps even unknowable, or too costly to be pursued. Sophisticated techniques are therefore applied to a time series to identify repeating patterns within the series on which forecasts are then based. These methods are not generally used by professional economists but they often generate surprisingly good short-term forecasts.

Anticipation surveys

Another approach is to survey decision-makers' intentions and anticipations. Surveys provide valuable evidence of perceptions and expectations relating to business conditions. Responses are subjective but they provide early signals of changes in economic trends. In other words, the main advantage of this approach is that survey data become available in advance of comparable historical data, on which other forecasting methods are based.

The survey method has been followed extensively for decades by the Stellenbosch Bureau for Economic Research (BER) which regularly undertakes surveys of business and consumer opinion. The following are its most important publications:

- *Manufacturing Survey:* A concise quarterly overview of the latest developments in the South African manufacturing industry, including the results of the BER's latest in-depth survey of manufacturing firms nationwide. (The full report is available to subscribers only.)

- *Retail Survey:* A quarterly report that contains the results of the BER's latest market research on the behaviour of South African consumers – their confidence, spending patterns, attitudes and expectations. (The full report is available to subscribers only.)

- *Building and Construction Survey:* A quarterly report of current conditions, constraints and trends in the building and construction sector, as well as forecasts. Building contractors, quantity surveyors and architects are surveyed and house price indices and the BER's building cost index are also included. (The full report is available to subscribers only.)

- *Economic Outlook:* A detailed annual forecast of the South African economy for the next five to six years. (The full report is available to the BER's Macro Service clients only.)

- *Economic Prospects:* A quarterly report that contains forecasts of the South African economy for the coming 18 to 24 months. (The full report is available to subscribers only.)

- *RMB/BER Business Confidence Index:* A quarterly survey and publication sponsored by RMB.

- *FNB/BER Consumer Confidence Index:* A quarterly survey and publication sponsored by FNB.

- *Kagiso Purchasing Managers' Index (PMI):* A monthly survey and publication sponsored by Kagiso. Based on the widely used and highly regarded PMI produced by the National Association of Purchasing Managers in the USA, this index, which is compiled in collaboration with the Institute of Purchasing and Supply South Africa (IPSA), is closely monitored in the financial markets as well as in the business world in general.

- *Ernst & Young Financial Services Survey:* A quarterly survey of current and expected conditions in the financial services sector, sponsored by Ernst & Young.

- *FNB Building Confidence Index:* A quarterly survey of current and expected conditions in the building industry sponsored by FNB.

- *BER Inflation Expectations Survey:* A quarterly survey of inflation expectations commissioned by the South African Reserve Bank. The results are an important input in the regular meetings of the SARB's Monetary Policy Committee.

The results of all these surveys are regularly reported in the media and keenly awaited in the financial markets. Details on all the publications are available on the Bureau's website *(www.ber.sun.ac.za).*

A variation of this type of approach is used by the South African Chamber of Commerce and Industry (SACCI) to compile its monthly Business Confidence Index (BCI) which regularly receives wide coverage in the media. The BCI is not an opinion/perception-based index. In other words, it does not reflect what business is saying but what it is doing and experiencing. Instead of undertaking regular opinion surveys, business people are asked from time to time to identify key economic variables and these variables are then monitored on a monthly basis. In 2010 the BCI comprised the following indicators:

- average monthly weighted exchange rate of the rand against the US dollar, the euro and the British pound, as well as the volatility of the rand exchange rate

- consumer inflation rate for urban areas

- real predominant prime overdraft rate

- volume of retail sales

- rate of change in real credit extension to the private sector

- average monthly weighted US dollar price of gold and platinum
- volume of merchandise imports
- volume of merchandise exports
- new vehicle sales
- liquidations of companies and close corporations
- volume of manufacturing production
- real value of private sector building plans passed
- all-share price index of the JSE Ltd

The BCI is a composite weighted index which combines these 13 indicators. Index numbers are explained in Section 6.1.

Consensus of observers approach

A further variation of the anticipatory approach, which is followed widely in the private sector and also used in the media, is the consensus of observers approach. Instead of eliciting opinions from business people or consumers, the opinions of forecasters or other experts are gauged. An economist, for example, will gauge the opinion of other analysts (including other economists) who are regarded as having expert knowledge on the prospective course of key economic variables such as real GDP, the consumer price index, interest rates, exchange rates, fixed investment, exports and imports. Forecasting in South Africa also invariably entails visits to the SARB and the National Treasury to gauge the prospective course of monetary policy and fiscal policy. The media, however, often collect the forecasts of a panel of economists and publish the average forecasts of a variety of economic indicators, as well as the highest and lowest estimates. For a number of years *Sake24* (published in *Beeld*, *Die Burger* and *Volksblad* newspapers) has run an annual forecasting competition among professional economists in South Africa. Every month more than 30 economists submit their forecasts of key macroeconomic variables which are then published in the newspapers. Once the actual outcomes are known, the forecasts are evaluated statistically to identify the FinMedia24 'economist of the year'. Reuters conducts a similar monthly poll which is published in its *EconoMeter*. Again an annual winner is selected.

Econometric models

An econometric model consists of a number of identities and a set of functions which have been fitted to historical data, using various statistical techniques. Each function or equation represents the quantitative relationship(s) between the relevant economic variables, expressed in mathematical terms. An econometric model is thus a quantitative version of an economic model. This is in contrast with most of the other forecasting techniques, which are not based on economic theory.

Econometric models differ enormously in size. The model may be a single equation which links the level of GDP to the money stock and/or government spending. It may also consist of hundreds or even thousands of equations aimed at predicting a similar level of variables for a country or a group of countries. However, larger models do not necessarily yield better results than relatively simple models.

Econometric models are widely used in South Africa in both the public and private sectors. Among the best-known models are the quarterly and annual models of the SARB and the Stellenbosch Bureau for Economic Research. The BER uses its models to compile its *Economic Outlook and Prospects*, referred to earlier, while the results of the SARB's models are important inputs in the regular meetings of the Bank's Monetary Policy Committee. Econometric models, however, are not used for forecasting purposes only. Many of the models are used primarily for structural analysis and policy simulations (eg to estimate the possible impact of particular policy measures).

Chapter 5

Employment and unemployment

One of the main macroeconomic objectives is to fully employ the available factors of production, particularly labour. Put differently, the aim is to keep the unemployment rate as low as possible. Aggregate data on employment and unemployment are therefore of particular interest to economists, policy makers, politicians, business people and other observers. In the United States of America (US), for example, monthly figures on total employment in the US economy often have a significant impact on financial markets and the direction of economic policy. However, in a developing country such as South Africa, with its large and growing informal sector and large volumes of legal or illegal immigration, it is virtually impossible to obtain accurate information on the levels of employment or unemployment or, for that matter, the size of the population.

5.1   Population data

The basic point of departure in compiling data on employment and unemployment is the total population of the country. This is where the problems start. In South Africa population censuses were undertaken every five years or so from 1980 to 2001 by Stats SA, but the only consensus among analysts seems to be that they were all inaccurate.

The censuses conducted in 1980, 1985, 1991, 1996 and 2001 yielded estimates of the total population of 29,2 million, 33,2 million, 38,0 million, 40,6 million and 44,8 million respectively. The original figure for 1996 (37,9 million) took most observers by surprise since the South African population had been estimated at approximately 42,0 million in mid-1996 (based on the 1991 census). Many analysts seriously questioned the accuracy of the data and after a prolonged debate the official figure was raised to 40,6 million. In mid-2009 the population was estimated at 49,3 million. The next census is scheduled for 2011.

Counting the population is no easy task. Various physical problems are experienced in reaching all the inhabitants, and individuals or families often deliberately try to avoid being registered (or counted). During the apartheid era, for example, many people did not wish to be counted and certain areas were virtually inaccessible to enumerators. Nowadays there are many illegal immigrants from other African countries who also do not wish to be identified for fear of repatriation, while tax evaders might also not wish to divulge personal information. Another problem with the South African population series is that Transkei, Bophuthatswana, Venda and Ciskei were excluded from their respective dates of independence to 1994.

A detailed analysis of population data and trends falls beyond the scope of this book. Suffice it to note that population data are important and that unreliable data on the level and growth of the population have serious implications for estimates of employment and unemployment as well as for other economic indicators (eg per capita data). Population censuses also yield a host of information about various characteristics of the population.

5.2   Economically active population

To estimate unemployment we require some indication of how many people are willing and able to work. The **unemployment rate** is then obtained by expressing the number of people who are willing and able to work but who do not have jobs as a percentage of the total number of people who are willing and able to work.

The total number of people who are willing and able to work is called the **labour force** or **economically active population** (EAP). The EAP consists of workers in the formal sector of the economy plus self-employed persons and employers plus informal sector workers plus unemployed persons. The EAP thus includes all people who are in work or unemployed. It is derived from the total population figure. Given the total population, the EAP depends on factors such as:

- the age distribution of the population – the greater the proportion of the population in the 15 to 64 age group (ie **the working-age population**), the greater the labour force will be
- retirement rules and the availability of social security – compulsory retirement and the availability of social pensions and other forms of social security tend to reduce the labour force
- social, cultural, religious or other conventions about the role of women in society
- the availability of household appliances, childcare centres and other institutions which enable women to take up paid employment outside the home
- the level of development and structure of the economy

The fraction, proportion or percentage of the population of working age (ie 15 to 64 years) who are economically active is called the **labour force participation rate** (LFPR). Thus

$$\text{LFPR} = \frac{\text{labour force (or economically active population}}{\text{population of working age (15 to 64 years)}}$$

The LFPR can be expressed as a percentage by multiplying the above fraction or ratio by 100. Separate LFPRs can be estimated for each gender and for specific age groups, for different population groups and for different geographic areas.

In South Africa, the LFPRs tend to differ between the different population groups. For example, in the first quarter of 2010 the LFPR for South Africa was estimated at 54,6%. The estimates for the different population groups were 58,9% for Indians/Asians, 51,2% for black Africans, 65,4% for coloureds and 69,5% for whites. The overall LFPRs for males and females were estimated at 61,9% and 47,9% respectively. On the basis of these estimates the South African labour force (or EAP) in the first quarter of 2010 was estimated at 17,1 million.

5.3   Employment

Employment data are important. Such data can, for example, be compared to the EAP to estimate unemployment, while trends in employment in different sectors or industries indicate important structural changes in the economy. Employment data are also used to calculate productivity, earnings per worker and other economic indicators. In the United States, the monthly release of employment data is one of the major events on the economic calendar (see Box 5-1).

Unfortunately, South African employment data are notoriously unreliable. They do not cover all sectors of the economy, definitions often change, and Transkei, Bophuthatswana, Venda and Ciskei were excluded while they were independent.[1] Historically, one of the best series of data pertaining to total employment in the formal sector of the South African economy was the **standardised employment series**, originally generated in 1984 by Roukens de Lange and Van Eeghen in an attempt to address the shortcomings of the existing data. The series (which included employment in agriculture and domestic service) was updated on occasion, but not regularly. Although the series is only available up to 1998, such employment data provide important information about trends and structural changes in the economy. Some of these trends and changes can be illustrated by calculating the percentage shares in total employment of the various sectors. Table 5-1 shows the **relative shares** of the various sectors in 1950, 1960, 1970, 1980 and 1998. This is an example of a **percentage classification table**. When interpreting a percentage classification table containing time-series data, it is important to note that a decline in a particular **percentage contribution** does not necessarily indicate an **absolute** decline, since the total might have increased. By the same token, an increase in the percentage contribution of a particular item does not necessarily indicate an absolute increase. It is therefore advisable to provide the absolute values of the totals along with the percentage contributions. In this way the person using the data can always derive the absolute changes and avoid arriving at incorrect conclusions.

---

1.   For a summary of some of the problems pertaining to South African employment data, see Barker, F. 2007. *The South African labour market*, 5th edition, Pretoria: Van Schaik:37-40.

BOX 5-1: AN INFLUENTIAL SET OF ECONOMIC INDICATORS

Probably the most keenly awaited and influential release of economic indicators in the world, particularly in the financial markets, is the monthly *Employment Situation Report* published by the US Bureau of Labor Statistics. It is a very timely report, released just a week after the end of the month being reviewed, and is rich in detail about the US labour market and household earnings.

The report is so important because it gives the first indications of what is happening to employment, unemployment and household income in the USA and where the largest economy in the world is heading. It is closely monitored by the investment community and policy makers and no other indicator can move equity and bond markets like the data on employment and unemployment contained in the report. In fact, the report is so important to participants in the financial markets that dealers, brokers and economists often plan their holidays around its release.

The report contains the results of two separate surveys: the *Current Population Survey* (CPS), a household survey, and the *Current Employment Statistics* (CES) survey, an establishment survey. The two surveys are similar in nature to the *Quarterly Labour Force Survey* and the *Quarterly Employment Statistics* released by Stats SA and discussed in the text.

The key data are those pertaining to unemployment (generated by the CPS) and the monthly change in non-agricultural employment (generated by the CES). However, since the two surveys approach the labour market from different perspectives, they sometimes yield conflicting results. The possible impact of these and other economic indicators on the financial markets are discussed in Chapter 9.

Stats SA publishes quarterly estimates of employment in its *Quarterly Employment Statistics (QES)* and *Quarterly Labour Force Survey (QLFS)*. The *QES* is based on a survey of enterprises that is aimed at obtaining data on employment and earnings in the formal non-agricultural sector of the economy. The agricultural sector and the informal sector (including domestic work) are excluded. Approximately 22 000 enterprises are surveyed each quarter by means of a questionnaire and the data are published in *Statistical release P0277*, approximately three months after the end of the quarter for which the survey was conducted. The *QES* replaced the earlier *Survey of Employment and Earnings (SEE)* in 2005. The *QES* covers more employees than the *SEE* had (all those registered for income tax).

**Table 5-1: Employment shares of the main (formal) sectors
of the economy, selected years**

Sector	Percentage share of total employment				
	1950	1960	1970	1980	1998
Agriculture	26,9	22,2	17,4	13,3	11,1
Mining	12,9	12,9	10,7	10,2	5,9
Manufacturing	13,5	13,8	17,6	19,3	18,2
Electricity	0,6	0,7	0,7	1,0	0,9
Construction	2,5	2,7	5,2	5,3	3,8
Trade	9,6	11,0	12,0	12,5	13,2
Transport and communication	6,5	6,8	5,9	6,6	4,3
Financial services	1,5	2,6	3,1	3,9	7,9
Other services	26,0	27,3	27,4	27,9	34,7
Total	**100,0**	**100,0**	**100,0**	**100,0**	**100,0**
Total (absolute numbers in thousands)	3 787	4 651	6 164	7 560	7 423

Sources: Statistics South Africa, *South African labour statistics*, 1995, Section 2.8; Barker, F. 2003. *The South African labour market*, 4th edition, Pretoria: Van Schaik:80.

The *QLFS*, however, is a survey of households/dwellings to obtain data on employment and unemployment. In contrast to the *QES*, the informal sector is also covered. Approximately 30 000 households are surveyed each quarter by a permanent field force of Stats SA. The results are published in *Statistical release P0211*, approximately one month after the end of the quarter during which the survey was conducted. The *QLFS* is the main source of data on unemployment and the informal sector and will be discussed again later.

The *SARB* also publishes Stats SA employment data in index form in its *Quarterly Bulletin*. The absolute numbers in the base year are also provided, thus enabling users to estimate the absolute numbers for the months, quarters or years in question.

Table 5-2 contains data on formal sector employment in South Africa in December 2009. Employment data such as those in the table and the accompanying earnings data (not shown here) are important inputs in the estimation of the South African GDP.

Table 5-2: Employment in the formal non-agricultural sector in December 2009

Sector	Number	Percentage of total
Mining and quarrying	485 079	6,0
Manufacturing	1 183 599	14,5
Electricity, gas and water supply	58 797	0,7
Construction	413 385	5,1
Wholesale and retail; repair of motor vehicles, motor cycles and personal and household goods; hotels and restaurants	1 666 510	20,4
Transport, storage and communication	359 356	4,4
Financial intermediation, insurance, real estate and business services	1 796 329	22,0
Community, social and personal services	2 198 289	26,9
Total	**8 161 344**	**100,0**

Source: Statistics South Africa, Quarterly Employment Statistics (P0277), December 2009 (released on 23 March 2010).

The employment data generated by Stats SA (and the accompanying data on earnings (see Section 8.2)) are subject to a number of shortcomings, including changes in definitions, possible undercounting in mining and other sectors employing contract workers, the omission of small-scale agriculture, small self-employed manufacturers and new firms and undercounting of rural and informal sector employment. These problems have unfortunately given rise to discontinuities and sharp changes in employment data, which in turn have impaired the credibility of the data.

Formal and informal employment

As mentioned in Section 2.7, the informal sector (sometimes also called the unrecorded economy, shadow economy, underground economy, subterranean economy or hidden economy) became very important in South Africa in recent decades. There are primarily three reasons that people engage in informal sector activity:

- They do not want to pay tax.
- They cannot find employment in the formal sector.
- They are engaged in illegal activities.

Although there is no precise definition of the informal sector, Table 5-3 provides a good indication of the types of activity that are involved.

Table 5-3: Informal sector activities

Legal/socially acceptable	Illegal/socially unacceptable
Producers	**Producers**
Self-employed artisans, shoemakers, dressmakers and tailors, home brewers, craft and curio makers	Dagga producers, counterfeiters
Distributors	**Distributors**
Hawkers, flea-market traders, petty traders, carriers, runners, shebeeners	Pickpockets, burglars, robbers, embezzlers, confidence tricksters, gamblers, drug traffickers, black marketeers
Service providers	**Service providers**
Taxi operators, money lenders, musicians, launderers, repairers, shoe-shiners, barbers, photographers, herbalists, traditional healers, backyard mechanics, pawnbrokers	Hustlers, pimps, prostitutes, smugglers, bribers, protection racketeers, loan sharks

Source: W B Vosloo. 1994. 'The small firm as a vehicle for entrepreneurship', in *Entrepreneurship and Economic Growth*, Pretoria: HSRC:171.

As formal employment in South Africa stagnated and declined in the 1980s and early 1990s, increasing attention was paid to the informal sector as a source of employment and income. In 1989 and 1990 Stats SA conducted surveys to estimate employment and income in the informal sector and in 1994 estimates of the value of informal sector activity were included in the official national accounts for the first time. From October 1993 Stats SA conducted an annual *October Household Survey (OHS)* which included questions relating to the informal sector (see also Section 5.4 below). The *OHS* replaced the much criticised *Current Population Surveys*, which were undertaken from 1977 to 1991, as well as the separate surveys of the informal sector. The 1993 survey, however, did not include Transkei, Bophuthatswana, Venda and Ciskei (which still existed at the time) and its results were therefore not fully comparable with those of the subsequent surveys. The *OHS* was discontinued in 2000 and replaced by a *Labour Force Survey*. The last *OHS* was conducted in 1999 and the first *Labour Force Survey (LFS)* in February 2000. From the third quarter of 2008 the bi-annual *LFS* was replaced by the *Quarterly Labour Force Survey (QLFS)*.

Table 5-4 provides an example of the type of data on the informal sector generated by the *QLFS*. Some of the data are also provided by population group, gender, region, industry and occupation. During the first quarter of 2010 employment in the informal sector was estimated to be 15,7% of total employment in the South African economy, the remainder being in the formal non-agricultural sectors (70,1%), agriculture (5,1%) and private households (domestic work, 9,1%).

Table 5-4: Employment in the informal sector, Quarter 1, 2010

Industry	Number employed (thousands)	Percentage of total
Mining	2	0,1
Manufacturing	195	9,7
Utilities	2	0,1
Construction	257	12,8
Trade	944	47,0
Transport	193	9,6
Finance	148	7,4
Community and social services	260	13,4
Total	**2 001**	**100,0**

Source: Statistics South Africa, Quarterly Labour Force Survey, Quarter 1, 2010 (Statistical release P0211) (released on 4 May 2010). Percentages do not add up to 100 due to rounding.

Employment coefficient

Formal employment in South Africa tended to stagnate and decline in the 1980s and 1990s. To a large extent this was the result of the decline in economic growth experienced during this period. There is, however, the possibility that a smaller proportion of additional jobs was created for each percentage point growth in real GDP during this period than during the previous decades. A useful (albeit quite crude) indicator which can be used in this regard is the **employment coefficient** or **production elasticity of employment**. This indicator, which measures the degree of responsiveness of employment to economic growth, is calculated by simply dividing the percentage change in formal employment by the real GDP growth rate for successive periods of about five years (or periods covering full business cycles).

The reason that a fairly long period should be used to estimate the employment coefficient is that employment does not react immediately to changes in production. When demand increases, the required increase in production is usually achieved by utilising the existing workers more effectively, working overtime, and so on. If the expansion in demand proves to be of a more or less permanent nature, new workers are recruited, but even then it might take some time before additional workers are actually employed. The opposite tends to happen when demand and production decrease. Employers usually retain their employees initially and only start reducing the numbers once it becomes obvious that demand and production are not going to recover. Another problem is that employers might be locked into employment contracts that cannot be terminated quickly or without incurring significant retrenchment costs. The upshot of all this is that there tends to be a lag of up to two years between changes in production and changes in employment. Changes in employment and production thus have to be compared over fairly long periods before any meaningful conclusions can be drawn.

The South African employment coefficient remained quite stable (at about 0,5) from 1950 to 1990 but a significant (and worrying) change occurred in the 1990s. Economic growth was very low in the early 1990s but not much lower than during the 1980s. However, whereas formal employment still increased during the 1980s, it actually fell in absolute terms in the 1990s. As a result it was not even possible to calculate an employment coefficient for this period (since a negative value cannot be extrapolated and therefore does not make sense). The employment position improved in the new millennium, but at the time of writing the employment coefficient was still significantly lower than 0,5.

Note also that even an employment coefficient of about 0,5 implies that real GDP has to grow at an average annual rate of 4% to accommodate an average annual growth of 2% in the labour force.

Labour absorption capacity

Another indicator of the employment performance of the economy is the (marginal) **labour absorption capacity**, which can be defined as the ratio or percentage of new entrants to the labour force that are able to find employment in the formal sector of the economy:

$$\text{labour absorption capacity (\%)} = \frac{\text{increase in formal employment}}{\text{increase in labour force (EAP)}} \times 100$$

The labour absorption capacity of the South African economy is estimated to have declined from an average of almost 75% during the period 1965-1970 to about 12,5% during the period 1985-1989. This means that, on average, only between 12 and 13 out of every 100 new entrants were able to secure formal employment in the latter period. In the early 1990s the labour absorption capacity actually became negative, since formal employment declined in absolute numbers from 1989 while the labour force continued to grow at an estimated rate of more than 300 000 per year. In the new millennium there was a sharp improvement but at the time of writing there were no data on which a reliable estimate could be based.

Note that the labour absorption capacity (a marginal or incremental concept) differs from the **labour absorption rate** published by Stats SA. The latter is calculated as the ratio between the number of employed people (in both the formal and informal sectors) and the total working-age population. In the *QLFS* for the first quarter of 2010 this figure (which is also known as the employment-to-population ratio) was estimated at 40,8%.

5.4   Unemployment

Unemployment is easy to define but difficult to measure, particularly in a developing country such as South Africa. An **unemployed person** is someone who seeks but cannot find employment. Those who choose to be unemployed (for reasons such as age, full-time study or a marked preference for leisure) and those who have given up hope that they will ever find employment (the discouraged) are not classified among the unemployed.

The **unemployment rate** is obtained by expressing the total number of unemployed persons as a percentage of the total number of available workers (ie as a percentage of the economically active population or labour force).

Two definitions of unemployment are used to generate statistics on unemployment: a **strict definition**, formulated by the International Labour Organisation and generally used in international comparisons of unemployment in developed countries, and an **expanded definition** which is more suitable to developing countries and which was used from 1994 to 1998 to officially estimate unemployment in South Africa. In 1998, however, Stats SA reverted to using the strict definition as the official definition.

According to the **strict definition** unemployed persons are those people within the economically active population (ie aged 15 to 64) who: (a) did not work during the seven days prior to the survey interview (the reference week), (b) were available to start work during the reference week, and (c) actively looked for work or tried to start a business in the four weeks prior to the survey interview. The three conditions are thus: without work, currently available for work and seeking work. Note, however, that if the person had worked for at least an hour during the reference week, he/she is not classified as unemployed. The requirement for being classified as employed is therefore not particularly strict!

The **expanded definition** of unemployment excludes criterion (c) above. In other words, whereas a person had (according to the strict definition) to have taken steps recently to find a job, the expanded definition only requires a desire to find employment. The expanded definition thus includes discouraged work-seekers. A discouraged work-seeker is defined as a person who was not employed during the reference period, was available to work or start a business but did not take active steps to find work during the last four weeks because of any of the following: no jobs were available in the area, the person had been unable to find work requiring his/her skills or had lost hope of finding any work.

Prior to 1994 the strict definition was used by Stats SA to estimate unemployment in South Africa, with the result that the official estimates were generally criticised as being too low. The subsequent switch to the expanded definition eliminated much of the earlier criticism against the official estimates, although some observers regarded the new estimates as being too high. In 1998 Stats SA reverted to using the strict definition as the official definition.

Once the number of unemployed persons has been estimated, this number has to be expressed as a percentage of the EAP or labour force to obtain an unemployment rate. This adds another source of error since the estimation of the EAP is no easy task (as explained briefly in Section 5.2).

Different sets of information can be used to estimate unemployment, for example: **census data**, which contain information about the economic status of the population; data on persons **registered as unemployed** with the Department of Labour; and **sample survey data** generated by surveying a number of households. These sets of data form the basis of different possible approaches to estimating unemployment: the census method, the registration method and the sample survey method. At present the last is the only real source of unemployment data in South Africa. But first we shall discuss the other two methods.

The census method

In every population census there are some questions aimed at determining the economic status of the population. The problem, however, is that the focus of the census is on estimating the population rather than on obtaining information about employment and unemployment. Estimates of the latter are a byproduct of the exercise and it is doubtful whether enough effort is made to obtain accurate data in this regard. Another drawback is that census data are only generated every five or ten years. Nevertheless, census data provide a wealth of information which researchers can use in conjunction with other data to generate profiles of unemployment.

The registration method

A second potential source of data on unemployment is the statistics on registered unemployment obtained from monthly returns submitted by the different placement centres of the Department of Labour and other agents of the Department. A person is classified as a registered unemployed person if that person is of working age, out of work, available for work and registered as a work-seeker with the Department or its agents. However, since September 1998 data on registered unemployment are no longer published by the Department of Labour.

In any event, the main problem with data on registered unemployment is that registration is voluntary. Only a small portion of unemployed persons take the trouble to register, mainly only those who are eligible for unemployment benefits (on condition that they are registered as unemployed) and those who hope that the Department will be able to place them in employment. Data on registered unemployment therefore did not reflect the **level** of unemployment in the country. Nevertheless, **changes** in registered unemployment were traditionally regarded as an important indicator of trends in the labour market and in the economy at large. In fact, the number of registered unemployed persons (seasonally adjusted and on an inverse scale) was regarded as one of the best coincident indicators of the South African business cycle. When this number increased, it was regarded as an indication that a downswing or recession was being experienced while a decrease in the number was regarded as a sign that economic conditions were improving.

Some countries still use the registration method, either on its own or in conjunction with the sample survey method, which is the one preferred and recommended by the International Labour Organisation (ILO), which tries to standardise the definition and measurement of unemployment internationally as far as possible.

The sample survey method

Until the late 1970s little was known about the level, rate or growth of black unemployment in South Africa. The only available data were generated by private researchers through surveys conducted in various towns, cities and regions. In October 1977 the Department of Statistics started conducting monthly *Current Population Surveys* on a sample basis to obtain estimates of black unemployment. These surveys were later extended to include coloureds (July 1978) and Asians (September 1982). However, due to a number of shortcomings the surveys were discontinued in 1990. In 1993 the Central Statistical Service (as Stats SA was then known) took a significant further step by conducting the first *October Household Survey (OHS)*. This survey was aimed, inter alia, at providing certain insights into and perspectives on the most important elements of the country's unemployment profile. As mentioned in Section 5.3, the survey also replaced the previous surveys of the informal sector. The results (which excluded the former independent national states, which were still in existence at that stage) were published in May 1994 in *Statistical release P0317*. Similar sample surveys covering the whole of present-day South Africa were subsequently conducted annually in October, until 1999.

In February 2000 Stats SA conducted its first *Labour Force Survey (LFS)*, which generated a wide variety of data on employment and unemployment in South Africa. The *LFS* was 'a twice-yearly rotating panel household survey, specifically designed to measure the dynamics of employment and unemployment in the country'. The results were published by Stats SA in *Statistical release P0210*.

For the purposes of the *LFS*, both the strict and expanded definitions of unemployment were used, with the former being regarded as the official definition of unemployment in South Africa. The *LFS* generated a variety of unemployment data by gender, population group, province, age, level of education and previous occupation.

In an attempt to improve the quality and timeliness of employment and unemployment data Stats SA replaced the *LFS* in the third quarter of 2008 with the *Quarterly Labour Force Survey (QLFS)*. This is a quarterly survey of approximately 30 000 households (or dwellings). Each quarter 25% of the dwellings in the sample rotate out of the sample and are replaced by new dwellings. With the introduction of the new survey Stats SA for the first time employed a trained permanent field force to survey the households on a continuous basis. The release of the data was also speeded up significantly. At the time of writing the data became available approximately a month after the end of the quarter (compared to a lag of at least six months in the case of the earlier *LFS*).

The *QLFS* generates a variety of data on employment and unemployment, including employment by industry, sex and occupation, formal and informal employment by industry, unemployment by sex, province and population group, and characteristics of the unemployed and the not economically active population.

As a result of the changes in surveys and in the questions and definitions used, the results of the various surveys are not comparable. However, with the introduction of the *QLFS* there was an overlap with the *LFS* and data from the latter were revised back to 2000 to make them more comparable with those generated by the *QLFS*. The unemployment rate based on the expanded definition of unemployment is, however, no longer published. Fortunately, this rate can be calculated from the published data. This is done by adding the number of discouraged work-seekers to the number of unemployed persons as well as to the labour force and then expressing the expanded unemployment number as a percentage of the enlarged labour force. For example, in the first quarter of 2010 the labour force (1) was 17 113 million, the number of unemployed (2) was 4 310 million and the number of discouraged work-seekers (3) was 1 839 million. The published unemployment rate based on the strict definition (25,2%) was obtained by expressing (2) as percentage of (1). To obtain the unemployment rate based on the expanded definition, (3) has to be added to both (2) and (1), and (2) + (3) then has to be expressed as a percentage of (1) + (2):

- Unemployment = 6 149 million (4 310m + 1 839m)
- Labour force = 18 952 million (17 113m + 1 839m)
- Unemployment as percentage of labour force = 32,4%

Table 5-5 contains data on unemployment in South Africa from 2008 to 2010, while Table 5-6 provides some details on unemployment in South Africa during the first quarter of 2010. Note the variations in the labour force participation rate. For example, the unemployment rate in KwaZulu-Natal is particularly low (relative to the other provinces), but the *LFPR* in that province is also very low relative to Gauteng and the Western Cape.

Underemployment

Some workers are neither unemployed nor fully employed and should therefore be classified as being **underemployed**. Two types of underemployment are distinguished: **visible underemployment** and **invisible underemployment**. The former occurs when a person involuntarily works less than full time (ie fewer than the normal hours, days, weeks or months). Recall that anyone who worked for a minimum of one hour during the reference period is classified as employed. The visibly underemployed include part-time workers, casual workers and seasonal workers who would prefer to be in full-time employment, as well as urban unemployed who temporarily stay with their families on farms and help with the work. Underemployment can also be linked to efforts by employers to circumvent labour legislation or avoid trade union influence by employing large numbers of part-time or casual workers (eg via labour brokers) instead of a smaller number of full-time workers.

Table 5-5: Unemployment in South Africa (expressed as a percentage of the labour force), 2000-2010

Month/quarter and year	Strict definition	Expanded definition
September 2000	23,3	30,0
September 2001	26,2	34,5
September 2002	26,6	34,6
September 2003	24,8	34,7
September 2004	23,0	33,7
September 2005	23,5	32,8
September 2006	22,1	30,9
September 2007	21,0	31,4
3rd quarter 2008	23,2	27,6
3rd quarter 2009	24,5	31,1
1st quarter 2010	25,2	32,4

Sources: Statistics South Africa, Labour Force Survey: Historical revision September series, 2000 to 2007 (released 23 March 2009), Quarterly Labour Force Survey (Statistical release P0211), various issues.

Table 5-6: Labour force participation and unemployment in South Africa, Quarter 1, 2010

	LFPR (%)	Unemployment (%)	
		Strict definition	Expanded definition
Total	54,6	25,2	32,4
Women	47,9	27,3	35,9
Men	61,9	23,4	29,2
Black African	51,2	29,7	n.a.*
Coloureds	65,4	21,8	n.a.*
Indian/Asian	58,9	9,2	n.a.*
Whites	69,5	6,1	n.a.*
Western Cape	68,2	20,3	22,0
Eastern Cape	43,9	29,8	41,5
Northern Cape	52,3	27,8	31,6
Free State	56,4	27,2	33,6
KwaZulu-Natal	46,7	19,3	30,6
North West	48,0	26,3	35,0
Gauteng	70,6	27,1	30,4
Mpumalanga	54,0	29,3	37,8
Limpopo	37,2	26,8	40,0

*   n.a. = not available

Source: Statistics South Africa, Quarterly Labour Force Survey, Quarter 1, 2010 (Statistical release P0211, released 4 May 2010).

This is termed the **casualisation** of the work force. (A related, but different, concept is **clandestine employment**, which refers to the undeclared employment of workers (eg illegal immigrants) to evade social security contributions and other aspects of labour legislation. Such employment is an example of informal or unrecorded employment.)

Whereas visible underemployment can be regarded as inadequate employment as a result of an insufficient amount of work, **invisible underemployment** is the result of a misallocation of labour (eg as a result of an under-utilisation of skills or low productivity). An example would be a qualified engineer working as a shop assistant. The existence of underemployment complicates the definition and measurement of unemployment. Attempts have been made periodically by private researchers and Stats SA to estimate the extent of underemployment in South Africa but no reliable estimates are available. Suffice it to note that this is but one of the many complications encountered when employment and unemployment are estimated.

5.5   International comparisons

International comparisons of economic data are always subject to a number of errors. This is particularly true of labour market statistics, in spite of persistent efforts by the ILO to standardise such statistics. In fact, even the ILO explicitly warns analysts that most of the data published on unemployment are not comparable from one country to another since they are drawn from different sources or based on different definitions. With regard to the definition of unemployment there may be differences, for example, in respect of age limits, reference periods, criteria for seeking work and treatment of persons temporarily laid off. Other differences include different approaches towards counting home workers, domestic servants, part-time staff, people with more than one job, as well as differences in the treatment of self-employed persons and those engaged in informal sector activity. As far as sources are concerned, most countries nowadays use the sample survey method, but some still use the registration method. One should therefore always check the definitions and sources before drawing conclusions from international comparisons of unemployment data.

Unemployment data may also be subject to government manipulation. In the 1980s, for example, the Conservative government in the United Kingdom changed the way in which unemployment was measured no less than 23 times in an attempt to bring the unemployment rate down to a politically acceptable level (*The Economist*, 3 March 2007:36).

Chapter 6

Inflation

Since World War II most countries have experienced sustained, frequently rapid, price increases and as a result there is a great interest in the inflation phenomenon in general and in inflation data in particular. Many other economic variables (eg wages, salaries, interest rates and rent) are either directly or indirectly linked to price increases and it is therefore important to measure inflation as accurately as possible. With the adoption of inflation targeting by the South African government in 2000 the measurement of inflation assumed even greater importance.

To measure inflation, which is defined as a sustained increase in the general price level, a yardstick of the general price level and an appropriate period for measuring changes in this yardstick have to be selected. Various price indices therefore have to be examined. But before this can be done, the more general topic of index numbers has to be investigated.

In this chapter we start with a brief explanation of index numbers, followed by discussions of price indices in general and various specific price indices. It is also explained how these indices can be used to calculate inflation rates, which are by definition rates of change. Some examples are provided and the advantages and disadvantages of different price indices and different measurement periods are discussed. In the process, some of the most common errors in calculating and interpreting inflation rates are also pointed out.

6.1   Index numbers

As mentioned above, inflation is defined as a sustained increase in the general price level. The general price level, however, is not directly observable. The quantities of goods and services are expressed in a variety of physical units (eg tonne, kilogram, litre, metre, watt, carat) and their prices are often not directly comparable. Some way therefore has to be found to combine the prices of a wide variety of goods and services in a single number. The solution is to use index numbers and to construct a price index. The topic of index numbers is wide-ranging and in this section we confine ourselves to those aspects that are required for an understanding of the compilation and interpretation of general or composite price indices.[1]

An index number indicates the level of a single or composite variable in relation to its level at another time, during another period, at another place and so on. The most significant economic changes are those occurring over time. For our purposes, therefore, an index number can be defined as the ratio between the value of a variable or group of variables at a given time or during a specified period and its value at a base time or during a base period, the latter being normally taken as 100.

For example, if a loaf of bread costs R8,00 in 2009, the base period of the comparison, and R10,00 in 2010, the index number for 2010 is calculated as

$$\frac{R10,00}{R8,00} \times 100 = 125$$

It is immediately apparent from the index number of 125 that the price of a loaf of bread increased by 25% from 2009 (the base period) to 2010. Likewise, if 2009 is the base period of an index and the index number for 2011 is 135, it is immediately apparent that the value of the variable or group of variables concerned increased by 35% between 2009 and 2011.

An **index** is a series of index numbers with a fixed frequency (eg month, quarter, year). A **specific index**, such as the index of maize production, contains a single component (or variable). A **general** or **composite index**, such as the index of industrial production or the consumer price index, is obtained by combining various variables or specific indices in one index.

The construction of a general or composite index involves five basic steps:

- the choice of items or components (the basket or regimen)
- the choice of a base period
- the assignment of weights to the different items or components
- the collection of the data
- the calculation of the index numbers

Choice of items to be included in the basket or regimen

The choice of a list of items to be included in a general or composite index is crucial. This list is usually referred to as the **basket** or **regimen**. The choice of items usually depends on the relative significance of each potential item and its measurability.

---

1.   For more detail on index numbers, see PJ Mohr, *et al*, 1995. *The practical guide to South African economic indicators*, Johannesburg: Lexicon.

Choice of base period

The base period is the reference point of any index and the index number for the base period is normally set at 100. When using or interpreting any index, one first has to determine the base period.

Base periods have to be chosen carefully because different results can usually be obtained by varying the base period. The main criteria used in selecting a base period include the following:

- The base period should be relatively **recent** because as many as possible of the index components have to be included in both the current and base period. The more recent the base period, the more comparable the current figures are with those of the base period.

- The base period should preferably fall in an economically **stable** or **normal period**. Abnormal periods (eg periods of abnormally high or low inflation or economic growth) should be avoided, otherwise a distorted picture could be obtained.

- Since many indices are published at regular intervals it is always useful, for comparison purposes, if they have a **common base period**.

- **Census**, **survey** or **sample years** are often used as base periods because comprehensive data are available for the relevant variables in such years. This information can then be used to determine the weights to be used in constructing the index.

The assignment of weights to the different items

To construct a meaningful composite index, the various items or components have to be weighted. In other words, a weight has to be assigned to each item according to its relative importance. In a price index, for example, the importance of each price is determined by the proportion of income spent on the product concerned. These weights usually add up to 1 or 100. A choice also has to be made between current period weights (the **Paasche method**), fixed base-period weights (the **Laspeyres method**) or a combination of the two (eg the **Fisher method**). In economics the choice is usually between the Paasche and Laspeyres methods, that is, between variable (current) weights and fixed (base-period) weights.

The collection of the data and the calculation of the index numbers

These aspects will be dealt with when particular price indices are discussed.

A cautionary note

Note that an index number is a **relative** measure only. In other words, it only indicates the extent to which the phenomenon measured has changed when compared with some earlier period. An index number does not give any indication of the actual **level** of the variable. Index numbers are arbitrary and can be manipulated to yield various results, for example, by changing the basket, base period, weights or formula. Index numbers therefore always have to be interpreted with caution.

6.2   Price indices

A composite price index is a device used to measure the cost of a group of goods and services (the basket or regimen) as a ratio of their cost in the base period, the latter usually being taken as 100.

$$\text{Price index number} = \frac{\text{cost of basket in current period}}{\text{cost of basket in base period}} \times 100$$

A composite price index number is calculated by comparing the weighted average price of a selected basket of goods and services to the weighted average cost of the same basket in the base year. Apart from **explicit price indices**, such as the consumer price index (CPI) and producer price index (PPI), **implicit price deflators** can also be derived from the ratio between nominal (current-price) and real (constant-price) magnitudes. Implicit price deflators are dealt with separately in Section 6.7.

To construct a composite price index, the different steps outlined in the previous section have to be followed.

- **Basket (or regimen) selection**. It is usually impossible to include all relevant items in the calculation of a price index. A representative sample of goods and services to be included therefore has to be determined.

- **Base year selection**. In the case of price indices, international prescriptions or recommendations (eg by the International Monetary Fund and the United Nations) are frequently the decisive factor. To facilitate international comparisons common 'round' base years (eg 1995, 2000, 2005) are usually chosen and sample surveys to determine the appropriate weighting of the different items also tend to be conducted in these years. It should be noted, however, that it is always possible to technically shift base years for comparison purposes. The technique for doing this is explained in Box 6-1.

- **Weighting**. The next step is to assign weights to the various items in the basket, since not all items are equally important. For example, a 10% increase in the price of pencils is less important than a 10% increase in the price of basic foodstuffs or a 10% increase in the price of motor vehicles. The relative importance of the individual items is usually estimated by surveying the spending patterns of

BOX 6-1: SHIFTING THE BASE PERIOD OF AN INDEX
AND LINKING TWO INDICES

To compare different indices or to examine the movements in a particular index over a long period, it is often necessary to shift the base period of an index. The same logic applies to constant-price time series which are also expressed in base-year values.

Suppose, for example, that (in February 2008) an economist wished to shift the base period of the annual consumer price index (CPI) from 2000 (as it was published at that stage) to 2005. Each index value would have to be transformed to the new base period (2005). This is done by simply dividing each original index number by the 2005 number and multiplying the result by 100. The results are shown below:

Year	CPI (2000 = 100)	Calculation	CPI (2005 = 100)
2001	105,7	(105,7/128,0) x 100	82,6
2002	115,4	(115,4/128,0) x 100	90,2
2003	122,1	(122,1/128,0) x 100	95,4
2004	123,8	(123,8/128,0) x 100	96,7
2005	128,0	(128,0/128,0) x 100	100,0
2006	134,0	(134,0/128,0) x 100	104,7
2007	143,5	(143,5/128,0) x 100	112,1

This simple procedure is known as **technical shifting**. It should not, however, be used indiscriminately. Technical shifting can, for example, be applied to a fixed-weight (or Laspeyres) index such as the CPI only if the same weights have been used to calculate all the index numbers. Once the CPI has been reconstructed on the basis of new weights, as in South Africa in 2009, a completely new index (with a new base period) is created. This is a **fundamental shift** of the base period and the new index is strictly speaking not comparable with the previous index which has been technically shifted to the new base period. In practice, however, technical shifting is often used.

A simple and useful (although also theoretically flawed) technique for linking two differently based indices is illustrated below. This technique, which is in fact merely an extension of technical shifting, is called **splicing** or **chaining**.

Splicing (or combining two differently based indices) is quite simple but it can only be done if the old and the new series have at least one overlapping period. This is normally the case when an index is revised. The CPI figures prior to and after 2008 can be used to illustrate the technique – 2008 was the new base year after the CPI revision. As mentioned above, the technique is essentially the same as technical shifting.

Year	Old index (2000 = 100)	Revised index (2008 = 100)	Spliced index (2008 = 100)
2004	123,8		77,4
2005	128,0		80,0
2006	133,9		83,7
2007	143,5		89,7
2008	160,0	100,0	100,0
2009		107,1	107,1

For 2008 and 2009 the spliced (or chained) index numbers are identical to the new (revised) index numbers. For the years 2004 to 2007 the spliced index numbers are obtained by technically shifting the base period to 2008, as illustrated earlier. These numbers are obtained by dividing the original numbers by the index number for 2008 and multiplying the answer by 100. For 2004 the new number is (123,8/160,0) x 100 = 77,4, and so on.

consumers (in the case of the CPI), businesses, government, or whatever the case might be. See the discussion on the consumer price index in Section 6.3.

- *Price collection*. The systematic gathering of information on prices (usually on a monthly basis) is a major task. See the discussion on the consumer price index in Section 6.3.

- *Calculation of price index numbers*. The two principal price indices in South Africa, the CPI and the PPI, are both calculated according to the Laspeyres formula, which uses fixed weights for the different items. The main advantage of this kind of index is that a series of Laspeyres index numbers have a common denominator or base and are therefore comparable in the strict sense. Moreover, the calculation of a Laspeyres index requires less information than any other technique. However, because fixed weights are used, a Laspeyres price index tends to overstate price increases and understate price decreases and therefore has an upward bias. In other words, the use of a Laspeyres price index tends to overstate inflation when consumption patterns shift in response to changes in relative prices. The general problem is that the relevant basket and/or weights may become inappropriate (eg as a result of changes in relative prices or quantities, the introduction of new items, the disappearance of existing items and quality changes). New indices therefore have to be constructed from time to time by changing the basket, weights and base period.

In practice the basic Laspeyres formula also has to be adapted because volume or quantity (Q) data are not always available. The adapted formula used for constructing price indices is as follows:

$$I_t = \frac{\Sigma P_0 Q_0 (P_t/P_0)}{\Sigma P_0 Q_0} \text{ where}$$

I_t = index number in period t
Σ = 'the sum of' (summation sign)
P_0 = price in base period
Q_0 = quantity in base period
$P_0 Q_0$ = value in base period = value of weight
P_t = price in period t

The adapted formula only requires value data ($P_0 Q_0$) for the base period in addition to price data for the base period (P_0) and for each subsequent period (P_t).

Problems associated with price indices

As mentioned above, Laspeyres index numbers tend to be **biased upwards**. Because fixed weights are used, too much importance may be attached, for example, to goods whose volumes have decreased because they have become relatively more expensive. However, as long as there are no drastic changes in the composition of the basket, the degree of bias is small.

Another problem is **quality changes**. What is a quality change and how is it measured? For example, can the price of this year's Honda Civic 1.8i 5-door Exi be directly compared with the price of last year's model? There are no simple solutions to this problem.

New products also create all kinds of problems. In recent years, for example, the introduction of the Internet, cellular phones, iPods, Blu-Ray players, laptops, notebooks and blackberries has had a major influence on spending patterns. How should these changes be accommodated? What impact do they have on the comparability of price index numbers?

Another problem is the difference between **advertised** (or catalogue) **prices** and **actual transaction prices**. For example, discounts are often varied in response to changes in market conditions.

A similar type of problem, which is associated in particular with the PPI, stems from the fact that certain goods such as specialised machinery and equipment, ships and aircraft are often **custom-made**. How are the data about the prices of these goods to be collected and processed?

Finally, it should always be remembered that a price index is an **average** and as such it often conceals more than it reveals.

6.3   The consumer price index

The CPI is an index of the prices of a representative basket of consumer goods and services. It is calculated and published monthly by Stats SA. The CPI is probably the most frequently used (and abused!) of all the economic indicators in South Africa.

Retail prices have been recorded and used to calculate price index numbers in South Africa since 1895. A price index: cost of living (food, fuel, light and rent) was calculated annually from 1895 to 1910. This was followed by a variety of retail price indices and eventually (in 1958) by the consumer price index. The price data for a particular month are those collected during the first three weeks of the month. The index number is published towards the end of the following month (usually on the fourth Wednesday) in *Statistical release P0l4l* (available at *www.statssa.gov.za*). Seasonally adjusted monthly CPI figures are published in the *SARB Quarterly Bulletin*.

Additional information

Although it is the total CPI which generates most interest and is used most frequently, a whole range of indices is published each month. The CPI is published for five expenditure groups, 42 urban areas, and more than 40 groups and subgroups of goods and services. A separate CPI for pensioners is also published. Some of these additional CPIs will be referred to again later. Note, however, that these additional data do not allow for comparisons of price **levels** between different provinces or expenditure groups. They can only be used to calculate **rates of change**, the reason being that the actual cost of the basket in the base period may differ significantly between provinces, expenditure groups etc. Thus, if the index for a particular province increases much more rapidly than the indices for other provinces, it does not necessarily follow that the actual cost of living is greater in the province experiencing the rapid rate of increase. This is yet another example of the important distinction between **levels** and **rates of change**.

Base period

At the time of writing 2008 served as the base year. The immediately preceding base years were 2000, 1995 and 1990.

Basket (regimen) and weights

The CPI is a fixed-weight or Laspeyres index. The basket of goods and services (or regimen) and the weights accorded to the different goods and services are based on detailed surveys of household income and expenditure (the *Income and Expenditure Survey*). At the time of writing the latest survey was that conducted from September 2005 to August 2006. Surveys are conducted approximately every five years and after each survey a new index is constructed with a new basket and set of weights. The next survey is scheduled for 2011, with the results to be published in 2013 or 2014. After that, however, Stats SA intends to introduce new CPI weights every three years (instead of every five years).

In South Africa the basket currently comprises 416 goods and services, and the weights are based on the spending patterns of representative samples of households in the different urban areas. Table 6-1 shows the weights accorded to different kinds of goods and services in South Africa in constructing the most recent CPIs. At the time of writing, goods comprised 54,2% of the basket and services 45,8%. Note the importance of housing and transport. Some salient features of the revision of the basket in 2008 are discussed in Box 6-2.

CPI TRIVIA
For many years canaries were included in the CPI basket in Italy. In 2000, however, the canary was replaced by the motorcycle helmet.

Table 6-1: Weights of different kinds of goods and services in the South African CPI, 1995, 2000 and 2008

Group	1995 Weight	2000 Weight	2008 Weight
Food	18,2	20,99	14,27
Non-alcoholic beverages	0,82	1,10	1,41
Alcoholic beverages	1,18	1,40	3,29
Cigarettes, cigars and tobacco	0,95	1,14	2,29
Clothing and footwear	4,76	3,25	4,11
Housing	24,07	22,14	20,69
Fuel and power	3,11	3,49	1,87
Furniture and equipment	3,94	2,53	3,22
Household operation	4,69	4,82	2,64
Medical care and health expenses	5,95	7,15	1,47
Transport	14,74	14,84	18,80
Communication	3,06	2,98	3,22
Recreation and entertainment	2,38	3,31	3,48
Reading matter	0,74	0,39	0,71
Education	2,04	3,48	2,19
Personal care	3,06	3,67	2,20
Other goods and services	6,49	3,32	14,14
Total	**100,00**	**100,00**	**100,00**

Source: Statistics South Africa.

BOX 6-2: REVISION OF CPI IN 2008

As mentioned in the main text, the reweighting of the CPI in 2008 was based on the *Income and Expenditure Survey (IES)* conducted between September 2005 and August 2006. This was a much more thorough survey than the earlier ones, despite the fact that the sample size was 20% smaller than the previous *IES*.

Two criteria were used to select goods and services to be included in the basket. The spending on a product had to be a significant proportion of total household expenditure *and* the product had to be purchased by a large number of households. In this way cheap (albeit important) products (eg matches) were eliminated, as were expensive items bought by a minority of households (eg caravans, boats). A separate basket was compiled for each province and all the products included in at least one provincial basket were included in the national basket. The provincial baskets range from 356 products (Limpopo, Northern Cape) to 392 products (Western Cape) and the national basket contains 416 products (down from the previous 1 200 products).

Spending patterns also change over time due to technological progress and other reasons. For example, VHS recorders and cassettes were excluded from the basket, while minibus taxi fares, funeral costs, restaurant and take-away meals, sports events tickets, DVD players and discs, Internet service provider fees and laptop computers were included.

An important change occurred as far as the estimation of **housing costs** is concerned. Home loan (mortgage) interest rates were excluded and replaced by owners' equivalent rent (OER). The latter is the opportunity cost of housing, that is, the cost to the owner of living in the home rather than renting it out (in other words, the rent that could have been earned if the house had been rented out). The basic reason for excluding interest rates is that they represent the cost of debt rather than the cost of living. The switch to OER also eliminated the need to calculate a separate CPIX (CPI excluding mortgage interest rates) for inflation-targeting purposes. From the introduction of inflation targeting in 2000 to 2008, CPIX had been used as the basis for setting the inflation targets. (However, to accommodate contracts that stipulate CPIX as the inflator, Stats SA continues to publish a CPI excluding OER.) The switch to OER is one of the requirements of the International Labour Organisation (ILO), the body which establishes international norms for the construction of CPIs. Another of these norms which Stats SA has adhered to since 2008 is to classify the contents of the basket according to the COICOP (Classification of individual consumption by purpose), instead of the previous ITC (International trade classification).

Collection of price data

Once the basket and weights have been selected, the prices of the goods and services have to be collected. In a comprehensive index such as the CPI, price collection is a major task. An average of around 100 000 prices are collected each month. As far as goods are concerned, Stats SA sends a national team of fieldworkers to each sampled retail store to record actual prices every month. A team based in Stats SA's head office collects prices for services. As mentioned earlier, the prices are collected during the first three weeks of the month.

The prices of almost all goods in the basket are ascertained monthly but the prices of many services are collected less frequently. Some prices (eg rent of dwellings, local bus fares and taxi fares) are collected every three months, while other prices (eg doctor's fees, toll fees, university and school fees, postal tariffs, medical aid contributions) are collected annually, except if a clearly identifiable extraordinary adjustment occurs. Other prices (eg water, electricity and television licences) are collected at different intervals. These practices should be borne in mind when CPI data are interpreted because they tend to result in stepped rather than smooth increases. It is also one of the reasons that movements in the CPI should preferably be judged over periods of at least 12 months (see Section 6.4).

Formula

As mentioned previously, the CPI is a fixed-weight or Laspeyres index. The actual formula used is the adjusted version of the Laspeyres index provided in Section 6.2.

Interpretation and uses

Although the index number for any particular month is a summary of thousands of individual information items, the number in itself is not particularly useful. This is because the index number only indicates the ratio between the weighted average price of the basket of goods and services in that month and the price that prevailed in the base period. The figure becomes really useful only when it is compared with those of more recent periods.

The most common use of the CPI is to calculate inflation rates. This is dealt with in detail in Section 6.4. In addition, the CPI can also be used to inflate or deflate other time series or indices, as explained in Box 6-3, or to adjust prices, wages, salaries, rent and other variables to changes in the price level (eg as an escalator when index-linking is practised).

While the CPI is potentially a useful indicator, it is unfortunately also subject to indiscriminate use or abuse. For example, the practice of linking prices, wages, salaries, rent and other variables to the CPI (either formally or informally) increases the inflationary bias of the economy. This is because such index-linking virtually ensures that any price increase is automatically passed on in the form of further increases. The CPI is also often used indiscriminately to deflate time series or other indices. As explained in the next section, a variety of inflation rates can be calculated from a specific set of index numbers. This creates the opportunity for abuse by politicians and others (including economists!). Monthly variations in the CPI have also become important in speculative financial markets simply because they are regarded as important by the majority of participants in these markets.

BOX 6-3: DEFLATING A TIME SERIES OR INDEX

Deflating a time series or index means converting a nominal (current-price) time series or index to a real (constant-price) time series or index. In other words, the effect of price increases is removed. **Inflating** is the opposite of deflating.

Consider the following example. The figures in the first column of the table below show the average monthly earnings (in **nominal** terms) of South African manufacturing workers between 2000 and 2008. The second column shows the CPI for each of these years. The values in the last column are **real** values, obtained by dividing each nominal value by the corresponding price index number and multiplying the result by 100. For example, for 2000 the real value is obtained as (R4 698/62,5) x 100 = R7 516,8 (rounded to R7 517). The figures in the last column thus show the average monthly earnings at constant (2008) prices (ie in real terms). See also Tables 8-1 and 8-2 in Chapter 8.

Year	Average monthly earnings in manufacturing at current prices (R)	CPI (2008 = 100)	Average monthly earnings at constant (2008) prices
2000	4 698	62,5	7 517
2001	5 216	66,1	7 891
2002	5 653	72,1	7 840
2003	5 980	76,3	7 837
2004	6 575	77,4	8 495
2005	6 972	80,0	8 715
2006	7 152	83,7	8 545
2007	7 957	89,7	8 871
2008	8 855	100,0	8 855

The process of **inflating** can be illustrated by working from right to left in the above table. The real value is multiplied by the CPI and the result divided by 100 to obtain the nominal value. Thus, for 2004 we have (R8 495 x 77,4) ÷ 100 = R6 575. As mentioned earlier, inflating is simply the reverse of deflating.

The first column in the table above shows that the average **nominal** monthly earnings increased every year. The last column shows what happened to average real earnings per worker in manufacturing between 2000 and 2008 (ie to the purchasing power of the nominal earnings). While nominal earnings increased each year, real earnings fell in four of the years (2002, 2003, 2006 and 2008). The cumulative increase in real earnings between 2000 and 2008 was 17,8% (= [(R8 855 ÷ R7 517) – 1] x 100). Using the formula explained in Chapter 3, the average annual increase in real earnings in manufacturing between 2000 and 2008 can be obtained. The result is 2,07%.

Advantages and disadvantages

The CPI is an **explicit** price index that is calculated **directly** (in contrast to an implicit or derived deflator), becomes available rapidly, is relatively accurate and is not revised. A lot of care, time and effort are devoted to its construction and it is probably the most reliable of all the various price indices and arguably one of the most reliable of all the main economic indicators.

The CPI is subject, however, to all the standard defects of an explicit price index based on fixed, base-year weights. For example, it is upwardly biased because changes in the composition of consumer expenditure are ignored. Another, less serious, defect is that not all consumer goods and services are included. However, the coverage of the South African CPI is very broad, also by international standards. It should nevertheless always be borne in mind that the CPI is not directly applicable to any individual household. It is an **average** figure which pertains to a mythical 'average household' which is as fictitious as the family with 1,6 children.

The fact that the CPI data include indirect taxes such as VAT is a contentious issue. As a result, any shift from direct taxes to indirect taxes is reflected in an increased CPI, *ceteris paribus*. In other words, increased indirect taxation causes an increase in the CPI, which may subsequently be advanced as a reason for further price or wage increases. Some observers therefore argue that all taxation should be excluded from the CPI, as is the practice in certain other countries. The counter argument is that the aim of the CPI is to measure the cost of goods and services to the consumer and that indirect taxes should therefore be included in the index.

6.4   Calculating an inflation rate

The inflation rate should preferably always be annualised, that is, expressed as an **annual rate**. In fact, since inflation is a process of sustained price increases, the rate should preferably be measured over a period of not less than one year. All the prices included in the CPI and other price indices are also not measured every month – certain prices are actually only adjusted and measured once a year. There are thus both principles and technical considerations that make it inadvisable to measure inflation over very short periods (eg monthly).

In practice, however, great interest is shown in the latest available monthly and quarterly price indices. On the one hand, participants in speculative financial markets often attach great value to these figures (mainly because most other participants attach great value to them!), with the result that they are frequently discussed and analysed in the media. Politicians, on the other hand, seek figures from which they can make political capital. Government spokespersons require figures that indicate an improvement, while opposition spokespersons tend to select figures that indicate a deterioration. Policy makers want to prove that their policies are appropriate. Economists want to prove that their forecasts were good, and business people require information on the latest trends for planning purposes.

Even serious, objective observers often wish to analyse the movements in the latest monthly or quarterly figures over relatively short periods, but this should only be done with due regard to the underlying trend over longer periods.

Once the latest CPI data are published, a variety of methods can be used to calculate an inflation rate. Some of these methods are now illustrated with the aid of South African CPI data for 2008 and 2009 presented in Table 6-2.

Month on same month of previous year

The most common practice in South Africa is to compare the index number for a particular month with the index number for the corresponding month of the previous year. The result is then expressed as a percentage change. For example, if we compare the index value for December 2009 (ie 109,2) with that of December 2008 (102,7), an inflation rate of 6,3% is obtained. The calculation is as follows:

$$\frac{109,2 - 102,7}{102,7} \times 100 = 0,063 \times 100 = 6,3\%$$

or

$$(\frac{109,2}{102,7} - 1) \times 100 = (1,063 - 1) \times 100 = 0,063 \times 100$$
$$= 6,3\%$$

Table 6-2: The consumer price index and inflation in South Africa, 2008-2009

Month	Consumer price index (2008 = 100)		Inflation rate (%)
	2008	2009	
January	95,4	103,1	8,1
February	96,0	104,3	8,6
March	97,4	105,7	8,5
April	98,0	106,2	8,4
May	98,7	106,6	8,0
June	100,1	107,0	6,9
July	101,4	108,2	6,7
August	102,0	108,5	6,4
September	102,6	108,9	6,1
October	102,8	108,9	5,9
November	102,9	108,9	5,8
December	102,7	109,2	6,3
Average for year	**100,0**	**107,1**	**7,1**

Source of basic data: Statistics South Africa.

This is the method used to calculate the inflation rate reported in the media each month. The method covers a period of 12 months and therefore indicates what happened to prices during the most recent 'year'. However, inflation rates calculated according to this method are subject to considerable fluctuations. For example, an increase in the petrol price or the rate of value-added tax may suddenly raise the inflation rate in a particular month. A year later the opposite can happen when the impact of the original increase is eliminated. A major drawback of a year-on-year comparison is thus that it suffers from the **base effect** – what happened one year ago has as much impact as what happened in the latest period. Another problem with this method is that all prices are not measured every month. This may give rise to stepped rather than relatively smooth increases in the CPI from month to month. Economists often refer to 'technical reasons' or 'statistical noise' when explaining sudden jumps or falls in the rate of increase in the CPI.

Annual average on annual average (or 12-month moving average)

When the inflation rate for a calendar year is calculated, the usual procedure is to compare the average of all the monthly indices in a particular year with the corresponding average for the previous year. In our example the annual averages for 2008 and 2009 are given in the last row of Table 6-2. The percentage change shown in the last column of the last row is obtained as follows:

$$\frac{107,1 - 100,0}{100,0} \times 100 = 7,1\% \ (\text{or} \ (\frac{107,1}{100,0} - 1) \times 100 = 7,1\%)$$

Note that this figure differs from the result obtained by simply comparing the figures for December 2009 and December 2008. The reason is that the figure of 7,1% is based on all 24 monthly figures in Table 6-2. In this way, short-term fluctuations in the index figures for particular months are eliminated. This method therefore gives a better indication of the intensity of the inflation process over a longer period. Moreover, this method is not restricted to calendar years. Any 12-month average (eg from July to June) may be compared with the previous 12-month average (also from July to June) in order to calculate an inflation rate. This is probably the most satisfactory method, since it covers a longer period than the previous method and also eliminates the effect of technical factors. However, to determine possible short-term changes in the inflation rate, this method has to be supplemented by other methods, such as the comparison of a month on the same month of the previous year, as well as the additional two methods outlined below.

Month on previous month at an annual rate

Another practice is to compare a particular month's figure with that of the immediately preceding month and to express the change at an annual rate. This is done as follows: obtain the ratio of the two consecutive monthly figures; raise this to the power 12 (for the 12 months of the year); subtract 1; and multiply by 100 to obtain a percentage. For example, comparing the figure for December 2009 with that of November 2009 yields an annual rate of 9,3%:

$$[(109,2/108,9)^{12} - 1] \times 100 = (1,0336 - 1) \times 100 = 3,4\%$$

The corresponding rate for November 2009 (compared to October 2009) was 0,0%. This rate is clearly subject to large fluctuations. In fact, for certain months (eg December 2008) this method yields a negative inflation rate, since the CPI is sometimes lower in a particular month than in the previous month. Calculating an inflation rate by comparing the CPI for two consecutive months is therefore not significant, unless the CPI data have been **seasonally adjusted.**

Seasonally adjusted monthly index numbers are published quarterly by the South African Reserve Bank in its *Quarterly Bulletin*. Table 6-3 contains the seasonally adjusted monthly CPI figures as well as quarterly averages for 2008 and 2009.

Table 6-3: Seasonally adjusted consumer price index, 2008-2009

Month	Quarter	Seasonally adjusted consumer price index (2008 = 100)	
		2008	2009
January		95,4	103,1
February		96,3	104,7
March		97,3	105,6
	I	**96,3**	**104,5**
April		98,0	106,2
May		98,9	106,8
June		100,0	106,9
	II	**99,0**	**106,6**
July		101,1	107,8
August		101,7	108,2
September		102,4	108,7
	III	**101,7**	**108,2**
October		102,6	108,7
November		103,1	109,1
December		103,1	109,6
	IV	**102,9**	**109,1**

Source: South African Reserve Bank.

Comparing the seasonally adjusted figure for December 2009 with that of November 2009 yields an annual rate of 5,6% (compared to the 3,4% obtained on the basis of the unadjusted figures):

$$[(109,6/109,1)^{12} - 1] \times 100 = (1,0564 - 1) \times 100 = 5,6\%$$

The corresponding rate for November 2009 (compared to October 2009) was 4,5% compared to the 0% obtained on the basis of the unadjusted figures. The inflation rates based on seasonally adjusted monthly changes are thus more meaningful, but a significant degree of variation often remains. At most, therefore, inflation rates based on successive monthly index numbers can only supplement inflation rates calculated according to the first two methods explained in this section.

Quarterly average on previous quarterly average at an annual rate

Similar conclusions apply to inflation rates based on quarterly average CPI data. Some economists compare the average CPI for a particular quarter with the average for the previous quarter to identify possible short-term changes in the inflation rate. The unadjusted quarterly averages for 2009 (based on the figures in Table 6-2) were: 104,4 (I); 106,4 (II); 108,5 (III); and 109,0 (IV). The increase between two successive quarters at an annual rate is calculated as follows: obtain the ratio of the two consecutive quarterly averages; raise this to the power 4 (for the four quarters of the year); subtract 1; and multiply by 100 to obtain a percentage. For example, by using the figures for the last two quarters of 2009, an annual rate of 2,6% is obtained:

$$[(109,0/108,5)^4 - 1] \times 100 = (1,019 - 1) \times 100 = 1,9\%$$

The corresponding change between the second and third quarters was 7,3%. This rate is also subject to significant fluctuations. Once again the problem can be alleviated by using seasonally adjusted data. For example, using the **seasonally adjusted** averages in Table 6-3, an annual rate of 3,4% is obtained by using the figures for the last two quarters of 2009:

$$[(109,1/108,2)^4 - 1] \times 100 = (1,034 - 1) \times 100 = 3,4\%$$

The corresponding change between the second and third quarters was 6,1%. The results of seasonally adjusted data are still subject to significant fluctuations, but less than the unadjusted data. (The same technique can, of course, be applied to compare the average of any three consecutive monthly figures to the average of the previous three monthly figures. For example, the average for September, October and November can be compared to the average for June, July and August and so on.)

Using the methods outlined above, six different inflation rates (or rates of change in the CPI) could therefore be calculated when the CPI for December 2009 became available. These results (with the corresponding results for the period to November 2009 in brackets) were as follows:

- month on same month of previous year: 6,3% (5,8%)
- last 12 months on previous12 months: 7,1% (7,4%)
- month on previous month at annual rate: 3,4% (0,0%)

- 3 months on previous 3 months at annual rate: 1,9% (3,8%)
- month on previous month at annual rate (seasonally adjusted): 5,6% (4,5%)
- 3 months on previous 3 months at annual rate (seasonally adjusted): 3,4% (5,7%)

The SARB also publishes a table in its *Quarterly Bulletin* which contains annual and monthly inflation rates for the CPI and its main components.

6.5   Subindices of the CPI

As mentioned in Section 6.3, Stats SA also publishes various subindices of the CPI. These subindices all contain useful information, but are used less frequently than the overall CPI and receive less attention in the media.

Expenditure groups

Because the spending patterns of different expenditure groups vary, Stats SA publishes different CPIs for five expenditure groups. At the time of writing the five expenditure group categories or quintiles, defined according to the total annual expenditure per household obtained in the 2005/6 *Income and Expenditure Survey*, were as follows (in 2005/6 prices):

- Very low expenditure group: up to R14 564
- Low expenditure group: R14 565 up to R23 278
- Middle expenditure group: R23 279 up to R36 755
- High expenditure group: R36 756 up to R79 152
- Very high expenditure group: R79 153 and more

Since the expenditure patterns vary between the groups, different weights were assigned accordingly to the CPIs for the different groups. For example, food had a weight of 37,45 in the consumer basket of the very low expenditure group in urban areas, compared to 9,17 for the very high expenditure group. Because of the differences in the weights, the inflation rates for the different expenditure groups may vary considerably if the prices of different categories of goods and services are not increasing at roughly similar rates. The information provided by these different subindices is very useful when **changes** in the cost of living of different expenditure groups have to be estimated (eg during wage negotiations). However, as explained earlier, the data can only be used to compare **changes** in the CPI. They cannot be used to compare differences in the **level** of the cost of living.

Geographic areas

As mentioned in Section 6.3, Stats SA also publishes different CPIs for the nine provinces, consisting of a total of 16 primary urban areas and 26 secondary urban areas. Again it is important to note that the data can be used to compare **changes** in the CPI only. They cannot be used to draw any conclusions about differences in the **level** of the cost of living between the different provinces. Even the changes in the CPI cannot be compared accurately since each province has its own particular CPI basket.

Traditionally the South African CPI focused on the metropolitan areas. The geographic coverage of the CPI was later extended to include a number of 'other urban areas'. In May 2003 the geographic coverage was extended further by publishing CPIs for both the **rural areas** and the **total country**. No pricing surveys are undertaken in the rural areas but the weights used are based on information for the rural areas obtained from the *Survey of Income and Expenditure of Households*. The prices are those collected in the secondary urban areas.

The **headline inflation measure**, which also serves as the basis for calculating the inflation target, is the CPI for all urban areas (previously the CPI for historical metropolitan and other urban areas).

Apart from the detail published regularly in *Statistical release P1041*, a host of further detail for each province is available on request from Stats SA.

Administered and regulated prices

From June 2005 Stats SA also published price indices for administered prices, regulated prices and administered prices that are not regulated. An **administered price** is defined as a price that is set consciously by an individual producer or group of producers and/or any price that can be determined or influenced by government without reference to market forces. **Regulated prices** are those administered prices that are monitored and controlled by government policy. The indices for administered and regulated prices tend to increase much faster than those for market-based prices.

It should be clear at this stage that there is a wide range or suite of CPIs, not a single figure (or set of figures).

6.6   The producer price index

A second well-known price index is the PPI. However, as will be explained below, the PPI became less relevant in 2008, when exported commodities were added to the PPI basket and imported commodities were no longer explicitly included in the overall basket. At the time of writing the PPI was being revised in an attempt to eliminate some of its shortcomings.

Whereas the CPI measures the cost of goods and services to the consumer, the PPI measures prices at the level of the first significant commercial transaction. Prices of imported goods are measured at the point where they enter the country, while manufactured goods are priced when they leave the factory. Likewise, exported goods are measured when they are sold for the first time.

There are actually three separate PPIs, one for the domestic output of South African industry groups (including exports), one for imports and one for exports, with the first one serving as the 'headline' PPI. The data in these series are used by the private sector for contract price adjustments, and as deflators in the compilation of the national accounts (ie to transform nominal values into real values).

Like the CPI, the PPI is also estimated and published on a monthly basis by Stats SA. The price information refers to the first seven days of the month, except in the case of mining and most of the agricultural products, where the information refers to the average prices for the month. The prices of all items exclude VAT. The index number is published in *Statistical release P0142.1*, usually on the fourth Thursday of the following month (ie the day after the release of the CPI). Seasonally adjusted monthly data are published by the SARB in its *Quarterly Bulletin*. The basic data are available at *www.statssa.gov.za*.

The PPI is also a Laspeyres (ie fixed-weight) price index. The **basket** and **weights** are based on statistics of production and foreign trade. The weights are calculated according to value added. At the time of writing 2000 was still the **base period** of the PPI, but the weights were mostly based on the value added in 2004/05.

The prices of more than 1 000 goods are collected directly from producers by means of a postal enquiry. Approximately 2 325 manufacturers, 2 325 exporters and 2 325 importers are included in the sample of respondents. Prices are also obtained from government departments and other organisations that determine or collect prices required for the index. At the time of writing an average of 13 000 price quotations were collected each month from approximately 2 700 outlets by means of 1 500 distinct questionnaires.

Some prices are not collected every month, but at three-month intervals. Certain goods are priced in January, April, July and October; others in February, May, August and November; and the remainder in March, June, September and December. As a result, some prices remain unchanged from one month to the next, while some of those that do change increase or decrease in a stepped fashion. This has to be borne in mind when interpreting the PPI. Ideally, movements in the PPI should be interpreted over a period of at least a year.

All the methods explained in Section 6.4 can also be applied to the PPI to calculate an inflation rate. Table 6-4 shows the results of comparing the PPI for each month of 2009 with that of the corresponding month of 2008 to calculate rates of change over 12 months. Note the decline in PPI inflation during the course of the year, eventually resulting in **deflation** (ie falling prices) from May to November.

Subindices

As mentioned earlier, there are actually three broad PPIs, one for the domestic output of South African industry (including exports), one for imported commodities and one for exported commodities. In addition, separate data are published for 28 groups, 61 subgroups and more than 120 selected materials (eg in the construction industry).

Table 6-4: South African PPI, 2008-2009 (2000 = 100)

Month	(a) 2008	(b) 2009	% change from (a) to(b)
January	164,9	180,0	9,2
February	167,2	179,4	7,3
March	170,6	179,6	5,3
April	174,1	179,2	2,9
May	182,7	177,2	–3,0
June	187,5	179,9	–4,1
July	192,5	185,2	–3,8
August	193,6	185,8	–4,0
September	186,7	179,8	–3,7
October	185,8	179,7	–3,3
November	183,4	181,2	–1,2
December	181,3	182,5	0,7
Average for year	**180,8**	**180,7**	**0,1**

Source: Statistics South Africa.

Differences between the PPI and CPI

The PPI and CPI are both explicit price indices. Some of the differences between the two have already been referred to. The main differences are the following:

- The PPI estimates the cost of production, in contrast to the CPI which estimates the cost of living.
- The CPI pertains to consumer goods and services, while the PPI pertains to goods only (including capital and intermediate goods and exported commodities).
- Price information is obtained from different sources and different weighting systems are used. Where items overlap, their weights differ significantly between the PPI and the CPI. For example, foodstuffs have a much larger weight in the CPI than in the PPI.
- VAT is included in the CPI, but excluded from the PPI.

Links between the PPI and CPI

Traditionally, movements in the PPI were scrutinised carefully, since they often gave an indication of where the CPI was heading. Because the PPI measured the cost of production and included imported capital and intermediate goods, a significant change in the rate of increase in the PPI usually provided an indication that the rate of increase in the CPI would also change at a later stage. For example, when the rand depreciated against the major currencies, the prices of imported capital and intermediate goods also tended to increase, along with the prices of imported consumer goods. These increases were reflected immediately in the PPI and, after a time-lag of some months, also in the CPI. However, after the revision of the PPI in 2008, these links became much weaker, mainly because imports are no longer included explicitly in the 'headline' PPI, while exports (which have little or no relevance for consumer prices) are included. Under the new weighting system exported commodities also have a greater impact on movements in the 'headline' PPI than before. The implication is that an increase in international commodity prices (eg mineral prices) is reflected in an increase in the PPI, even though it has little or no relevance for inflation in South Africa. As mentioned earlier, Stats SA was revising the PPI in an attempt to make it more meaningful.

6.7   Implicit price deflators

Apart from explicit price indices such as the CPI and PPI, a variety of implicit price deflators can also be used to calculate inflation rates. An **implicit price deflator** is derived by dividing a nominal (or current-price) magnitude by the corresponding real (or constant-price) magnitude. It can be expressed as a quotient, or as an index, by multiplying the quotient by 100. The deflator is called an implicit deflator because it is **implied** by (or derived from) the difference between the value of the magnitude expressed at current and constant prices respectively.

A price deflator can be derived for any magnitude that is estimated at both constant and current prices. The best-known examples are the GDE deflator, GDP deflator and GNI (or GNP) deflator. These deflators are not published separately but can easily be derived from the published national accounting data.

GDE deflator

The gross domestic expenditure deflator (GDE deflator) is an implicit index of the domestic price level and is obtained by dividing the GDE at current prices (or nominal GDE) by the GDE at constant prices (or real GDE).

$$\text{Thus: GDE deflator} = \frac{\text{GDE at current prices}}{\text{GDE at constant prices}}$$

The index can be expressed as a ratio or as a percentage (by multiplying the ratio by 100). The base year of the index is the base year for estimating the value of GDE at constant prices.

Table 6-5 provides an example of calculating the GDE deflator. Column (a) shows the annual GDE at current prices for the period 2002 to 2009, while column (b) shows the corresponding values of GDE at constant 2005 prices. Column (c) shows the ratio between the first two columns and, in column (d), the figures in column (c) have simply been multiplied by 100 to express them as a percentage (with 2005 = 100). The fact that the GDE deflator for 2005 is 100 is no accident, since GDE at constant prices must be equal to GDE at current prices in the base year. The GDE deflator for 2002 is obtained by dividing the current price value (R1 126 162 million) by the constant price value (R1 317 641 million). This yields 0,855 (ratio) or 85,5 (index). In the last column an inflation rate is derived by calculating the percentage change between the successive annual values of the GDE deflator. Thus, for 2003 the rate is the percentage increase between the 2002 value (85,5) and the 2003 value (89,8):

$$\frac{89,8 - 85,5}{85,5} \times 100 = 5,0\% \text{ (or } (\frac{89,8}{85,5} - 1) \times 100 = 5,0\%)$$

All the other figures and rates are obtained in the same way.

Table 6-5: Calculating the GDE deflator, 2002-2009

Year	GDE at current prices (Rm) (a)	GDE at constant 2005 prices (Rm) (b)	GDE deflator (ratio) (a)/(b) (c)	GDE deflator (index) ((c) x 100) (d)	% change in GDE deflator (e)
2002	1 126 162	1 317 641	0,855	85,5	–
2003	1 242 787	1 383 661	0,898	89,8	5,0
2004	1 419 502	1 490 735	0,952	95,2	6,0
2005	1 578 472	1 578 472	1,000	100,0	5,0
2006	1 810 678	1 714 312	1,056	105,6	5,6
2007	2 076 262	1 824 753	1,138	113,8	7,8
2008	2 352 714	1 885 686	1,248	124,8	9,7
2009	2 443 950	1 851 377	1,320	132,0	5,8

Source of basic data: SARB Quarterly Bulletin, March 2010.

To understand the derivation of the GDE deflator, it is important to realise that GDE at constant prices (real GDE) is not simply obtained by dividing or deflating GDE at current prices (nominal GDE) by a single index. What actually happens is that the various components of GDE at current prices are each converted separately to constant prices, using a wide variety of methods and indices. This is a complicated process. Fortunately, all we need to know is that, once the process has been executed (with a view to calculating real growth), the difference between nominal GDE and real GDE yields an index which we can use to calculate an inflation rate for the economy as a whole.

Since GDE is a broadly based aggregate, the GDE deflator is often regarded as an appropriate basis for calculating an inflation rate for the economy as a whole. Recall that GDE consists of the total spending by households, firms and the government on final goods and services (including imports). Whereas the CPI and PPI pertain to limited baskets only, the GDE deflator pertains to the prices of all final goods and services purchased in the economy.

GDP deflator

Most of the national accounting data are published at both constant and current prices, with a view to calculating real growth rates. This allows for the calculation of a wide range of deflators. Probably the best-known of these is the GDP deflator. Thus, although the main purpose of the transformation of GDP at current prices to GDP at constant prices is to measure economic growth, it also yields a measure of inflation, since the difference between nominal GDP and real GDP indicates what has happened to prices since the base year.

The GDP deflator is derived in the same way as the GDE deflator (as explained in Table 6-5). Like the GDE deflator, the GDP deflator is a much broader based index than the CPI or the PPI. However, it has one potential drawback. Since GDP includes exports and excludes imports, it follows that the GDP deflator reflects changes in export prices, while excluding changes in import prices. From an inflation point of view, however, import prices (such as the price of imported oil) are important, while export prices (such as the price of gold) are of little significance. Thus, when the price of gold falls, it pushes down the rate of increase in the GDP deflator. The GDP deflator may therefore indicate that the inflation rate decreased, while the rate of increase in prices in the domestic economy may actually have increased or been constant. Likewise, changes in import prices are not reflected in the GDP deflator (since GDP excludes imports) but they have a definite bearing on domestic price levels. As long as export prices and import prices are increasing at the same rate (ie when the terms of trade remain unchanged (see Chapter 7)), this shortcoming of the GDP deflator does not present a serious problem. But when export prices and import prices are increasing at significantly different rates, the inflation rate calculated on the basis of the GDP deflator can be misleading. This is one of the reasons for the occasional divergence between the annual rates of change in the GDP deflator and the other explicit and implicit price indices (see Table 6-6).

On account of this problem, the GDE deflator and the GNI deflator (which is explained below) are preferred to the GDP deflator. Note that the problem is related to the shortcomings of real GDP as a basis for measuring economic growth (discussed in Section 3.2).

GNI deflator

The GNI deflator is obtained by dividing GNI at current prices by GNI at constant prices. The main shortcoming of the GDP deflator (that it includes export prices and excludes import prices) does not apply to the GNI deflator. This might seem strange, since the only difference between GNI and GDP is the net primary income to the rest of the world. In other words, GNI also includes exports and excludes imports. However, when converting nominal (current-price) GNI to real (constant-price) GNI, an adjustment is made for changes in the terms of trade (ie the ratio between export prices and import prices (see Section 7.4)). As a result, real GNI thus measures the volume of exports in terms of the volume of imports that it can be exchanged for (see also the discussion in Section 3.2). This means that the GNI deflator is a better measure of the domestic price level than the GDP deflator when the terms of trade fluctuate (which they often do in the case of South Africa). For the same reason, real GNI is a better basis for measuring economic growth (from a welfare point of view) than real GDP (see Section 3.2).

Advantages of implicit price deflators

The following are some of the main advantages of implicit price deflators, compared to explicit price indices such as the CPI and PPI:

- Implicit price deflators such as the GDE deflator, GDP deflator and GNI deflator provide a more comprehensive coverage of the price level than the explicit price indices.

- Implicit price deflators are well suited to international comparisons because of the greater standardisation of concepts and uniformity of methods of estimation in the national accounts than in respect of the CPI and PPI.

- The implicit price deflators are based on current weights (ie they are Paasche indices) and therefore reflect actual expenditure, in contrast to the CPI and PPI which are based on fixed base-period weights. Any possible substitution effects as a result of changes in relative prices are therefore reflected in the deflators (but not in the CPI and PPI).

The formula for an implicit price deflator is

$$\frac{\sum P_t Q_t}{\sum P_0 Q_t}$$

compared to the (Laspeyres) formula for a fixed-weight index (eg the CPI) which is

$$\frac{\sum P_t Q_0}{\sum P_0 Q_0} \times 100$$

where $\sum$ = summation sign
P_0 = price in base period
Q_0 = quantity in base period
$P_0 Q_0$ = value in base period
P_t = price in current period
Q_t = quantity in current period
$P_t Q_t$ = value in current period

Disadvantages of implicit price deflators

Implicit price deflators also have some disadvantages compared to explicit price indices, including the following:

- Consumers, politicians and policy makers are primarily interested in the prices of a limited basket of consumer goods and services (as measured by the CPI) and do not particularly care about what is happening to the prices of other final goods and services (eg the prices of capital goods) which are captured in the deflators.

- Strictly speaking, the implicit price deflators only measure pure price changes between the base period and the current period. Comparisons for periods other than between the current period and the base period reflect changes in the composition of output or spending as well as price changes. This is because current-period weights are used, which implies that there is a different basket in each period.

- The data from which implicit price deflators are derived are only available on a quarterly basis, with a time lag, and are always subject to revision.

The implicit price deflators therefore offer no real alternative to anyone interested in timely estimates of inflation which are not revised. Although useful for analytical purposes, the implicit price deflators are of little use to economists who have to forecast inflation.

6.8   Comparison between different measures of inflation

Table 6-6 shows the annual inflation rates for the period 2002–2009 calculated on the basis of each of the main indices explained in this chapter. Although these figures never all yield exactly the same results for any particular year, the differences are usually not very large and they tend to cancel out over time. This is illustrated by the figures in the last row of the table which show the compounded annual average increases in the five indices over the period as a whole (calculated using the formula provided in Chapter 3). Economists usually consider all these indices when analysing the inflation process. However, for consumers (and therefore also for politicians) the CPI is by far the most important index since it relates more closely to their cost of living or the purchasing power of their incomes than any of the other indices.

6.9   Reporting on and interpreting inflation data

Each month the release of the latest CPI and PPI data and the accompanying information about inflation generates tremendous interest in the media and in the financial markets. The way in which these data are reported leaves much to be desired. The main problem is the tendency to confuse **levels** and **rates of change**.

Table 6-6: Comparison of annual rates of increase in various explicit
and implicit price indices, 2002-2009

Year	Annual rate of increase in				
	CPI	PPI	GDP deflator	GNI deflator	GDE deflator
2002	9,1	14,2	10,5	9,7	9,5
2003	5,8	2,3	5,6	5,0	5,0
2004	1,4	2,3	6,3	6,0	6,0
2005	3,4	3,7	5,5	5,0	5,0
2006	4,6	7,7	6,5	5,4	5,6
2007	7,2	10,9	8,3	7,4	7,8
2008	11,5	14,3	9,2	8,9	9,7
2009	7,1	0,0	8,0	6,8	5,8

Source of basic data: SARB Quarterly Bulletin, March 2008, March 2010.

For example, when the rate of increase in the CPI falls, it is often reported as a drop in the CPI. This is, of course, incorrect since the **level** of the CPI usually increases every month. In Table 6-2, for example, we saw that the level of the CPI increased during every month of 2009 except October and November. The annual **rate of increase** in the CPI fell in every month from March to November. The fall in the annual rate of increase in the CPI from 8,0% in May to 6,9% in June was typically reported as a 'drop in the CPI from 8,0% to 6,9%'.

This erroneous reporting is not confined to non-economists. Even economists, who should know better, are often guilty of incorrect or sloppy reporting in respect of rates of change (see Box 6-4).

BOX 6-4: SOME TYPICAL EXAMPLES OF SLOPPY OR ERRONEOUS REPORTING ON PRICE INDICES AND INFLATION

'Lowest PPI in 30 years raises fear of deflation', front-page headline in *Business Day*, 26 June 2003.

'PPI val soos 'n klip', front-page headline in *Sake-Beeld*, 26 June 2003. The report started as follows: 'Produsentepryse het verlede maand soos 'n klip tot die laagste vlak in meer as 30 jaar geval...' (Actually the PPI increased at an annual rate of 1,1%.)

'Die verbruikersprysindeks (VPI) het in April vir die eerste keer in langer as drie jaar tot onder 5% gedaal.' Sake 24, 27 May 2010:21.

'Le Roux and Rossouw also expect sharp declines in January's consumer price index (CPI).' *Rapport*, 22 February 2009 (translated).

This type of reporting also serves to further confuse ordinary citizens, many of whom already distrust the official inflation statistics. When a decline in inflation is reported, consumers are often up in arms because their experience is that prices are still increasing. While this dissatisfaction should be attributed partly to a failure to realise that the overall inflation rate is an average rate for the country as a whole, much of the confusion again stems from the inability to distinguish between **levels** and **rates of change**. Like economic growth, inflation is an exponential phenomenon with every change occurring off a new base. Thus, if the price of a good increased from R1,00 to R1,10 in Year 1 and from R1,10 to R1,20 in Year 2, the rate of increase dropped from 10% to 9,1% between Year 1 and Year 2. To many a consumer, however, the (absolute) increase is still the same and therefore the inflation rate should also be the same.

Another frequent interpretation error is to forget that the prices of some of the items in the regimen or basket may have remained unchanged, or even dropped, in absolute terms. For example, if the petrol price falls, the running cost of transport to the average household may fall in absolute terms (ie the actual level may fall). Given the large weight of transport cost in the CPI, this may have a significant impact on the level of the CPI and therefore also on the rate of increase since the same month of the previous year.

Despite all the criticisms and misinterpretations, the CPI is one of the most reliable of all economic indicators. Interpreted and used correctly it is also one of the most useful.

Chapter 7

International transactions

In an increasingly integrated and globalised world economy indicators relating to international transactions are particularly important. In the current international environment the economic performance of a country is often determined by the strength of its economic links with the rest of the world, while both the scope for and the direction of economic policy are frequently governed by these links. In this chapter we focus on some of the important indicators pertaining to international transactions, particularly the balance of payments and exchange rates.

7.1   The balance of payments

The balance of payments is a systematic statistical summary or record of all economic transactions between residents[1] in the reporting country (eg South Africa) and the rest of the world during a particular period (quarter or year). It includes all transactions by individuals, firms and government agencies and covers the exchange of physical goods, services, assets, gifts and all financial claims.

Nowadays, more than ever before, it is impossible to understand an economy without understanding its relationship with the rest of the world, and for such an understanding balance of payments data are essential. Like a company's income statement, the balance of payments is much more than a mere collection of figures. The balance of payments is a reflection of the economic position of a country and it is one of the most important bases for economic policy formulation. In South Africa, for example, it is often impossible to understand the direction and thrust of monetary policy without an understanding of the balance of payments.

Although the account is called a **balance** of payments, it records the value of transactions over a given period and therefore consists of **flow** concepts rather than stock concepts.

---

1.   *Residents* are defined as those who enjoy permanent domicile in the country in question, and comprise individuals, corporate entities and government bodies. Foreign subsidiaries and branch offices are regarded as residents of their host countries but diplomatic and military staff, tourists and other foreign visitors are considered to be residents of their countries of origin.

Even in the case of assets or liabilities it is not the **level** of the assets or liabilities (ie a stock) but the **change in their value** (ie a flow) that is reflected in the balance of payments.

All transactions that lead to a **receipt of payments** from foreigners (ie non-residents) are entered as **credits** (+) in the balance of payments and all transactions that lead to a **payment** to foreigners are entered as **debits** (–). Some examples of the treatment of individual transactions are provided in Box 7-4 at the end of this section. To understand the balance of payments one has to disregard any notion that credits are good and debits bad. In any case, every international transaction is recorded twice in the balance of payments, once as a credit and once as a debit (see Box 7-2).

Compiling the balance of payments is no easy task. In an attempt to standardise balance of payments data, the IMF publishes a *Balance of payments manual* which contains recommended concepts and definitions and rules for recording different types of transactions. In June 1999 the classification of the South African balance of payments was revised drastically to conform to the requirements of the 1993 edition of the *Balance of payments manual*.

The balance of payments consists of five subaccounts: the **current account**, the **capital transfer account**, the **financial account**, **unrecorded transactions** and the **official reserves account**. Transactions in goods and services, factor or primary income and current transfers are recorded in the current account, while transactions in assets, such as shares, stocks, bonds and fixed property, and other financial transactions are recorded in the financial account, previously called the capital account. Current or income transactions are recorded in the current account, while capital or asset transactions are recorded in the financial account. The capital transfer account is a smaller, relatively insignificant account. The official reserves account is the balancing item in the balance of payments, at least in principle. The unrecorded transactions serve to balance the whole account in practice.

South African balance of payments statistics are published quarterly (one quarter in arrears) in the *SARB Quarterly Bulletin*. The South African balance of payments data for 2008 and 2009 are summarised in Table 7-1.

In Table 7-1 the increase in gross gold and other reserves in 2008 is shown as a positive number, while the decrease in the reserves in 2009 is preceded by a minus sign (indicating a negative number). For the balance of payments to actually balance, these signs should be reversed. In other words, a decrease in the reserves should be indicated as a + (to balance the minus in the rest of the account), while an increase should be indicated as a – (to balance the plus in the rest of the account). This aspect is discussed further in Box 7-1 towards the end of this section.

We now take a closer look at the main accounts and the individual items in the balance of payments.

Table 7-1: South African balance of payments, 2008 and 2009 (R millions)

	2008	2009
Current account		
Merchandise exports, fob*	655 759	503 656
Net gold exports	48 534	52 776
Service receipts	105 352	100 681
Income receipts	48 254	34 075
less Merchandise imports, fob*	−739 852	−554 161
less Payments for services	−138 684	−123 579
less Income payments	−122 129	−87 593
Current transfers (net receipts +)	−18 909	−22 428
Balance on current account	**−161 675**	**−96 573**
Capital transfer account (net receipts +)	**208**	**216**
Financial account		
Net direct investment	100 291	34 845
Net portfolio investment	−134 865	92 469
Net other investment	130 713	−21 646
Balance on financial account	**96 139**	**105 668**
Unrecorded transactions	**91 394**	**7 726**
Change in net gold and other foreign reserves owing to balance of payments transactions	**26 066**	**17 037**
Change in liabilities related to reserves	−7 761	−2 724
SDR allocations and valuation adjustments	74 214	−38 647
Net monetisation (+)/demonetisation (−) of gold	158	45
Change in gross gold and other foreign reserves	**92 677**	**−24 289**

*   fob = free on board.

Source: SARB Quarterly Bulletin, March 2010.

Current account

As mentioned earlier, the value of all transactions in goods and services is recorded in the current account. The first item, **merchandise exports**, includes the trade in all physical goods, which consist of raw materials as well as intermediate and final goods. It is important to note that exports of capital goods also fall into this category and not under capital movements (which pertain to financial rather than real capital). The value of exported goods is determined free on board (fob), which means that the value put on an article includes the cost of its production as well as the cost of its transportation to the national border of the exporting country (including airports), but excludes the cost of transportation between countries.[2]

The second item, **net gold exports**, refers to net foreign sales of **commodity gold** (see Box 7-1). Prior to 2004 net gold exports included changes in the gold holdings of the South African Reserve Bank, other banking institutions and the gold mines, but in 2004 the definition was amended in accordance with the IMF's *Balance of Payments Manual* and the data were revised retrospectively to 1981. Nowadays there is a clear distinction between monetary gold and non-monetary (or commodity) gold. **Monetary gold** is gold owned by the monetary authorities and held as an international reserve asset. **Non-monetary gold** is simply a commodity (held by mines, jewellers and other non-central bank entities). International transactions in non-monetary (commodity) gold are recorded in the current account of the balance of payments. The item 'net gold exports' thus refers to commodity gold only. The treatment of monetary gold is explained later.

BOX 7-1: THE DECLINING IMPORTANCE OF GOLD

The South African economy has long been associated with gold. Large parts of the South African economy developed around the gold mining industry and over the years gold was an important source of exports, income, employment and tax revenue. For many years gold also played a pivotal role in the international monetary system.

All this has changed, however. Annual gold production in South Africa peaked at 1 002 tons in 1970 and subsequently declined fairly steadily. Sporadic sharp increases in the gold price spurred the industry from time to time but production declined to such an extent that South Africa was overtaken by China as the world's leading producer in the new millennium. Precise estimates vary a little, but by 2009 South Africa (220 tons) was ranked third alongside the United States (220 tons) and behind China (330 tons) and Australia (223 tons). At that stage South African gold production was significantly lower than in 1922.

Despite the changing fortunes of gold and the gold mining industry, certain indicators relating to the metal still receive prominence in the media and elsewhere. For example, the latest gold price is still reported many times each day on radio and television and net gold exports are still recorded separately from other merchandise exports in the balance of payments, despite having been overtaken by platinum and coal as the country's leading export commodity. It is important to realise, however, that gold has largely lost its monetary role and that the South African gold mining industry is no longer the force it used to be.

---

2.   Whereas the national income and product accounts discussed in Chapter 2 measure the creation of value added (to avoid double counting), the balance of payments measures the movement of value across national borders. The balance of payments therefore records trade in assets and second-hand goods, which are excluded in the national income and product accounts (except for the value of commissions or other forms of value added associated with such trade).

Apart from trade in goods, the current account also records the trade in **services**. Trade in services includes the transportation of goods and passengers between countries, travel, construction services, financial and insurance services, various business, professional and technical services, as well as personal, cultural and recreational services and government services. Travel allowances and money spent by tourists on food and accommodation while travelling in foreign countries all fall in this category. The third item on the balance of payments represents the total value of all **service receipts** during the period concerned.

The fourth item is **income receipts**, which refer to income earned by South African residents in the rest of the world. There are two categories of income flow: compensation of employees and investment income. Compensation of employees includes wages, salaries and other benefits earned by individuals from countries other than those in which they are resident (ie from the rest of the world). Investment income includes dividends, interest, profits and other forms of income earned from the provision of financial capital. It is important to note that investment income is recorded in the current account, not the financial account. Thus, when a South African purchases shares in a British company on the London Stock Exchange the value of the shares purchased is recorded in the financial account but any subsequent dividend receipts are recorded as income receipts in the current account of the South African balance of payments. In such a case there is therefore a definite link between transactions recorded in the financial account and current account respectively. Likewise, all interest and dividend payments on foreign investment in South Africa are also recorded in the current account of the South African balance of payments (as income payments). Thus, the larger the foreign investment in the country, the larger the income payments tend to become. Note that income receipts in the balance of payments are equivalent to the **primary income from the rest of the world** identified in the national accounts (see Section 2.8).

The fifth, sixth and seventh items in the current account of the balance of payments, **merchandise imports**, **payments for services** and **income payments**, are calculated on the same basis as merchandise exports, service receipts and income receipts respectively. The main difference, of course, is that the income or expenditure flows are in the opposite direction, that is, from South African residents to the rest of the world. Income payments are equivalent to the primary income to the rest of the world identified in the national accounts.

Merchandise exports, net gold exports and merchandise imports together constitute the **trade account**, also called the goods account, a subaccount of the current account which records imports and exports of goods only (including gold). The difference between the exports and imports of **goods only** is called the **trade balance.** For example, from Table 7-1 the South African trade balance for 2009 can be calculated as R503 656 million plus R52 776 million minus R554 161 million = R2 271 million. The South African trade balance has tended to be positive during the postwar period. In other words, the value of South African merchandise exports (including gold) has tended to be greater than the value of the country's merchandise imports. Against this, however, payments for services and income payments always exceed service receipts and income receipts by a significant amount with the result that the balance on current account is often negative (ie in deficit).

The last item in the current account of the balance of payments is **current transfers**. This entry includes such items as social contributions and benefits and taxes imposed by governments, as well as private transfers of income, such as gifts, personal, immigrant and other remittances and charitable donations. In the South African balance of payments the amount paid usually exceeds the amount received by a significant amount. Note that in the case of transfers, money, goods or services are transferred without receiving anything tangible in return (ie without any *quid pro quo*). These are therefore unrequited transfers.

The **balance on current account** is the net total of all the various items. The current account of the South African balance of payments is sometimes in deficit and sometimes in surplus. Deficits have to be financed in some way or another. For example, during the period 1985-1993 South Africa was subject to international financial sanctions and had to repay its foreign debt and therefore could not afford to run current account deficits. Economic policy thus had to be aimed at ensuring current account surpluses. From 1994 onwards, however, current account deficits could once again be financed by net inflows on the financial account and such deficits often occurred in subsequent years.

Since all the items in the balance of payments are recorded in **nominal** terms (ie at current prices), all the balances are therefore also expressed at **current** prices. Unlike the national production, income and expenditure accounts, the balance of payments cannot be deflated to obtain a set of real values. This creates somewhat of a problem since a comparison of nominal balances over time does not really make sense. The solution is to express the balance as a ratio or percentage of another economic aggregate such as GDP. For example, in 2007 and 2008 current account deficits of R144 553 million and R161 675 million respectively were recorded in South Africa. On the face of it there was thus a worsening of the position on the current account (an increase in the deficit of more than 11%) between 2007 and 2008. To a certain extent this conclusion is correct, since the larger deficit had to be financed. However, expressed as a percentage of nominal GDP, the deficit actually decreased, from 7,2% to 7,1%.

It is important to realise that current account data by themselves have no real meaning. For example, a current account deficit may be good or bad, depending on the circumstances and the underlying causes of the deficit. A current account deficit is often regarded as an indication that a country is living beyond its means (ie spending more than it is earning). But the deficit may also indicate that the country has strong growth potential and that other countries are willing to grant the necessary credit to finance imports of capital goods required to achieve economic growth. Likewise, a current account surplus is often seen as an indication of a strongly competitive economy. A surplus, on the one hand, may be the result of a sluggish economy or of deliberate policy measures to keep imports low (eg barriers to imports or measures aimed at restricting economic activity). In South Africa, for example, the relatively rapid expansion during the 1950s and 1960s was characterised by current account deficits and concomitant net inflows of foreign capital. On the other hand, the introduction of financial sanctions in the 1980s and the commitment to repay foreign debt in the wake of the 1985 debt standstill forced the authorities to apply restrictive policies to keep imports low and to generate current account surpluses which could be used to repay the debt. Current account surpluses were thus recorded during a period of low, even negative, growth. After 1994, however, current account deficits were again recorded along with relatively high economic growth.

Capital transfer account

The capital transfer account, which was created in 1999, is relatively insignificant, as can be gauged from the data in Table 7-1. Capital transfers are offsetting transactions to the transfer of ownership of fixed assets, transfers of funds associated with the acquisition or disposal of fixed assets (such as a grant by a foreign government earmarked for a housing project in South Africa), debt forgiveness and transfers by migrants (ie the value of household or personal effects as well as financial claims and liabilities transferred by migrants from their former to new countries of residence).

Financial account

The second main subaccount of the balance of payments is the financial account, which records international transactions in assets and liabilities. This account was formerly called the capital account and is sometimes referred to as 'transactions in external assets and liabilities'.

The financial account has three main components: direct investment, portfolio investment and other investment. **Direct investment** includes transactions related to the acquisition of share capital in foreign countries by establishing new businesses, or through mergers and takeovers. The purpose of the investor must be to gain control of or meaningful say in the management of the enterprise in which the investment is made, for example by purchasing a substantial portion of the shares of a foreign company or by setting up a foreign branch or subsidiary. For balance of payments purposes a 'substantial portion' is defined as at least 10% of the shares. Direct investment comprises not only the initial equity transaction establishing the relationship between a direct investor and an enterprise, but also all subsequent transactions between affiliated enterprises. Transactions in real estate also form part of direct investment. Apart from the net amount of direct investment, separate figures are provided in respect of liabilities (ie direct investment by foreigners in South Africa) and assets (ie direct investment by South Africans in the rest of the world). Note that an increase in liabilities represents an inflow of foreign capital (in the financial sense), while an increase in assets represents an outflow. An increase in liabilities therefore has a positive sign in the balance of payments, while an increase in assets has a negative sign. In other words, an increase in liabilities is recorded as a credit, while an increase in assets is recorded as a debit. Likewise, a decrease in liabilities is recorded as a debit, while a decrease in assets is recorded as a credit. The same principle applies in respect of portfolio investment and other investment, the next two components of the financial account.

Portfolio investment refers to the purchase of assets such as shares (equities) or bonds where the investor is interested only in the expected financial return on the investment. In other words, the investor is not aiming to gain control of or have a meaningful say in the management of the enterprise in which the investment is made. Portfolio investment includes international equity and debt securities not classified as direct investment. In addition to long-term debt and equity securities, money market debt instruments and tradeable financial derivatives are also included in portfolio investment. This type of investment, which has been significant in South Africa in recent years, is potentially very volatile, as illustrated clearly in Table 7-1.

Other investment is a residual category which includes all financial transactions not covered under direct investment, portfolio investment or reserve assets. It includes trade credits, loans, currency and deposits and other assets and liabilities. When a South African importer purchases foreign goods, the transaction is often financed through short-term credit obtained abroad. Likewise, South African exports to other countries may also be financed through credit granted to the foreign importer. Such trade credits constitute a significant portion of other investment. See also Box 7-2.

The **balance on financial account** is shown separately and is obtained by adding net direct investment, net portfolio investment and net other investment (see Table 7-1).

The flows recorded in the financial account can be public or private. In the detailed tables published quarterly in the *SARB Quarterly Bulletin*, direct investment, portfolio investment and other investment are split into different categories according to the institutions involved. These are:

- monetary authorities
- public authorities
- public corporations
- banking sector
- private non-banking sector

In the case of direct investment the monetary authorities and public authorities are not applicable.

BOX 7-2: FOREIGN DEBT

Borrowing from the rest of the world gives rise to an inflow of foreign exchange but it also adds to the country's foreign debt, an indicator that is closely monitored in the financial markets and elsewhere. South Africa experienced its own foreign debt crisis in September 1985, which had serious implications for the economy for a number of years.

In the *SARB Quarterly Bulletin* South Africa's foreign debt is expressed in both US dollars and rand. To obtain an indication of the relative size of the debt and to enable international comparisons, each country's foreign debt is usually

- expressed in a common currency (eg US dollars)
- expressed as a percentage of GDP
- expressed as a percentage of its exports of goods and services

Any debt has to be serviced. The debt service in this case is the sum of interest payments and principal repayments (amortisation) due on outstanding foreign debt. The **debt service ratio** is then obtained by expressing the debt serviced as a percentage of the country's exports of goods and services. This ratio provides an indication of the affordability of the foreign debt.

Unrecorded transactions

The fact that a double-entry accounting system is used for the recording of balance of payments transactions (see Box 7-3) means that, in principle, the net sum of all credit and debit entries should equal the change in the country's net gold and other foreign reserves. However, this does not happen in practice. The errors and omissions that occur in compiling the individual components of the balance of payments and the net effect of differences in coverage, timing and valuation are entered as unrecorded transactions. In practice, therefore, unrecorded transactions serve to ensure that the balance of payments actually balances. As shown in Table 7-1, the total value of unrecorded transactions, which pertain to the current, capital transfer and financial accounts, can be quite significant.

Official reserves account

The last element of the balance of payments is the official reserves account. A country's official reserves consist of gold, special drawing rights (SDRs) issued by the IMF, the country's IMF reserve position and foreign exchange reserves. The foreign exchange reserves are held in the form of foreign bank notes, demand deposits with foreign banks and other claims on foreign countries which can readily be converted into foreign bank demand deposits. In South Africa the official reserves are called **gold and other foreign reserves**. As in many other countries, a portion of South Africa's official reserves is held in the form of gold. When necessary, some of the gold may be sold to obtain foreign currency (such as US dollars, Japanese yen, pounds sterling and euros).

The combined current account, capital transfer account and financial account balances and unrecorded transactions yield the change in the country's **net** gold and other foreign reserves owing to balance of payments transactions.

In principle, the **change in the gold and other foreign reserves** constitutes the **balancing** item in the balance of payments as a whole. For example, if the current account closes with a deficit while there is an insufficient net inflow of capital to finance this deficit, the overall deficit is 'balanced' by a drop in the reserves. If, however, the combined current, capital transfer and financial account balances and unrecorded transactions are in surplus, the reserves will rise, as was the case in 2008 and 2009 (see Table 7-1). The overall balance of payments should always balance because every transaction is recorded twice – once as a debit and once as a credit. In other words, double-entry bookkeeping is applied (see Box 7-3 and the examples in Box 7-4). In practice, however, there are a number of unrecorded transactions. As mentioned earlier, the value of these unrecorded transactions has to be included to ensure that the balance of payments actually balances.

The change in the country's **gross** gold and other foreign reserves during a particular period is obtained by adding three further items to the change in the **net** reserves. These are the change in the liabilities related to reserves, SDR allocations and valuation adjustments and the net monetisation or demonetisation of gold. The change in the liabilities related to reserves is the net result of the official short-term loans obtained specifically to bolster the reserves and any repayment of such loans. The second item consists of valuation adjustments and allocation of SDRs by the IMF. SDRs are a form of credit which may be used when balance of payments difficulties are experienced. The valuation adjustments have to be made because the gold reserves are valued at a market-related price. The gold reserves are valued at a price taken at 14:30 on each valuation date. The prevailing exchange rate is then used to convert the resultant amount in dollars to rand. As explained earlier, a clear distinction is drawn nowadays between monetary gold and commodity gold. When a central bank increases its holding of monetary gold by acquiring commodity gold (eg newly-mined gold) it is deemed to have monetised gold. Likewise, when a central bank releases monetary gold for non-monetary purposes it is deemed to have demonetised gold. The last of the three items shows the net monetisation (+) or demonetisation (–) of gold.

In 2009, for example, the country's net gold and other foreign reserves increased by R17 037 million as a result of balance of payments transactions (see Table 7-1). Liabilities related to reserves decreased by R2 724 million during the year, while SDR allocations and valuation adjustments amounted to a negative figure of R38 647 million, mainly as a result of the appreciation of the rand against the major currencies. Together with a small (R45 million) monetisation of gold, this yielded a total decrease of R24 289 million in the country's **gross** gold and other foreign reserves.

Transactions recorded in the current, capital transfer and financial accounts are entered into for business or profit reasons or for altruistic or political reasons (in the case of transfers).

These transactions are therefore called autonomous transactions, and are sometimes also referred to as items above the line. In contrast, transactions in official reserves are called accommodating transactions or items below the line.

BOX 7-3: WHY THE BALANCE OF PAYMENTS ALWAYS BALANCES

The balance of payments always balances in formal or accounting terms. In any economic transaction (including international transactions) one party provides a good, a service or a financial asset, while the other party provides something in exchange, usually the money to be paid for the good, service or financial asset in question.

The balance of payments is based on the principles of double-entry bookkeeping. Each transaction appears twice, once as a credit and once as a debit. Most transactions appear once in the current or financial account and once in the foreign reserves account. This is because each transaction in the current or financial account corresponds, in principle, to a transaction in the foreign exchange market. There are some exceptions, as explained in Box 7-4.

In recording transactions in both the current and financial account all inflows of goods, services or asset titles are recorded as **debits** (–), and all outflows of goods, services or asset titles are recorded as **credits** (+). To understand this, the impact of any transaction on the foreign exchange market has to be considered. Any outflow of goods (ie exports), services or asset titles (eg as a result of foreign investment in the country) which creates a demand for the domestic currency on the foreign exchange market and a supply of foreign exchange (ie of other countries' currencies) implies a credit (+) item on the balance of payments. Conversely, any inflow of goods (ie imports), services or assets (eg as a result of investment abroad) creates a supply of domestic currency and a demand for foreign exchange (ie for other countries' currencies) and therefore leads to a debit (–) item on the balance of payments.

In the official reserves account a use of reserves is recorded as a credit item and an addition to the reserves as a debit item. This may seem confusing. To understand this accounting convention, one should view money drawn from the official reserve account as a supply of foreign exchange or an outflow from the official reserves account to the rest of the balance of payments. Hence it is treated as a credit or 'export-type' transaction in the official reserves account. Likewise, an addition to the reserves is recorded as a debit. Such additions may be regarded as a use of foreign exchange or an inflow to the foreign reserves account from the rest of the balance of payments. Hence they are treated as debit or 'import-type' transactions in the official reserves account.

The examples in Box 7-4 illustrate how double-entry accounting is applied to the balance of payments.

BOX 7-4: SOME EXAMPLES OF HOW TRANSACTIONS ARE RECORDED IN THE BALANCE OF PAYMENTS

The following brief list of examples provides some indication of how various transactions are recorded in the South African balance of payments.

- *Kumba, a major South African iron ore producer, exports iron ore to the value of R100 million to China.* This is recorded as merchandise (or goods) exports in the current account (ie as a credit). The contra entry depends on the way in which the transaction is financed. If the exports are paid for in cash, or financed by trade credit granted by a foreign bank, the foreign exchange reserves will increase by R100 million (ie a debit in the official reserves account). If the exports are financed through trade credit granted by a South African bank, the contra entry will be a debit in the financial account (ie an increase in assets).

- *An American tourist spends R100 000 while staying at the One and Only Hotel on the Victoria and Alfred Waterfront in Cape Town.* This is recorded as services receipts (ie an export of services) in the current account (as a credit) and as a corresponding increase in the foreign exchange reserves (as a debit in the official reserves account).

- *SABMiller purchases machinery to the value of R500 million from a German company to expand its plant at Rosslyn.* This is recorded as merchandise (or goods) imports in the current account. (All imports and exports of capital goods are recorded in the current account.) The contra entry again depends on how the transaction is financed. If the machinery is paid for in cash or through a loan (trade credit) granted by a South African bank, the foreign exchange reserves will decrease (shown as a credit in the official reserves account). If the transaction is financed through trade credit granted by a foreign (eg German) bank, the contra entry will be a credit in the financial account (ie a corresponding capital inflow or increase in liabilities). When the loan is repaid, there will be a debit in the financial account (ie a capital outflow or decrease in liabilities) and a corresponding credit in the official reserves account (ie a decrease in foreign exchange reserves).

- *Sasol pays dividends to the value of R600 million to foreign shareholders.* This is an example of investment income recorded in the current account as income payments (ie a debit). The contra entry is a credit in the official reserves account (a decrease in foreign exchange reserves).

- *The Nelson Mandela Children's Fund receives a donation of R10 million from a British donor.* This is recorded as a positive unrequited current transfer in the current account (ie as a credit). The debit entry is the corresponding increase in foreign exchange reserves (recorded in the official reserves account). Note that the recipients of transfers do not have to provide anything in return. It is sometimes jokingly said that all that is required in return for such a transfer is a smile or a thank you note.

- *The South African government donates medical equipment to the value of R10 million to Rwanda.* This is an unrequited transfer which has no impact on the foreign exchange market. The transaction represents an export of goods (ie a credit in the current account, under merchandise exports) and the corresponding debit is recorded under transfers.

- *A South African resident purchases shares to the value of R1 million in Microsoft, the American computer software company.* This is recorded as a portfolio investment (an increase in assets) in the financial account. The South African resident obtains a foreign asset which is entered as a debit since the funds leave the country. The contra entry is a credit in the official reserves account (ie a decrease in foreign exchange reserves).

- *Steinhoff (a South African company) spends R100 million on purchasing an existing factory in Poland.* This is a transfer of the ownership of an existing asset. In contrast to the earlier example of SABMiller purchasing capital goods in Germany, there is no movement of capital goods across national borders. The transaction is recorded as a debit in the financial account under direct investment and as a corresponding credit in either the financial account or the official reserves account, depending on how the transaction is financed.

- *The South African Treasury raises R1 billion through the sale of a ten-year bond to financial institutions in Europe.* This is recorded as a credit under portfolio investment in the South African financial account and as a corresponding debit in the official reserves account (ie an increase in foreign exchange reserves).

7.2   Foreign trade statistics

The Customs and Excise section of the South African Revenue Service (SARS) releases preliminary foreign trade statistics each month (during the last week of the following month). These statistics, which are reported regularly in the media, pertain to trade in merchandise (ie goods) only.

Further data on South Africa's international trade, including the destination of exports and the origin of imports, as well as the composition of foreign trade, are available at the SARS website *(www.sars.gov.za)*.

South African exports consist mainly of primary goods (emanating from the mining industry and the agricultural sector), while the country's imports consist mainly of capital and intermediate goods, which together constitute about 80% of total imports. Table 7-2 confirms these facts.

Table 7-2: South African exports and imports by commodity, 2009

Products	Exports % of total	Imports % of total
Precious metals and stones	24,8	0,9
Base metals	14,8	4,3
Mineral products (oil, coal, ore etc)	20,1	21,8
Agricultural produce, food and beverages	9,2	6,7
Pulp and paper products	2,0	1,8
Transport equipment	8,6	8,9
Motor vehicle components	0,0	5,5
Machinery and appliances	8,6	26,1
Chemical products, plastics and rubber	7,4	13,1
Textiles, clothing, footwear and accessories	1,0	4,1
Miscellaneous manufacturing	0,8	1,6
Other	2,6	5,2
Total	**100,0***	**100,0**

*   Export shares do not add up to 100 due to rounding.

Source: National Treasury, *Budget Review 2010*:25.

South Africa's main trading partners were traditionally the developed industrial countries. Although the actual ranking changed from time to time, Germany, the United Kingdom, the US and Japan were by far the most important sources of South African imports and destinations of South African exports. In recent years, however, Asian and African countries have also become important trading partners. Figures for the direction of international trade are also published by the IMF in its quarterly and annual *Direction of Trade Statistics*. Table 7-3 gives an indication of the direction of South Africa's foreign trade in 2007. It shows the country's main trading partners ranked by the total merchandise trade (exports plus imports) with each country.

A significant feature of South African exports in recent years has been the rapid increase in exports to the rest of Africa. In 1990, for example, these exports amounted to only $1 496 million (or 6% of total exports) but by 2007 the amount had increased to $9 416 million (or 14,8% of total exports). Countries such as Zambia, Zimbabwe and Mozambique had become among the most important destinations of South African exports.

Table 7-3: South Africa: major destinations of exports and origins of imports, 2007*

Country**	Exports to the country (Rm)	Imports from the country (Rm)	Exports plus imports (Rm)
Germany	35 894	65 516	101 410
United States	52 865	43 033	95 898
China	29 303	60 264	89 567
Japan	49 472	36 929	86 401
United Kingdom	34 466	27 075	61 541
Netherlands	20 276	8 982	29 258
France	9 132	18 803	27 935
Italy	10 048	15 601	25 649
India	9 484	12 506	21 990
Korea	8 162	12 604	20 766

*   Data are for merchandise exports and imports only.

** Countries are ranked according to the total value of trade with South Africa (merchandise exports and imports).

Source: South African Revenue Service: Division of Customs and Excise *(www.sars.gov.za).*

Box 7-5 contains information about an important indicator of global trade (and economic activity).

BOX 7-5: THE BALTIC DRY INDEX

The Baltic Dry Index (BDI) is an important barometer of global trade and also an important leading indicator of international economic activity. It is issued daily by the London-based Baltic Exchange and, interestingly enough, relates to shipping *prices* rather than cargo *volumes*. The index tracks worldwide international shipping prices of various sizes of dry bulk cargoes such as coal, iron ore, grain and building materials.

Since the supply of cargo ships is highly inelastic (virtually fixed), the price of shipping depends on demand, with a marginal change in demand having a potentially large impact on price. The price of shipping thus provides an excellent unbiased or objective indication of the volume of global trade, in contrast to other indicators that may be manipulated to serve narrow interests, or be subject to speculative activity.

The BDI was introduced in 1985 and reached a record high level of 11 793 points on 20 May 2008. However, by 5 December 2008 it had dropped by 94%, to 663 points, the lowest since 1986. In view of what actually happened during this period, these data clearly indicate the value and sensitivity of the index.

7.3   Measures of openness

In a world in which international trade is becoming increasingly important and in which a country's international economic links have an important bearing on the performance of the economy and the direction of economic policy, analysts are often interested in the degree of **openness** of an economy. The openness of a country's economy indicates the extent of a country's involvement in the global economy, particularly international trade. In practice this is often measured by expressing the value of exports, the value of imports, or the combined value of imports and exports as a percentage of GDP. Although the use of exports for this purpose is fairly uncontroversial, the inclusion of imports is problematic, since imports do not form part of GDP. It is always preferable to express a variable as a ratio or percentage of an aggregate of which it forms a part. Even with exports there is somewhat of a problem, since the import component of exports is included in the aggregate export figures. In other words, not all the value added to exported goods and services occurs domestically and therefore forms part of GDP. Expressing exports as a percentage of GDP thus inevitably also involves some imports being expressed as a ratio of an aggregate of which they do not form part. As a result it is quite possible to obtain a degree of openness of more than 100% for countries which import a lot and re-export most imports. Such cases, however, are the exception rather than the rule. The main examples are Hong Kong (which now forms part of China) and Singapore. For these trading centres the value of imports also exceeds the value of GDE, since most of the imports are destined for re-export (with little value added) rather than for consumption or investment in the domestic economy. Since exports are not included in GDE, a percentage of greater than 100% is thus possible. In Hong Kong, for example, exports were 193,9% of GDP and imports 201,1% of GDE in 2009.

The most sensible approach, nevertheless, is to use (a) exports as a percentage of GDP, (b) imports as a percentage of GDE (which usually includes most imports) or (c) an average of (a) and (b). Such indicators of the openness of selected countries are shown in Table 7-4.

As shown in the table, the measured degree of openness can vary significantly from country to country. Large economies such as Japan and the US are relatively closed economies, mainly as a result of their size. In other words, while the absolute **levels** of their exports and imports are extremely high, they are low **relative** to their respective GDPs and GDEs. Moreover, these economies (like most others) have tended to become more open in recent years. The low percentages for Brazil can partially be explained by its traditional inward focus, although this has already changed significantly in the present era of globalisation. At the other end of the spectrum, Malaysia and Singapore and Hong Kong (not shown in the table) serve as major international trading centres and have measured degrees of openness close to or in excess of 100%. As explained earlier, this is due to the large volume of imports relative to the size of the domestic economy, coupled with the fact that most imports are destined for re-export. In other words, a large portion of imports and exports essentially constitute transit trade. Similar arguments apply to some other South-East Asian economies such as Thailand. Note that the Netherlands also has a high measured degree of openness. This is simply because the country is very small and also an important gateway to some other European countries. As far as South Africa is concerned, Table 7-4 indicates an average degree of openness. By international standards the South African economy is open but not particularly open.

Table 7-4: Measures of openness, South Africa and selected other countries, 2009

Country	(1) Exports as % of GDP*	(2) Imports as % of GDE*	(3) Average of (1) and (2)
France	23,0	24,4	23,7
Germany	40,8	38,0	39,4
Japan	12,5	12,3	12,4
Netherlands	69,3	66,9	68,1
United Kingdom	27,9	29,5	28,7
United States	11,0	13,4	12,2
Australia	19,9	20,3	20,1
Canada	28,7	29,9	29,3
New Zealand	30,9	31,8	31,4
Argentina	21,4	16,9	19,2
Brazil	11,3	11,3	11,3
Chile	38,1	32,9	35,5
India	20,6	24,1	22,4
Korea	49,9	47,9	48,9
Malaysia	96,9	96,0	96,5
Thailand	68,4	64,7	66,6
Botswana	33,6	40,2	36,9
Kenya	26,3	36,1	31,2
Nigeria**	44,3	30,9	37,6
South Africa	**27,1**	**27,7**	**27,4**

*   Exports and imports are of goods and services only.

** Figures for Nigeria are for 2008.

Source of basic data: International Monetary Fund, *International Financial Statistics.*

Although the ratios included in Table 7-4 are not insignificant, some observers argue that the **marginal import ratio** or **marginal propensity to import** should also be calculated. In some countries the import sector may be relatively small, but economic growth may require a large volume of imported goods (particularly capital goods). The marginal import ratio (ie the **change** in imports per unit of **change** in output or expenditure) may thus be high even if the **average** import ratio (ie the ratio between the **level** of imports and the **level** of output or expenditure) is relatively low. A country with a high marginal import ratio is particularly vulnerable (or open) to developments in the international sphere, South Africa being a good example.

7.4   Terms of trade

The terms of trade are a ratio between export and import prices. They are calculated by dividing an export price index by an import price index and expressing the result as an index by multiplying it by 100:

$$T = \frac{P_x}{P_y} \times 100 \text{ where}$$

T = terms of trade
P_x = export price index
P_y = import price index

The basic reason for the calculation of the terms of trade is that the **value** of export earnings and payments for imports depends on the **prices** of exports and imports as well as the **volume** of exports and imports. For example, when export prices decline, a greater volume of exports have to be produced and sold, merely to keep export earnings constant. Export prices are therefore important. But even more important than the absolute level of export prices is the **ratio between export prices and import prices** (ie the terms of trade). The terms of trade are an indication of the volume or quantity of imported goods that can be obtained per unit of goods exported. When the prices of a country's exports (in the domestic currency) are falling **relative** to the prices of the goods and services that it imports, also expressed in the domestic currency (ie when the terms of trade decline or deteriorate), the country actually becomes poorer. The reason is that the country then has to sell more of its export products and use more of its scarce factors of production simply to be able to afford the same volume of imports as before. On the other hand, if the terms of trade improve (ie if export prices increase relative to import prices), the country is better off than before since fewer exports are required to afford the same volume of imports as before (or more imports can be purchased with the same volume of exports). For example, if the ratio between the export price index and the import price index increases from 110 to 121 it means that the terms of trade have improved to the extent that an unchanged volume or quantity of exports will purchase a quantity of imports 10% greater than before, or that the same quantity of imports will now require 9% less exports to pay for them.

When a country's exports are dominated by an important product, changes in the price of that product can have a significant impact on the country's terms of trade and the welfare of the nation. Given the historical importance of gold, different terms of trade are still published for South Africa: one excluding gold and the other including gold. However, as mentioned in Box 7-1, gold is not nearly as significant nowadays as it was a few decades ago.

Terms of trade figures are published regularly by the South African Reserve Bank (SARB). The terms of trade are derived from the exports and imports of goods and services. Changes in the South African terms of trade (including gold) were provided (for selected years) in Table 3-2 in Chapter 3.

Remember that changes in the terms of trade have a significant impact on the differences between the growth in real GDP and real GNI as well as on the differences in the growth of the different implicit price deflators (GDE deflator, GDP deflator and GNI deflator) (see Sections 3.2 and 6.7).

7.5   Exchange rates

An **exchange** rate is the price of one country's currency (eg the South African rand) in terms of another country's currency (eg the US dollar). Exchange rates can be expressed directly or indirectly. Most countries use the **direct method**. With this method the exchange rate shows how much of the local currency (rand in the case of South Africa) has to be exchanged for one unit of a foreign currency (eg the US dollar). The direct method thus indicates the domestic price of the foreign currency. For example, if one has to pay R10 to obtain one US dollar, the direct quotation is thus that $1 = R10,00. With the **indirect method**, however, the exchange rate is expressed as the amount of foreign currency that is required to purchase one unit of the domestic currency. The indirect method thus indicates the foreign price of the domestic currency. In the above example, the indirect quotation is thus R1 = US$0,10. In other words, only 10 US cents are required to purchase one rand. The indirect method is simply the inverse of the direct method. The SARB uses the direct method when quoting exchange rates in the *SARB Quarterly Bulletin*. Both the direct and the indirect quotations are published daily in most newspapers. The international abbreviation for the South African rand is ZAR and for the US dollar it is USD. A typical quotation in the foreign exchange market would thus be 1USD = ZAR8,8342. All quoted exchange rates are **nominal bilateral** exchange rates, since they are expressed in **money** terms and involve the currencies of **two** countries.

Since many countries use the dollar as their national currency, it is always preferable to indicate which dollar is referred to. Each currency has a unique three-letter code (called the ISO code) in the foreign exchange market, for example, USD = US dollar; AUD = Australian dollar; NZD = New Zealand dollar; CAD = Canadian dollar; HKD = Hong Kong dollar; SGD = Singapore dollar; ZWD = Zimbabwean dollar; EUR = euro; JPY = Japanese yen and GBP = British pound. As mentioned above, ZAR is the ISO code for the South African rand.

Dealers in foreign exchange (mainly the large banking groups) normally quote four different rates at any particular time: a **selling rate** and three **buying rates** (the telegraphic transfer rate, the airmail rate and the surface mail rate). The rates published in the *SARB Quarterly Bulletin* are middle rates (ie weighted average daily rates of the banks at approximately 10:30). The difference between the buying rate and the selling rate is called the spread. Apart from the spread, the foreign exchange dealers also charge a separate fee or commission when foreign exchange transactions are conducted. When exchange rates are quoted, the spotlight inevitably falls on the exchange rate between the rand and the US dollar. However, although the dollar has historically been very important, and still is by far the most important international reserve currency, the euro is much more important for South Africa's foreign trade than the dollar. At the time of writing the euro constituted 34,82% of the basket of currencies that was used to estimate the effective exchange rate of the rand (which is explained later), while the dollar had a weight of only 14,88%.

Appreciation and depreciation

When more of one currency (say South African rand) is required than before to purchase one unit of another currency (say US dollar), the first currency has **depreciated** against the second currency (or the second currency has **appreciated** against the first). Because an exchange rate is a ratio between two currencies, exchange rate movements should always be interpreted with circumspection. For example, if the exchange rate changes from $1 = R9,20 to $1 = R9,30, the rand has depreciated against the dollar. Likewise, if the exchange rate changes from R1 = $0,1250 to R1 = $0,1200, the rand has also depreciated against the dollar. In both these examples the dollar appreciated against the rand.

It is important to note that there is no such thing as an increase or decrease (or appreciation or depreciation) of an exchange rate. At any given moment there are a host of different exchange rates and over a given period the rand may appreciate against some currencies while depreciating against others. When exchange rates and exchange movements are described, the currencies concerned should always be specified clearly. Statements such as 'the exchange rate has increased', 'the exchange rate has declined', 'the exchange rate has depreciated', 'the exchange rate is weak' or 'the exchange rate is strong' are devoid of meaning. The correct form is to state, for example, that 'the rand has depreciated against the dollar' (or in dollar terms), 'the dollar has appreciated against the rand' or 'the rand has appreciated against the euro'.

Moreover, in a world of floating exchange rates it is also inappropriate to use the terms 'devaluation' and 'revaluation'. Currencies depreciate and appreciate; they are not devalued or revalued. The only case where devaluation and revaluation will be appropriate is when a currency is pegged (fixed) against another currency or basket of currencies and the peg is adjusted.

Spot and forward exchange rates

A further important distinction is that between **spot exchange rates** and **forward exchange rates**. A spot exchange rate is the rate at which foreign exchange is bought and sold for immediate delivery, while a forward exchange rate pertains to foreign exchange bought and sold for delivery at a future date. For example, a three-month forward exchange (buying) rate for US dollars of $1 = R9,2648 quoted on 1 February means that a South African importer can ensure paying a rate of R9,2648 per dollar for a fixed amount of dollars on 1 May by buying the dollars forward. In practice the forward price (which is determined by the spot rate and the interest rate differential between the two countries) is usually higher than (at a premium to) or lower than (at a discount to) the spot price. Forward exchange transactions provide importers and exporters with an opportunity to cover themselves against the risk of future changes in the spot exchange rate.

Nominal and real exchange rates

The exchange rate quoted at any particular time (in money terms) is the **nominal exchange rate**. For analytical purposes a **real exchange rate** can also be calculated by taking price movements into account. For example, in the case of South Africa and the United States, the (bilateral) real exchange rate between the rand and the dollar is determined by adjusting the nominal exchange rate by the ratio of South African prices to United States prices. The underlying principle is that a proportionally higher increase in the domestic prices of South African products relative to the domestic prices of United States products will affect the **competitiveness** of the South African economy if this differential price movement is not neutralised by a corresponding adjustment of the exchange rate between the two currencies.

There is no consensus as to which prices or costs should be used to calculate real exchange rates (ie to ascertain the competitiveness of a country). A variety of price or cost indices can be used, each with its own advantages and disadvantages. These include consumer price indices, producer price indices, export price indices, import price indices and indices of unit labour costs (see Section 8.5). To keep things simple, consumer price indices are used in the following example of the calculation of a bilateral real exchange rate (ie a real exchange rate between two currencies).

Column (a) in Table 7-5 shows the average nominal exchange rates between the rand and the US dollar for the different years. In column (b) these rates are expressed as an index (with 2008 = 100). Column (c) indicates the ratio between the South African CPI and the US CPI (2008 = 100), expressed as an index. The South African CPI increased from 72,1 in 2002 to 107,1 in 2009 (see column (b) in Table 7-7). Over the same period the CPI for the USA increased from 83,6 to 99,6 (see column (c) in Table 7-7). Thus $CPI_{SA}/CPI_{USA} = (72,1/83,6 \times 100) = 86,2$ in 2002 and $107,1/99,6 \times 100 = 107,5$ in 2009.

Table 7-5: Calculating bilateral real exchange rates: an example

Year	Exchange rate SA cent/ US dollar (a)	Nominal R/$ rate (index) (2008 = 100) (b)	$CPI_{SA}/$ CPI_{USA} (2008 = 100) (c)	Real R/$ rate (index) (2008 = 100) (d)
2002	1 051,65	127,4	86,2	147,8
2003	756,47	91,7	89,2	102,8
2004	644,99	78,2	88,3	88,6
2005	636,23	77,2	88,2	87,5
2006	676,72	82,0	89,4	91,7
2007	705,44	85,5	93,1	91,8
2008	825,17	100,0	100,0	100,0
2009	843,72	102,2	107,5	95,1

Sources of basic data: SARB *Quarterly Bulletin* and US Bureau of Labor Statistics *(www.bls.gov).*

To obtain an index of the real exchange rate between the rand and the dollar, the index of the nominal exchange rate (column (b)) is divided by the price-ratio index (column (c)) and the result is expressed as an index by multiplying it by 100.

Column (a) in Table 7-5 shows that, on average, the rand appreciated against the US dollar in **nominal** terms between 2002 and 2005 – and subsequently depreciated against the dollar. In real terms, the rand also appreciated against the dollar from 2003 to 2005 as indicated by the figures in column (d). It then depreciated from 2006 to 2008, before appreciating again in 2009. (Note that the nominal exchange rates in columns (a) and (b) in the table indicate the prices of the dollar in rand terms, not the other way around. An increase in the value or index thus indicates an appreciation of the dollar against the rand while a fall in the value or index indicates an appreciation of the rand against the dollar. If the indirect method of quotation is used, the interpretation will be exactly the opposite.)

A real appreciation in the value of the rand against the dollar (ie a fall in the real R/$ rate in column (d)) implies that South African exports become relatively more expensive in the United States and that imports from the United States become relatively cheaper in South Africa, *ceteris paribus.* A fall in the real R/$ rate in column (d) to below 100,0 indicates an **overvaluation** of the rand in real terms, compared to the base year, while a value above 100,0 points to an **undervaluation**. In 2002 and 2003, for example, the dollar was overvalued (or the rand undervalued) in terms of price differentials compared to 2008. For the other years the dollar remained **undervalued** or the rand **overvalued** (on this basis) against the rand.

Consider the result for 2009. In 2009 the South African inflation rate (7,1%) was significantly higher than that of the USA, where prices actually fell marginally (by 0,4%). Compared to 2008, the dollar should therefore have appreciated against the rand in nominal terms by 7,5% (ie the difference between the two inflation rates) to maintain the real exchange rate between the two currencies. Instead it only appreciated on average by 2,2%, hence the real depreciation of the dollar (or appreciation of the rand) by approximately 5% (from 100,0 to 95,1).

Note that the index numbers **depend on the base year of the index**. Conclusions should therefore always be drawn very carefully. In this specific case the rand depreciated sharply against the dollar in 2008, making this year a particularly unsuitable base year for such calculations.

Effective exchange rates

For analytical purposes, real exchange rates such as those derived in Table 7-5 are more meaningful than nominal exchange rates. However, the exchange rate between the rand and the US dollar is a **bilateral** exchange rate which pertains only to trade between South Africa and the United States and to other transactions invoiced in dollars. Analysts often wish to obtain a picture of the average movement of the rand against the currencies of all our main trading partners to assess for example, the competitiveness of the country's exports. These currencies may be appreciating or depreciating against the US dollar. An overall measure of the movement of the rand against the major currencies is obtained by calculating an **effective exchange rate** (also called a **multilateral** exchange rate). The effective rate is a weighted average rate which is derived by weighting the exchange rates between the rand and the main currencies, using the different countries' shares in South Africa's foreign trade as weights. This measure of the overall value of one currency against a basket of currencies is also known as the **trade-weighted exchange rate**. However, since different sets of weights can be applied to the price indices, it is possible to estimate a range of effective exchange rates. The exercise to estimate an effective exchange rate is conducted regularly by the South African Reserve Bank and the results are published in the *SARB Quarterly Bulletin*. At the time of writing fifteen currencies were used for this purpose, with the euro (34,82), US dollar (14,88), Chinese yuan (12,49), British pound (10,71) and Japanese yen (10,12) having the largest weights. Recall from Table 7-3 in Section 7.2 that these currencies are those of some of South Africa's main trading partners.

Like **bilateral** exchange rates (ie exchange rates between two currencies), **effective** exchange rates can also be expressed in **nominal** and in **real** terms. The nominal effective exchange rate is obtained by using nominal exchange rates, while the real effective exchange rate is obtained by adjusting the nominal effective exchange rate by the effective foreign price ratio. The **effective foreign price ratio** is the trade-weighted ratio between South African prices and prices in the economies of our main trading partners. As mentioned earlier, different sets of prices can be used for this purpose. The SARB uses producer prices to calculate the real effective exchange rates published regularly in the *SARB Quarterly Bulletin*.

Table 7-6 shows the average annual nominal and real effective exchange rates for 2002 to 2009 (with 2000 as the base year). Note that the rates are indices rather than exchange rates *per se*. The higher the index number, the stronger the rand, and vice versa. The figures in the first column show that the rand appreciated in **nominal** terms against the basket of currencies from 2002 to 2005 and subsequently depreciated. The second column indicates that the **real** effective exchange rate also rose from 2002 to 2005. Although it tended to decline subsequently, most of the values still exceeded 100,0, pointing to an overvaluation of the rand (in real effective terms) compared to 2000 (the base year). See also Box 7-6.

Table 7-6: Effective exchange rates of the rand, 2002-2009*

Year	Nominal effective exchange rate (2000 = 100)	Real effective exchange rate (2000 = 100)
2002	66,54	82,55
2003	83,24	103,23
2004	90,84	110,13
2005	91,03	112,50
2006	85,68	108,87
2007	77,44	105,05
2008	64,17	94,09
2009	65,69	101,43

*   Rates are averages for the year.

Source: *SARB Quarterly Bulletin*, March 2008, March 2010.

BOX 7-6: EVEN THE EXPERTS CAN GET IT WRONG!

In the 83rd annual address of the Governor of the South African Reserve Bank in 2003 we find the following statements (on pp 2-3):

> The weakness of the US dollar was a major factor in a significant recovery of the external value of the rand. Having declined by 34 per cent on a trade-weighted basis during 2001, the nominal effective exchange rate of the rand recovered by 24 per cent in 2002 and by a further 12 per cent up to the end of July 2003... Similarly, the real effective exchange rate of the rand recovered markedly since the beginning of 2002. This index, which reflects the trade-weighted exchange rate of the rand deflated by the production price differential between South Africa and its main trading partners and competitor countries, rose by an estimated 16 per cent over the eighteen month period up to the end of June 2003.

When the nominal effective exchange rate of the rand declines, all or part of the decline may be the result of the fact that prices increased faster (on a trade-weighted basis) in South Africa than in the economies of our major trading partners. To determine what happened to the real effective exchange rate of the rand, the nominal effective exchange rate has to be adjusted (deflated) by the positive difference in the rate of increase in prices between South Africa and our trading partners.

This can be approximated by subtracting the inflation differential from the rate of decline in the nominal effective exchange rate. However, if the nominal effective exchange rate of the rand rises, as it did in 2002 and 2003, while South African inflation is still higher than in the other countries, the positive inflation differential has to be *added* to (and not subtracted from) the percentage increase in the nominal effective exchange rate in order to determine what happened to the real effective exchange rate. The latter thus rose by much more than the 16% mentioned in the last sentence of the quotation. In fact, the nominal improvement during the period alone was approximately 36% (24% + 12%). This example serves to underline how careful one needs to be when working with data on exchange rates, particularly real exchange rates.

Purchasing power parity

Another concept which is often used as an analytical tool to explain and predict movements in exchange rates is that of **purchasing power parity** (PPP). Two types of PPP can be distinguished: **absolute** PPP and **relative** PPP.

The **purchasing power parity** between any two countries is the number of units of the one country's currency (eg rand) which endows the holder with the same purchasing power (ie command over goods and services) as one unit of the other country's currency (eg US dollar). PPP can refer either to parity between a country (eg SA) and a specific trading partner (eg the USA), in which case it is a **bilateral** comparison, or to parity between the country and a group of trading partners, in which case it is a **multilateral** comparison.

According to the **absolute** PPP theory the 'equilibrium' exchange rate between two currencies is set by the ratio between the price levels in the two countries. Thus, if similar goods cost more in the United States than in South Africa (with prices in both countries expressed in dollars, using the prevailing exchange rates), the rand is **undervalued** relative to the dollar. Similarly, if dollar prices of goods are lower in the United States than in South Africa, the rand is overvalued against the dollar. Such comparisons can only be made if the actual prices in the two countries are known – price indices are insufficient to calculate an absolute PPP. A simple example of an absolute PPP is provided in the next sub-section. For another example, see Section 12.4 in Chapter 12.

The **relative theory** states that **changes** in exchange rates reflect **differences** in relative inflation **rates**. Relative **PPP** is thus concerned with the ratio of the 'equilibrium' exchange rate in a current period relative to the 'equilibrium' exchange rate in a base period. According to this theory, **PPP** is determined by the ratio of the domestic country's price index in the current period to the foreign country's price index in the same period, where both indices have a common base period. Thus, if dollar prices have risen at a slower rate in the United States than rand prices have risen in South Africa, the dollar should appreciate against the rand, compared to the exchange rate in the common base period.

Purchasing power parity exchange rates (ie relative PPPs) are calculated from the same information that is used to calculate real exchange rates. A PPP exchange rate is thus similar in many respects to a real exchange rate. The only difference is that, while a real exchange rate is expressed as an index, a bilateral PPP exchange rate can be expressed as an exchange rate. A bilateral PPP exchange rate is an 'ideal' or 'equilibrium' exchange rate in that it indicates what the exchange rate should be if purchasing power is to be maintained **relative to a certain base year**. The PPP rate can then be compared with the actual exchange rate to determine whether the currency concerned (eg the rand) is overvalued or undervalued against the other currency (eg the US dollar) in purchasing power terms (relative to the base year).

To illustrate the similarities and differences between PPP exchange rates and real exchange rates, we now use the same information as in Table 7-5 to calculate PPP exchange rates between the rand and the US dollar for the years from 2002 to 2009. The results are shown in Table 7-7.

Table 7-7: Calculation of bilateral PPP exchange rates between the rand and the US dollar, 2002-2009

Year	Nominal exchange rate (SA cent/ US dollar)	CPI (2008 = 100) SA	USA	PPP Index (CPI_{SA}/CPI_{USA}) (2008 = 100)	Exchange rate (SA cent/ US dollar)
	(a)	(b)	(c)	(d)	(e)
2002	1 051,65	72,1	83,6	86,2	711,30
2003	756,47	76,3	85,5	89,2	736,05
2004	644,99	77,4	87,7	88,3	728,63
2005	636,23	80,0	90,7	88,2	727,80
2006	676,72	83,7	93,6	89,4	737,70
2007	705,44	89,7	96,3	93,1	768,23
2008	825,17	100,0	100,0	100,0	825,17
2009	843,72	107,1	99,6	107,5	887,06

Sources of basic data: SARB Quarterly Bulletin and US Bureau of Labor Statistics (www.bls.gov).

The conclusions are essentially the same as those reached as a result of the data in Table 7-5. Note that the PPP index (column (d) of Table 7-7) is simply the ratio of the two price indices (column (c) of Table 7-5). The PPP exchange rate (column (e)) is obtained by multiplying the index in column (d) by the nominal exchange rate in the base year (825,17) and dividing the result by 100. To interpret the PPP (or 'ideal') exchange rates (column (e) of Table 7-7) they have to be compared to the actual exchange rates (column (a) of the table). Thus we see that in 2002 and 2003 the rand was **undervalued** against the dollar **(on the assumption that the rand was valued correctly in 2008, the base year)**. From 2004 to 2007 and in 2009 the rand was **overvalued** against the dollar (according to this yardstick). It has to be pointed out again, however, that the rand depreciated sharply in 2008 (the base year). This clearly illustrates the danger of comparisons based on **relative** PPP.

The notion of PPP exchange rates is subject to a variety of shortcomings and criticisms. There is, for example, no consensus on the choice of price index to be used to give empirical content to PPP theory. Any overall price index contains both non-traded and traded goods and these two sectors of the economy may be subject to different inflation rates. As with real exchange rates, unit labour costs are therefore often preferred to consumer or producer prices. The choice of base year is also problematic, particularly in a world in which inflation rates may fluctuate quite significantly. The most basic criticism, however, is that exchange rates are not affected simply by the prices of traded goods. Other factors such as barriers to trade (eg tariffs and quotas), technological developments, market sentiment and capital flows (particularly short-run capital flows) often have a decisive impact on exchange rate movements (as was the case in South Africa in 2008). No wonder that PPP is often referred to as 'pretty poor predictor'!

Big Mac index

Since 1986 the well-known British financial weekly *The Economist* has regularly published a light-hearted simplistic version of **absolute PPP** under the name of the Big Mac index. Instead of using the cost of a basket of goods and services (eg the CPI), a single good is taken as being representative of that basket, namely a McDonald's Big Mac hamburger, which is available, in similar shape and taste, in more than 100 countries. South Africa was excluded from the comparison until McDonald's opened its first outlet in this country in the mid-1990s.

The Big Mac PPP is the exchange rate that would leave hamburgers costing the same in the United States as abroad. Comparing the actual exchange rate with PPP then provides an indication of whether a currency is undervalued or overvalued compared to the US dollar. PPPs between other pairs of countries can also be determined using the Big Mac standard.

Table 7-8 contains some of the results of the survey conducted on 21 July 2010 (*The Economist*, 24 July 2010). The first column in the table shows the local currency prices of a Big Mac. The second column converts these prices into US dollars using the prevailing exchange rates. The third column shows the Big Mac PPPs. These are obtained by dividing the domestic price of a Big Mac by the price in US dollars ($3,73 in this case). This is what the exchange rate should be to make the dollar price of a Big Mac equal to the price in the domestic currency. For example, dividing the South African price of R18,50 by the American price of $3,73 gives a PPP of R4,96 per dollar.

The actual exchange rate on 21 July 2010 was $1=R7,54 (fourth column), implying that the rand was 34% undervalued against the US dollar at that stage (fifth column). By the same token the euro was 17% overvalued against the US dollar, the Swiss franc 66% overvalued, the Chinese yuan 48% undervalued, and so forth.

Table 7-8: The Big Mac index, 21 July 2010

Country	Big Mac prices		Implied PPP of the US dollar	Actual $ exchange rate	Local currency under (–)/over (+) -valuation (%) against $
	In local currency	In US dollars			
United States	$3,73	3,73	–	–	–
Australia	A$4,35	3,85	1,17	1,13	4
Britain	£2,29	3,48	0,61	0,66	–8
China	Yuan 13,20	1,95	3,54	6,78	–48
Euro area	€3,38	4,33	0,91	0,78	17
South Africa	R18,50	2,45	4,96	7,54	–34
Switzerland	CHF6,50	6,19	1,74	1,05	66

Source: www.economist.com/markets/bigmac.

As mentioned above, the Big Mac standard can also be used to calculate PPPs between other sets of currencies. For example, a Big Mac costs £2,29 in Britain and R18,50 in South Africa, implying a PPP exchange rate of R18,50 ÷ 2,29 = R8,08 to the British pound. The actual exchange rate was R7,54 ÷ 0,66 = R11,42 to the British pound, implying that the rand was 29,2% undervalued against the British currency in PPP terms at that stage.

Although the Big Mac index is a crude measure, it nevertheless often results in PPP estimates that are quite similar to those based on more sophisticated methods.

The Big Mac index is an innovative way of estimating PPP exchange rates. The publication of the latest Big Mac index regularly receives extensive coverage and it is often used as a guide to tourists planning to visit foreign destinations. But it is still a flawed index. The bulk of a burger's cost is determined by items such as wages, rent and electricity, which pertain to local inputs that are not traded internationally, and tend to be lower in poor countries. The more meaningful comparisons are therefore those between countries with similar levels of development and per capita income.

Do you really think you can get good conclusions from bad data?

Simon Kuznets

Once numbers get into print, they acquire a life of their own.

Terence Moll

Chapter 8

Wages, productivity and income distribution

This chapter deals with a variety of indicators related to wages, productivity and income distribution. The compensation of labour is by far the most important component of gross value added at factor cost (ie GDP viewed from the income side). For example, in 2009 the compensation of labour constituted 50,6% of South African gross value added at factor cost (or factor income). The other 49,4% was made up of rent, interest and profit. The remuneration of labour is both an important source of income in the economy and an important component of the cost of production. It is also often a very emotional issue, since it determines the living standards of workers as well as the costs of production and competitiveness of firms, particularly in labour-intensive industries.

8.1   Nominal and real income

The living standards of income earners and their families depend on the purchasing power of their incomes. When prices are changing, **nominal** incomes have to be adjusted for price changes to obtain **real** incomes, where nominal income refers to the amount received (in rand and cents) while real income refers to the purchasing power of the income (ie to what it will actually buy).

To derive real income from nominal income, the latter has to be deflated by a price index, using the technique explained in Box 6-3. Consumer price indices were originally constructed specifically for this purpose (ie to make it possible to derive real income from nominal income). Real income (eg a real wage) can be expressed in monetary terms (ie at constant prices) or as an index.

Consider the following example. Column (a) in Table 8-1 shows the hypothetical average nominal monthly wage earned by workers in a particular industry in 2006, 2007, 2008 and 2009. Column (b) shows the average consumer price index (CPI) in each of these years. The purpose of the exercise is to adjust the nominal wages in column (a) by the prices represented by the CPI in column (b) to obtain the real wages (which indicate the purchasing power of the nominal wages). This is done by dividing each nominal wage in

(a) by the CPI in (b) and multiplying the result by 100. The resultant values of the real wage in constant (2008) prices are shown in column (c). Note that the real wage increased between 2006 and 2007. This is because the percentage increase in the nominal wage was greater than the percentage increase in the price level. In 2008 the real wage was lower than in 2007. In 2009 the increase in the nominal wage was also not sufficient to compensate wage earners for price increases between 2008 and 2009 (reflected in a further decrease in the real wage). This resulted in wage earners being worse off in **real** terms in 2009 than in 2008 (the base year).

Table 8-1: Deriving real wages from nominal wages

Year	(a) Nominal wage (R)	(b) CPI (2008 = 100)	(c) Real wage (R) (= (a) ÷ (b) x 100)	(d) Real wage (index, 2008 = 100)
2006	10 000	83,8	11 933	102,9
2007	10 800	89,8	12 027	103,7
2008	11 600	100,0	11 600	100,0
2009	12 300	107,1	11 485	99,0

To facilitate the interpretation of the real wage, it is often also expressed as an index by taking the real value in the base year (2008) as 100. The index value for 2006 is obtained by dividing the real wage in 2006 (ie R11 933) by the value in the base year (R11 600) and multiplying the result by 100. The remaining items in column (d) are obtained in the same way.

The index of real wages can also be obtained by immediately transforming the nominal wage into an index, as illustrated in Table 8-2.

Table 8-2: Calculating an index of real wages: an alternative approach

Year	(a) Nominal wage (R)	(b) Nominal wage (index) (2008 = 100)	(c) CPI (2008 = 100)	(d) Real wage (index, 2008 = 100) (= (b) ÷ (c) x 100)
2006	10 000	86,2	83,8	102,9
2007	10 800	93,1	89,8	103,7
2008	11 600	100,0	100,0	100,0
2009	12 300	106,0	107,1	99,0

Column (a) in Table 8-2 contains the same information on the nominal wage as in Table 8-1. These data are then converted to an index by simply setting the value in 2008 equal to 100 and expressing all the other values as a percentage of this base value. For example, for 2006 the index value is obtained by dividing R10 000 by R11 600 and multiplying the result by 100. The result (86,2) is shown in column (b). Column (c) contains the same CPI data as in column (b) of Table 8-1. The CPI figures are then used to transform the index of nominal wages in column (b) to an index of real wages in column (d), in the same way as it was used in Table 8-1 to transform the nominal wage to a real wage (at constant 2008 prices). For example, the index value for 2006 (86,2) is divided by the CPI (83,8) and the result is multiplied by 100 to obtain the index value of the real wage of 102,9 in column (d). The other entries in column (d) are obtained in the same way.

8.2   Wage differentials

Apart from being interested in the **absolute** level of **wages**, in both **real** and in **nominal** terms, employees, employers and analysts are also interested in **wage differentials**, **relative wages** or the **structure of wages**. In other words, they want to know how the remuneration of an individual worker or group of workers compares to that of other individuals or groups. The main problem in this regard is to obtain accurate and comparable data on the remuneration of different individuals or groups. One official source of data on earnings is the *Quarterly Employment Statistics* (QES) published by Stats SA (as *Statistical release P0277*)) with a lag of approximately three months. These data, however, are averages for fairly large sectors or industries and subject to changes in definition or coverage. Although the data can serve as a useful benchmark, they have to be supplemented by other data before any meaningful conclusions can be reached in respect of the level of relative wages or changes therein.

**Table 8-3: Average monthly earnings in certain sectors of the
        South African economy, May 2010***

Sector	Average monthly earnings (R)
Electricity, gas and water supply	23 161
Transport, storage and communication	14 373
Community, social and personal services	13 664
Financial and business services	12 925
Mining and quarrying	11 639
Manufacturing	10 315
Construction	8 919
Wholesale and retail trade etc	7 802

*   Data include bonuses and overtime payment.

Source: Statistics South Africa, Quarterly Employment Statistics (P0277), June 2010 (released on 21 September 2010).

Table 8-3 provides an illustration of a comparison which can be drawn with the aid of the published official data. The table shows the average monthly remuneration of employees in different sectors of the South African economy in May 2010. Data are also available at constant prices to enable comparisons over time.

The deficiencies of the official data on wages and salaries and the need for comprehensive, up-to-date information (eg for wage bargaining purposes) created scope for private enterprise to collect and disseminate such data. Nowadays most employers and employee organisations (eg trade unions) subscribe to the information of a variety of private firms that specialise in this field.

8.3   Minimum living levels

Employers, trade unions and other interested parties often require information about what constitutes a 'living wage'. This is particularly relevant when a minimum wage or the remuneration of unskilled workers has to be determined. As a result there have been many attempts, in many countries, to define such a wage. The usual procedure is to estimate the amount of money required by an unskilled worker with an average size family to satisfy 'reasonable needs'. The problem, however, is that there is no consensus on what constitutes 'reasonable needs'. Should they be restricted to basic needs such as food, shelter, clothes, fuel and light? Or should they include some simple comforts as well? As one cynical observer once remarked, there are no limits to the 'living' which can include practically anything (or everything).

In South Africa the authoritative work in this regard was done by the Bureau of Market Research (BMR) at the University of South Africa. In an attempt to give empirical content to the concept of a living wage, the BMR developed two measures, the minimum living level and the supplemented living level. The **minimum living level (MLL)** indicated the minimum financial requirements of a family if they were to maintain their health and have acceptable standards of hygiene and sufficient clothing for their needs. The **supplemented living level (SLL)** provided for more items than the MLL. It was neither a subsistence nor a luxury budget. The BMR described the SLL as an attempt at determining a modest low-level standard of living. Unfortunately, due to the high cost of the survey, the BMR discontinued the compilation of the MLL and SLL in 2004.

8.4   Productivity

As mentioned earlier, the remuneration of labour is a significant element of the cost of production. The actual impact on costs depends on the relationship between the remuneration of labour and workers' contribution to production (ie their productivity). In this section and the next some of the important indicators in this regard are explained.

Productivity is a ratio which measures the amount of output that is produced with given amounts of factor inputs. The most widely used productivity concept is **labour productivity** which is the ratio between output and the labour input used to produce that output:

$$\text{Labour productivity} = \frac{\text{output}}{\text{labour input}} = \text{output per unit of labour input}$$

Labour productivity can be expressed as output per worker (obtained by dividing total output by total employment) or as output per hour (obtained by dividing total output by the total number of hours worked). At the macroeconomic level labour productivity is usually expressed as real GDP per worker.

Productivity figures can be calculated in volume terms or in monetary (value) terms, but they are usually produced as index numbers. Consider the following hypothetical microeconomic example. Column (a) in Table 8-4 shows output figures in volume terms for a steelworks in each of five consecutive years. Column (b) shows the average number of workers employed in each year. Dividing column (a) by column (b) yields the output per worker in volume terms in column (c). The figures in column (c) are then converted to an index by taking the tonnes per worker in Year 1 as 100,0 and expressing each other year's output as a percentage of the output in Year 1.

Table 8-4: Labour productivity in a steelworks

Year	Output per year (tonnes)	Number of workers	Output per worker	
			Tonnes	Index
	(a)	(b)	(c)	(d)
1	41 000	450	91,3	100,0
2	44 280	460	96,3	105,5
3	42 340	455	93,1	102,0
4	45 000	470	95,7	104,8
5	50 212	470	106,8	117,0

A productivity measure can be obtained for each individual factor input. For example, **capital productivity** is obtained by dividing output by the capital input (ie the capital stock). In other words, capital productivity is a measure of output per unit of capital input.

Labour productivity and capital productivity are both **partial** productivity measures, since they compare output against only one input at a time. Although convenient for quick and cursory analyses, partial measures do not provide a complete picture of productivity trends. One measure of productivity (eg labour productivity) can, for example, be raised by simply raising the quantity of the other input (eg capital). Consider the labour productivity figures in Table 8-4. The changes in the index in the last column are not necessarily attributable to the efforts of labour. For example, the increase in labour productivity between Year 4 and Year 5 could have been the result of an increase in the amount of capital per worker (ie the provision of additional or better machinery and equipment). This is referred to as an increase in the capital intensity of production (see Box 8-1).

Another disadvantage of partial productivity measures is that they do not isolate the impact of qualitative improvements in inputs, such as a higher level of education, technological progress and better resource allocation. To capture these effects, a further productivity concept was devised. **Multifactor productivity (MFP)** is a measure of the growth in output that is not explained by the growth in the quantity of inputs. MFP is therefore sometimes called a measure of the 'unexplained residual'. Multifactor productivity is also a ratio of output to input but in this case the input figure (the denominator) is the weighted average of the value of the labour input and the capital input. The sum total of all multifactor elements (such as worker and management skills and technology) are thus left as the items affecting the efficiency of the labour and capital inputs.

BOX 8-1: LABOUR AND CAPITAL INTENSITY OF PRODUCTION

Analysts are often interested in the ratio in which the two main factors of production, labour and capital, are combined in the production process as well as in the direction and magnitude of changes in this ratio. In other words, they are interested in the labour intensity or capital intensity of production. This is particularly important as far as employment creation and the significance of labour costs are concerned. If the production processes in an industry are highly capital intensive, an increase in production will result in a proportionally small increase in employment. Moreover, an increase in capital intensity will result in even fewer additional employees being required to generate additional production. In a country like South Africa, with large numbers of semi and unskilled workers and a shortage of capital goods, labour-intensive activities are generally preferred to capital-intensive processes. Unfortunately, for a variety of reasons (eg related to technology and industrial relations), capital intensity has grown in South Africa.

To measure capital intensity, data in respect of the capital stock are required. The SARB publishes estimates of the real fixed capital stock as at 31 December of each year in the *SARB Quarterly Bulletin*. The data are published for the economy at large, as well as by kind of economic activity and by type of organisation. The value of the capital stock at the end of a year is obtained by adding the net fixed investment during the year to the value of the capital stock at the beginning of the year. Net fixed investment is obtained by subtracting consumption of fixed capital (ie the provision for depreciation) from gross fixed investment during the year. Thus: capital stock as at 31 December = capital stock as at 1 January + gross fixed investment during the year – consumption of fixed capital.

Capital intensity can be measured by expressing the real fixed capital stock as a ratio of real output. This is called the average **capital-output ratio**. Capital-output ratios for calendar years can be calculated by using the data on the fixed capital stock and real GDP, for the economy at large as well as for the different kinds of economic activity. Average capital-output ratios for the economy at large are also published at the back of the *SARB Quarterly Bulletin* in a table titled *National accounts (selected data)*. Between 1970 and 2009 the average capital-output ratio for South Africa increased from 1,8 to 2,1. In other words, in 2009 2,1 units of capital were required to produce one unit of output, compared to the 1,8 units required in 1970. The ratio rose quite sharply in the 1970s and 1980s. In 1992 it was as high as 2,7 but it subsequently declined fairly consistently.

In economic analysis the focus is often on the **incremental capital-output-ratio (ICOR)**, which measures the ratio between the **change** in the capital stock and the change in output. In other words, it indicates the amount of **additional** capital (ie investment) required to produce an **additional** unit of output.

Another indication of capital intensity is the average **capital-labour ratio** which is the ratio between the real capital stock and the number of workers (expressed at constant prices). Data on this indicator are also included in the table referred to above. In 1970 the average capital-labour ratio (at constant 2005 prices) was R132 942. It increased to a maximum of R201 512 in 1983 and subsequently declined fairly steadily until 2003 (R161 034). However, it then increased again to reach R182 343 in 2009. Significantly more capital (in real terms) was therefore combined (on average) with each worker in 2009 than in 1970.

Like most other economic indicators, the distinction between **levels** and **rates of change** is extremely important when productivity data are interpreted, particularly at the international level. As mentioned earlier, the most common indicator of the level of productivity in a country is GDP per employed worker. There are, however, several difficulties associated with the comparison of productivity levels between countries, including the currency or exchange rate problem (see Section 12.3) and differences in the way in which output and input are measured. Some of these difficulties can be avoided by comparing the rates of change in productivity (ie productivity growth rates). However, productivity performance cannot be compared on the basis of growth rates only. For example, some developing countries have quite high productivity growth, but off a much lower base than in more mature economies. Finally, therefore, both the level of and the rate of change in productivity have to be taken into account, otherwise wrong conclusions may be drawn.

Also note that productivity can be increased in five possible ways:

- output increases while inputs remain constant
- output increases while inputs decline
- output increases faster than inputs
- output remains constant while inputs decline
- output declines at a slower rate than inputs

Labour productivity, for example, tends to vary during the business cycle simply because the quantity of labour input cannot be adjusted immediately to changes in output. When output falls during a recession, businesses cannot simply cut back on their workforces (eg because of employment contracts or because they do not wish to lose key personnel). The result is that measured productivity declines. During the ensuing boom the opposite occurs. Output rises rapidly but employment does not react immediately (because the existing labour force is underutilised initially and because it takes time to recruit new workers). Measured labour productivity can thus vary because of cyclical changes in output rather than changes in the efficiency with which labour input is utilised.

8.5   Unit labour cost

Productivity figures are frequently used in international comparisons of growth and competitiveness. Another indicator which is often used in international (and domestic) comparisons, in conjunction with productivity figures, is unit labour cost.

Unit labour cost is obtained by dividing the nominal cost of labour by real output. In other words, unit labour cost measures the average labour cost of producing one unit of output. For the economy as a whole, unit labour cost can be obtained by dividing total labour cost by real GDP. A comparison of trends in unit labour costs is more meaningful than a comparison of trends in wages because the former reflect changes in the amount of labour used in the production process as well as changes in the price of labour (ie changes in nominal wages or earnings).

Unit labour cost serves as an important indicator of cost pressures, competitiveness or the cost-efficiency of labour. There is an important link between productivity and unit labour cost. Unit labour cost is equal to the price of labour (earnings per worker) divided by labour productivity (output per worker). This can be explained as follows:

$$\text{Labour productivity} = Q/N, \text{ where } \quad Q = \text{output}$$
$$N = \text{number of workers}$$
$$\text{Unit labour cost} = wN/Q, \text{ where } \ w = \text{wage rate or earnings per worker}$$
$$N = \text{number of workers}$$
$$wN = \text{cost of labour}$$
$$Q = \text{output}$$

Unit labour cost (ULC) can be rewritten as follows:

$$\text{ULC} = \frac{wN}{Q} = \frac{w}{(Q/N)} = \frac{\text{earnings per worker}}{\text{labour productivity}}$$

In a dynamic context the growth rate in unit labour cost is approximately equal to the growth rate of earnings per worker minus the growth rate of output per worker.

$$\text{Thus } \frac{\Delta(\frac{wN}{Q})}{(\frac{wN}{Q})} \approx \frac{\Delta w}{w} - \frac{\Delta(\frac{Q}{N})}{(\frac{Q}{N})}$$

or

growth in unit labour cost ≈ growth in wages − growth in labour productivity

The above equation illustrates the important point that unit labour cost will remain unchanged if the percentage increase in wages is matched by a similar percentage increase in labour productivity. For example, if wages increase by 5% and labour productivity also increases by 5%, labour cost per unit of output will remain unchanged. However, if the increase in wages is proportionately greater than the increase in productivity, unit labour cost will increase and, depending on the importance of labour cost, total cost and prices will also tend to increase. The implication is that rapid increases in wages are not harmful, provided they are accompanied by proportional increases in productivity. By the same token, low productivity growth need not be a problem from an inflation or competitiveness perspective, provided wages are kept in check.

The above points can be illustrated with reference to the comparative experience of South Africa and Taiwan between 1975 and 1994. The first row in Table 8-5 shows the average annual percentage increase in labour productivity in the manufacturing sector in each of the two countries between 1975 and 1994. The second and third rows show the average annual percentage increases in nominal earnings per worker and in unit labour cost in manufacturing respectively. Note that wages in the manufacturing sector increased at approximately the same rate in the two countries during this period. The productivity performance, however, differed significantly and this was reflected in a large gap in the rate of increase in unit labour cost between the two countries. South Africa had a high inflation rate, while Taiwan had a high growth rate (and a high rate of increase in real earnings).

Table 8-5: Trends in labour productivity, nominal earnings and unit labour cost in manufacturing in Taiwan and South Africa, 1975-1994

	Taiwan	South Africa
Average annual increase in labour productivity in manufacturing (%)	5,9	0,6
Average annual increase in nominal earnings per employee in manufacturing (%)	13,9	14,1
Average annual increase in unit labour cost in manufacturing (%)	7,6	13,4

Source: Wefa Group, 1996, South African Competitiveness Monitor 1996: Volume 1 (International Comparisons), Pretoria: Wefa:35-36.

Relative movements in unit labour costs serve as important signals of international competitiveness in traded goods. If the increase in unit labour cost in a country is higher than in the economies of its international competitors, the situation might be temporarily absorbed by cutting profit margins or improving efficiency, but in the longer term deteriorating competitiveness will reduce exports, output and employment. Price competitiveness might also be restored temporarily by allowing the domestic currency to depreciate against other currencies (or to devalue the currency) but the initial benefit tends to be eroded quickly by price increases in the wake of the depreciation.

The SARB publishes quarterly and annual indices of productivity and unit labour cost for the economy as a whole as well as for the manufacturing sector in its *Quarterly Bulletin*. These data, however, are subject to large variations due to changes in the survey data (compiled by Stats SA) on which they are based.

8.6   Distribution issues

Distribution issues, especially those concerning the distribution of income among individuals, groups, sectors, regions and countries, have received increasing attention in recent decades. During the first two decades after World War II there was an almost exclusive preoccupation with macroeconomic aggregates such as total consumption, investment, government spending and national income, but in due course it was realised again that the distribution of national income may have a critical impact on the tempo, nature and geographic distribution of economic growth and development. At the same time existing distributions were increasingly questioned on ethical, social, political and economic grounds. Internationally, for example, such developments as decolonisation, political emancipation and the establishment of development economics as an autonomous field of study attracted close attention to the unequal distribution of economic activity between the First World and the Third World (or between the developed North and the underdeveloped South). This awareness was intensified, both domestically and internationally, by the development of instant communication, particularly televisual communication, which made everyone more conscious of what others have and do not have. New pressure groups were formed and they pressed their claims for a greater share of the proverbial cake or pie through collective bargaining, the law, public relations, political influence and even civil disobedience. These trends were intensified further by inflation and economic stagnation – everyone feels abused when real income is falling.

All the factors mentioned above have been present in South Africa. For example, the unequal distribution of income among the various population groups has long been an important social and political issue. The decline in total per capita real income after 1980 exacerbated the problem, since it meant that any particular group could only increase its share of the economic cake or pie at the expense of other groups. At the same time trade unionism grew apace while other pressure groups, including civil servants, teachers, nurses and even university lecturers, became increasingly vociferous.

From this brief introduction it should be clear that income distribution is an extremely important issue nowadays. One of the corollaries of the concern about income distribution is a large and growing need for statistical information on income distribution. Before discussing some of the available measures of income distribution, it should be pointed out, however, that the distribution of personal or household income is not the only distribution issue which interests economists. Others include the:

- division of national income between labour and capital
- distribution of economic activity between the various sectors of the economy
- distribution of economic activity between different geographic regions (eg the nine provinces in South Africa)
- distribution of economic activity between the public sector and the private sector

These distribution issues fall outside the scope of this book. The rest of this chapter focuses exclusively on the distribution of personal income among individuals and households.

The measurement of income distribution is a particularly difficult task. To compile a meaningful picture of the distribution of income one must have reliable information about the income of individuals or households during a particular period. Researchers therefore use data from population censuses or other survey data to estimate the distribution of income. Once the necessary information has been collected, certain measures or criteria have to be applied to estimate the degree of equality or inequality and to compare it with other distributions. A variety of such measures are used, with the Lorenz curve, the Gini coefficient and the quantile ratio being among the most popular.

Lorenz curve

The Lorenz curve (named after the American statistician Lorenz who developed it in 1905) is a simple graphic device which illustrates the degree of inequality in the distribution of the variable concerned.

To construct a Lorenz curve that reflects the distribution of income among the individuals or households in the economy, the latter first have to be ranked from poorest to richest. This is done on a **cumulative** percentage basis. In other words, we start with the poorest per cent of the population, the second poorest per cent and so on until we come to the richest per cent of the population. The **cumulative percentages of the population** are plotted along the horizontal axis. The vertical axis shows the **cumulative percentage of total income**. In other words, if the poorest per cent of the population earns 0,1% of the total income in the economy, that number will be plotted vertically above the first per cent of the population. If the second poorest per cent of the population earns 0,2% of the total income in the economy, it means that the first 2% earned a cumulative share of 0,3% (ie 0,1% plus 0,2%) of the income. This number (0,3) will then be plotted vertically above the 2 on the horizontal axis.

Table 8-6 shows a hypothetical distribution of income. To keep things simple, only the income shares of each successive 20% of the population are shown.

Table 8-6: A hypothetical income distribution

Percentage of		Cumulative percentage of	
population	income	population	income
Poorest 20%	4	20	5
Next 20%	6	40	10
Next 20%	10	60	20
Next 20%	20	80	40
Richest 20%	60	100	100

The first two columns in Table 8-6 contain the basic data. The last two columns are simply the cumulative totals. For example, these two columns show that the first 60% of the population (the poorest 60%) earn 20% of the total income.

The last two columns are then plotted as in Figure 8-1. The figure shows that the poorest 20% of the population earn 4% of the income, the poorest 40% of the population earn 10% of the income, and so on.

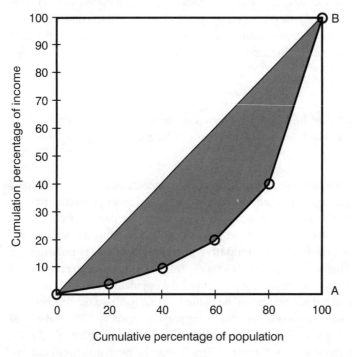

Cumulative percentage of population

Figure 8-1: A Lorenz curve

Note two other features of the diagram. The first is that the axes have been joined to form a square. The second feature is the **diagonal** running from the origin 0 (bottom left) to the opposite point B (top right) of the rectangle. The diagonal serves as a reference point. It indicates a **perfectly equal distribution** of income. Along the diagonal the first 20% of the population receives 20% of the total income, the first 40% receives 40%, and so on. Like the diagonal, any Lorenz curve must start at the origin 0 (since 0% of the population will earn 0% of the income) and end at B (since 100% of the population will earn 100% of the income).

The degree of inequality is shown by the deviation from the diagonal. The greater the distance between the diagonal and the Lorenz curve, the greater the degree of inequality. In Figure 8-1 the area between the diagonal and the Lorenz curve has been shaded. This **shaded area** is called the **area of inequality**. The greatest possible inequality will be where one person earns the total income. If that is the case, the Lorenz curve will run along the axes from 0 to A to B.

Since only the bottom triangle in Figure 8-1 has any real significance, the left-hand vertical axis and the top horizontal line may be left out. The scale on the vertical axis is then switched to the right-hand vertical line (between A and B). In other words, the Lorenz curve can be presented simply in a triangle, instead of in a square. The meaning and interpretation of the curve remain unchanged. The nearer the position of the Lorenz curve to the diagonal of the triangle, the more even the distribution. If the distribution is absolutely equal, the Lorenz curve will coincide with the diagonal. The further away the curve lies from the diagonal, the less even (or more uneven) the distribution.

A particular Lorenz curve reflects a distribution during a particular period or on a particular date. In other words, it can be constructed for cross-section data only, not for time-series data. To compare distributions over time (and to compare different distributions), different Lorenz curves have to be constructed and compared. Provided the curves do not intersect, such a comparison will reveal whether one distribution is more (or less) equal than the other. However, if they intersect, other criteria have to be considered. One of these is the Gini coefficient.

Gini coefficient

The **Gini coefficient** (or Gini ratio) is named after the Italian demographer Corrodo Gini, who invented it in 1912. It is a useful quantitative measure of the degree of inequality, obtained by dividing the area of inequality shown by a Lorenz curve by the area of the right-triangle formed by the axes and the diagonal. In Figure 8-1 the latter area is shown by the triangle formed by points 0, A and B.

The Gini coefficient can vary between 0 and 1. If incomes are distributed perfectly equally, the Gini coefficient is zero. In this case the Lorenz curve coincides with the line of perfect equality (the diagonal) and the area of inequality is therefore zero. At the other extreme, if the total income goes to one individual or household (ie if the incomes are distributed with perfect inequality), the Gini coefficient is equal to one. In this case the area of inequality will be the same as the triangle 0AB. In practice the Gini coefficient usually ranges between 0,30 (highly equal) and 0,70 (highly unequal). The Gini coefficient can, of course, also be expressed as a percentage, in which case it is called the **Gini index**.

Since the estimation of national income distributions is an arduous task, it is only undertaken sporadically (usually by private researchers or research teams). In fact, for some countries no Gini coefficients have been estimated. Estimates of income distribution are also subject to a larger margin of error than most other economic indicators. Nevertheless, Gini coefficients of income distribution are frequently used for analytical or policy purposes.

Table 8-7 contains a selection of Gini coefficients estimated for different countries in the post-war period. Although the figures are subject to a substantial margin of error, they do indicate some significant differences between different groups of countries.

Table 8-7: Gini coefficients for selected countries

Country/group of countries	Gini coefficient
Sub-Saharan Africa	
Ghana (2006)	0,428
Kenya (2005)	0,477
South Africa (2000)	0,578
Zimbabwe (1995)	0,501
East Asia and Pacific	
China (2005)	0,415
Korea (1998)	0,316
Malaysia (2004)	0,379
Thailand (2004)	0,425
Latin America	
Brazil (2007)	0,550
Chile (2006)	0,520
Colombia (2006)	0,585
Venezuela (2006)	0,434
Industrial countries	
Australia (1994)	0,352
Canada (2000)	0,326
Germany (2000)	0,283
United States (2000)	0,408

Sources: World Bank, *World Development Indicators*, 2010.

Two widely accepted conclusions emerge from Table 8-7. The first is that the Gini coefficients for industrial countries are generally much lower than for developing countries and the second is that the coefficient for South Africa is very high. South Africa and Brazil, both included in Table 8-7, are generally recognised as being the two large developing countries with the most unequal distribution of personal income. In fact, the late Michael McGrath, who was generally considered to be a South African authority on the subject, twice (1975 and 1991) estimated South Africa's Gini coefficient at 0,68, which ranks as among the highest ever recorded anywhere in the world.

Estimates of Gini coefficients vary considerably. For example, in Stats SA's survey of *Income and Expenditure of Households 2005/2006*, on which the CPI basket was based, a Gini coefficient with regard to disposable income from work and grants of 0,72 was reported. The Organisation for Economic Cooperation and Development (OECD) has also estimated high Gini coefficients for South Africa: 0,66 (1993), 0,68 (2000) and 0,70 (2008). Private researchers adjusted the Stats SA figure for social grants, free water, electricity and sanitation and direct taxes and arrived at a figure of 0,59, which is still quite high.

Gini coefficients can, of course, be estimated for the distribution of any variable among a group of individuals, households, firms etc. In South Africa, for example, Gini coefficients for the distribution of income are also estimated for each of the different population groups, the different provinces etc.

International comparisons of Gini coefficients should, however, always be treated with circumspection. The fact that Gini coefficients are not estimated at regular intervals for all (or most) countries effectively precludes inter-country comparisons for any particular period. Moreover, the quality of the data and some of the criteria applied in calculating the coefficient can also differ from country to country. For example, a distribution based on the individual as the unit is more unequal than a distribution of household data, since many individuals earn no income. Likewise, the distribution among employed workers will also differ from the distribution among households. Many of the studies done elsewhere (particularly in developing countries) were probably much more flimsy than those conducted in South Africa. While South Africa undoubtedly has a particularly skewed distribution of personal income, one cannot avoid the impression that the fact that this country's Gini coefficient is higher than those of other developing countries can probably be ascribed, at least partly, to more meticulous estimation (including more reliable data) than in comparable studies conducted in most other developing countries.

Terence Moll emphasised the low quality of studies aimed at estimating Gini coefficients, using Taiwanese studies as examples. He was particularly critical of cross-country comparisons of income distributions such as those in Table 8-7:

> A particularly dangerous trend is the appearance of many collections of cross-country distributional statistics on the developing world, crowned by the World Bank's annual indicators in *World Development Reports*. (T Moll, 1992, Mickey Mouse numbers and inequality research in developing countries, *The Journal of Development Studies 28(4), July*:691.)

The Gini coefficient is not the only quantitative yardstick for the estimation of the degree of equality (or inequality) of a distribution. It also has definite shortcomings. For example, in the case of intersecting Lorenz curves the same Gini coefficient can be obtained for different distributions. Various other distribution yardsticks have therefore been developed, including the Herfindahl index, the Dalton index, the Atkinson index and the Theil index. These indices fall beyond the scope of this book. It is important to bear in mind though that there is no perfect yardstick of equality (or inequality). No single criterion is therefore sufficient in itself. Whenever possible, various criteria should be investigated before choosing a specific measure or arriving at conclusions.

There is, however, another, relatively simple, way of expressing the inequality or equality of a distribution which is both easy to apply and to interpret.

Quantile ratio

A **quantile** is the collective term for quartiles, quintiles, deciles and percentiles, which divide a distribution into four equal parts, five equal parts, ten equal parts and a hundred equal parts respectively. A **quantile ratio** is the ratio between the highest x% and the lowest y% of a distribution. For example, in an income distribution a quantile ratio is the ratio between the percentage of income received by the highest x% of the population and the percentage of income received by the lowest y% of the population. The most popular practices in this respect are to compare the income received by the top 20% with that earned by the bottom 20% (ie the quintile ratio) and to compare the income received by the top 20% with that received by the lowest 40%. For example, using the data in Table 8-6 the

Table 8-8: Decile ratios for selected countries (no dates specified)

Country/group of countries	Decile ratio
Sub-Saharan Africa	
Ghana	16,1
Kenya	21,3
South Africa	35,1
Zimbabwe	22,0
East Asia and Pacific	
China	13,2
Korea	7,8
Malaysia	11,0
Thailand	13,2
Latin America	
Brazil	40,6
Chile	26,2
Colombia	60,4
Venezuela	18,8
Industrial countries	
Australia	12,5
Canada	9,4
Germany	6,9
United States	15,9

Source: United Nations Development Programme, *Human Development Report,* 2009.

ratio between the top 20% and the lowest 20% (the **quintile ratio**) is 15 (= 60 ÷ 4), while the ratio between the top 20% and the lowest 40% amounts to 6 (= 60 ÷ 10). The higher the quantile ratio, the greater the degree of inequality. Table 8-8 contains data on the ratio between the top 10% and the bottom 10% (ie the decile ratio) for the income distributions in the countries included in Table 8-7.

Note that the data in Table 8-8 exhibit a high (but not perfect) correlation with those in Table 8-7. Remember, however, that such data and comparisons are subject to a large margin of error. The figure for South Africa in Table 8-8, for example, appears to be on the low side.

It is quite wrong to try founding a theory on observable magnitudes alone. It is the theory which decides what we can observe.

Albert Einstein

… while econometric techniques have developed remarkably in the post-war era, it is far from evident that the statistics employed match the economic theory and available computing power.

Terence Moll

Chapter 9

Financial indicators

Every weekday there are short inserts on radio and television in which the latest economic (or market) indicators are presented. Although there is undoubtedly a great interest in these indicators, they are generally **financial** indicators rather than economic indicators, and then largely those which are of particular interest to speculators and other people who own or manage financial assets such as company shares (or equities), shares in unit trusts, bonds and foreign exchange accounts. This chapter deals with some financial indicators and other concepts. The focus is mainly on those which are of interest to economists rather than to speculators or portfolio managers, but some stock exchange and related indicators and concepts are also discussed.

9.1 Money and credit

Money is anything which is generally accepted as payment for goods and services or in the discharge of debt. This definition focuses on the essential function of money as a **medium of exchange** (or means of payment). Money can also serve as a **store of value** or **unit of account** (see Box 9-1).

BOX 9-1: WHAT MONEY IS NOT

Money is a popular subject. Money, it is said, talks, makes the man (or woman), and makes the world go around. The Bible says that the love of money is the root of all evil. Everyone is fascinated by money. Writers write about it, singers sing about it and people dream about having enough money to satisfy all their wants.

Money is, however, often confused with other things. It is therefore important to know what money is **not**. In particular, money is not income or wealth. Because income and wealth are often measured or expressed in money terms (eg in rand), they are frequently confused with money.

Income is the reward earned by the factors of production (labour, capital, natural resources and entrepreneurship) in the production process (in the form of wages, interest, rent and profit). The fact that income is usually calculated and paid in monetary terms is coincidental. Income is something completely different to money (which is essentially a medium of exchange or means of payment).

Money is also not synonymous with wealth. **Wealth** consists of assets that have been accumulated over time minus any possible liabilities. It can take many forms (eg savings deposits, shares, bonds, fixed property, paintings, oriental carpets, antiques). It can, of course, also take the form of money. Wealth, however, consists of a range of assets, of which money is but one. In fact, people who possess great wealth usually do not possess a great deal of money. They keep most of their wealth in other forms, particularly during high inflation, when money loses much of its function as a store of value.

Like many other economic variables, money is relatively easy to define but difficult to measure in practice. There is no unique operational definition of money which can be used to accurately measure the stock of money. Instead, there are different definitions which relate to the various functions of money. The South African Reserve Bank distinguishes between four monetary aggregates: M1A, M1, M2 and M3.

M1A is the narrowest aggregate and consists of coin and banknotes in circulation plus cheque and transmission accounts of the domestic private sector with monetary institutions. The components of this aggregate accord with the function of money as a medium of exchange. All the assets included in M1A can be used to effect payment to third parties. Although most people tend to think about notes and coin when thinking about money, the latter represent less than 14% of M1A and less than 3% of M3 (the broad definition of money – see below).

M1 is M1A plus other demand deposits held by the domestic private sector. It is a slightly broader aggregate than M1A but still relates to the function of money as a medium of exchange.

M2 is M1 plus other short-term deposits and medium-term deposits held by the domestic private sector. It is not a particularly significant aggregate, except that it is somewhat more stable than M1A and M1.

M3 is M2 plus long-term deposits held by the domestic private sector. M3 is the broadest and least liquid of the monetary aggregates and served as the basis for money supply guidelines set by the South African monetary authorities in the 1980s. The main advantage of M3 is that it is less susceptible to changes in individual portfolios as a result of financial innovations or to changes in expectations and the structure of interest rates.

Examination question: Define M1, M2 and M3.

Student's answer: They are freeways in and around Johannesburg – the M1 from south to north, the M2 from west to east and the M3…

Monetary aggregates are stock variables and are measured on the last day of each month and published in the SARB's *Release of Selected Monthly Data*. They are also published regularly in the *SARB Quarterly Bulletin*. Most economic analysts and policy makers regard the money stock as an important economic indicator. Monetarists, for example, see a direct link between the rate of increase in the money supply and the rate of increase in prices (ie the inflation rate). The monetary aggregates are also closely monitored in financial markets as possible indications of future trends in interest rates.

Another important financial indicator is **credit extension** by all monetary institutions, which is an important source of increases in the quantity of money. As in the case of the monetary aggregates, the data on credit extension are published in the SARB's *Release of Selected Monthly Data* as well as in the *SARB Quarterly Bulletin*. Various categories of credit extension are distinguished. The basic distinction is between credit extended to the domestic private sector and net credit extended to the government sector. About half of the credit to the domestic private sector is in the form of mortgage advances (to firms and households), while credit to households also accounts for about a half of the total credit extended to the private sector.

Data on credit extension are also closely monitored in the financial markets and the rest of the economy, along with the data on the monetary aggregates. For example, when the rates of increase in money and credit are decreasing, this might be seen as an indication that interest rates will tend to fall. However, when the rates of increase in money and credit are increasing quite rapidly, it is seen as an indication that the central bank will possibly raise interest rates or, at best, keep rates unchanged. Given the importance of interest rates in the financial markets, movements in money and credit are thus followed with great interest by the participants in these markets.

9.2   Interest rates

Interest is payment by a borrower to a lender for the use of funds. The **rate of interest** is the amount of interest payable over a certain period (usually a year) expressed as a percentage of the amount borrowed. The interest rate is thus the price a borrower has to pay to enjoy the use of funds which he or she does not own, and the return a lender enjoys for deferring his or her consumption or parting with liquidity. In somewhat cruder terms the interest rate is often defined as the price of money.

If the interest rate is 12% per annum, then for each R100 lent R12 is payable as interest at the end of a complete year, and for each part of R100 or part of a year a proportionate amount of interest is payable. **Simple interest** is calculated on the principal sum only, whereas **compound interest** is calculated on the principal plus any interest due at a date when it is agreed it should be added to the outstanding loan.

Simple interest is calculated by multiplying the initial or present value (*PV*) by the interest rate (*r*) and by the number of periods (*n*). Thus,

Simple interest $= PV \times r \times n$

For example, if R5 000 is borrowed at 12% for two years, the total interest payable would be

$$R5\ 000 \times \frac{12}{100} \times 2 = R1\ 200\ (\text{or R600 per year})$$

In the case of **compound interest** the interest is added to the initial amount after each period, instead of being paid to the lender. In this case the final or future value (FV) of the amount concerned is calculated as follows:

$$FV = PV\,(1 + r)^n$$

For example, if R5 000 is borrowed at 12% for two years and the interest is compounded annually, the total amount payable at the end would be

$$R5\ 000\,(1 + \frac{12}{100})^2 = R5\ 000\,(1,12)^2$$
$$= R5\ 000\,(1,2544)$$
$$= R6\ 272$$

In this case, therefore, the interest amounts to R1 272 (= R6 272 – R5 000) over the two years. The additional R72 is the 12% interest on the R600 interest payable after the first year.

Often an investment or loan stipulates an annual rate of interest compounded at shorter intervals (eg monthly). In such a case the total interest payable or receivable will be somewhat higher than it would have been if the interest had been compounded annually. The effective rate of interest can then be calculated by determining the future value at the end of the first year. Note, however, that for a monthly compounded rate the interest rate r in the formula becomes i/n, where i = nominal rate and n = 12 (the frequency). If the same amount (R5 000) and nominal rate (12%) are taken as in the previous example, then at the end of the first year

$$FV = PV\,(1 + \frac{i}{n})^n$$
$$= R5\ 000\,(1 + \frac{0,12}{12})^{12}$$
$$= R5\ 000\,(1,01)^{12}$$
$$= R5\ 000\,(1,1268)$$
$$= R5\ 634$$

This yields an effective rate of $\dfrac{5\ 634 - 5\ 000}{5\ 000} \times \dfrac{100}{1} = \dfrac{634}{5\ 000} \times \dfrac{100}{1} = 12,68\%$ per annum.

The subject of the basic formula $FV = PV(1 + r)^n$ can be changed to determine any of the other variables, should they be unknown.

For example, $PV = \dfrac{FV}{(1+r)^n}$

The calculation of the present value of a stream of expected future cash flows is called **discounting**, which is the opposite of compounding. In other words, the calculation of present values is the inverse of the calculation of future values. For example, the opportunity to receive R5 000 in two years' time while assuming an interest rate of 12% per annum compounded annually, is discounted to its present value as follows:

$$PV = \frac{FV}{(1+r)^n}$$
$$= \frac{R5\ 000}{(1,12)^2}$$
$$= \frac{R5\ 000}{1,2544}$$
$$= R3\ 985,97$$

The basic formula can also be used to determine r (if PV, FV and n are known) or n (if PV, FV and r are known). Nowadays all these functions are readily available features of simple financial calculators.

9.3   Some important interest rates and determinants of interest rates

Financial markets can be classified into two main categories: the money market and the bond (or capital) market. The **money market** is the market for lending and borrowing short-term financial instruments. The **bond market** is the market for lending and borrowing long-term financial instruments (with a term or outstanding maturity of more than one year). Money-market interest rates are thus short-term rates, while bond-market interest rates are long-term rates.[1]

Money market

Key interest rates in the money market include the repo rate, the prime overdraft rates, the Treasury bill rate, the JIBAR rates and call money rates.

The **repo rate** (short for repurchase rate) is the key element of the SARB's repurchase tender system. Under this system banks tender weekly for central bank funds through

---

1.   For more detail on the money market, bond market and other financial markets, see Van Wyk, K, Botha, Z and Goodspeed, I (eds). 2011. *Understanding South African Financial Markets* (4th edition), Pretoria: Van Schaik.

repurchase agreements. The repo rate is the interest rate at which the central bank is willing to extend credit to the banks. It is the key instrument of the monetary policy implemented by the SARB because it directly affects the cost of credit to the banking sector and therefore eventually to the general public as well.

A repo may be defined as the sale of an existing security (financial asset) at an agreed price, coupled with an agreement by the seller to purchase (buy back) the same security on a specified future date (normally seven days later) at the same price. The maturity value of the repo is determined in the initial agreement and consists of the price plus an agreed amount of interest. The interest represents the cost of obtaining the funds for a week.

In terms of the present accommodation policy of the Reserve Bank, repos are the main means whereby banks can obtain funds in order to comply with their cash reserve requirements. As a result of this refinancing system, repurchase agreements have become particularly important in South Africa. The underlying securities that may be used for this purpose include Treasury bills, Land Bank bills, Reserve Bank debentures and bonds of the Development Bank of Southern Africa, Eskom, Transnet, the South African National Roads Agency and the Trans-Caledon Tunnel Authority.

The **prime overdraft rate** (or simply **prime rate**) is the lowest officially announced rate at which a clearing bank such as Nedbank or Standard Bank will lend money to its clients on overdraft. Banks are free to set the prime rate at their own discretion but in practice competition usually forces the different banks to set the same prime rate, which tends to be adjusted whenever the repo rate is adjusted. The rate at which clients are charged on overdraft balances can vary from client to client (and from bank to bank), and can be higher or lower than the prime rate, depending on the client's credit status.

Treasury bills (TBs) are short-term government securities, usually 91-day bills. Treasury bills are issued per tender every week by the SARB on behalf of the National Treasury. Other TBs have tenors of 182 and 273 days. Because they are issued by tender no interest rate is indicated on TBs. The **Treasury bill rate** (TB rate) is the discount at which TBs are issued. The information printed on a TB consists only of its date of issue, expiry date and nominal value (payable to the holder at maturity). Note that the higher the price of a TB, the lower the yield is, and vice versa.

Another important interest rate (or rather set of interest rates) in the money market is the **Johannesburg Interbank Agreed Rate (JIBAR)**. JIBAR is a benchmark interest rate calculated as the average of the mid-rates of the negotiable certificates of deposit (NCDs) of the leading South African banks (excluding the highest and the lowest rate). An **NCD** is a financial instrument issued by a bank acknowledging the deposit of a specific sum of money for a fixed period and at a certain interest rate. Unlike an ordinary fixed deposit at a bank, an NCD can be sold before the maturity date in the secondary market. NCDs are mainly issued to attract deposits to supplement the funding requirements of a bank.

Four JIBARs are calculated for NCDs with maturities of one month, three months, six months and twelve months respectively.

Call money rates are the rates payable on large amounts held with banks which can be withdrawn on demand.

Bond (capital) market

Three main categories of financial instrument are traded in the capital market: interest-bearing securities (or bonds), shares and negotiable documents. In this section we focus on interest-bearing securities only. An interest-bearing security or **bond** is a contract between two parties entitling the holder to a certain amount (the nominal value) at a fixed future date as well as a fixed or variable rate of interest based on this value, usually payable six-monthly in arrears. The nominal value is the amount printed on the security. It is also called the par value, face value or redemption value and represents the amount accruing to the holder of the bond on the maturity date. The **coupon interest rate** (or **coupon rate**) is the (fixed or variable) interest rate that the issuer promises to pay the bondholder.

The first important interest rate in the bond market is the **rate on government bonds**. A **government bond** (or **gilt**) is an interest-bearing security issued by the central government for periods ranging from one to 25 years. (Bonds ranging from one to three years are classified as short term.) The bonds are usually issued in multiples of R1 million (at a fixed coupon rate). Once issued, these bonds can be traded in the secondary market at varying rates. The **running yield** of a bond is the annual income divided by (or as a percentage of) the buying price. The higher the price paid for a bond, the lower the return (or running yield) and the lower the price paid, the higher the return. This inverse relationship between the price of a bond and the yield on the bond plays a pivotal role in the bond market.

The next important set of rates in the bond market is the **rates on the bonds of public corporations** such as Eskom. Bonds issued by public corporations (**semi-gilts**) are similar in nature to those issued by the government. The rate at which these bonds are issued is largely a function of their marketability. In the secondary capital market the rates on public corporation bonds are higher than those on government bonds.

Other issuers of long-term interest-bearing bonds include **municipalities** and **private companies**. The less marketable and less secure these bonds are, the higher the interest rates are.

The yields on the various types of bond are reported regularly in the financial media.

The determinants of interest rates

Interest rates are determined by a variety of factors. Interest rates relate to what is going to happen in the uncertain future and therefore uncertainty plays an important role in their determination. The longer the term of a loan, the greater the uncertainty about what is going to happen and therefore the higher the interest rate tends to be. But this need not necessarily be the case, since the expected inflation rate also has to be taken into account. The higher the expected inflation rate, the higher interest rates will tend to be. But inflation may be expected to decline significantly in the long run, in which case long-term rates may be lower than short-term rates. Another important determinant is the ability of the borrower to repay the loan. The higher the risk of default or the lower the credit rating of the borrower, the higher the interest rate will tend to be. In the bond market, for example, the rates on government bonds are lower than those on bonds issued by parastatals (eg Eskom, Transnet), which in turn are lower than the rates on bonds issued by private companies.

By setting the repo rate, the Monetary Policy Committee (MPC) of the SARB plays a pivotal role in determining the level of short-term interest rates in South Africa and indirectly also impacts on the level of long-term interest rates. In setting the level of the repo rate the MPC takes a variety of indicators into account (see Box 9-2). In so far as these indicators affect the MPC's decision they may therefore all be regarded as determinants of South African interest rates.

BOX 9-2: INDICATORS THAT IMPACT ON THE MONETARY POLICY COMMITTEE'S INTEREST RATE DECISION

As mentioned in the text, the SARB's Monetary Policy Committee (MPC) takes a variety of indicators into account when deciding on the appropriate level of the repo rate. The following are among the most important of these indicators:

International economy

- GDP growth rates
- Business cycle indicators (particularly leading indicators)
- Inflation rates
- Crude oil prices
- Exchange rate developments
- Interest rate movements (particularly interest rate decisions of other central banks)
- International outlook for growth (incl forecasts)
- International outlook for inflation (incl forecasts)

South African economy

- Movements in CPI and all its components (eg food prices, price of petrol, price of electricity, other administered prices)
- Movements in PPI and all its components (eg food, imported commodities)
- Exchange rate developments

- Employment and unemployment
- Remuneration, productivity and unit labour cost
- Production (value added) and all its components
- Expenditure (GDE,GDP) and all components thereof
- Real-estate and equity prices
- Fiscal indicators (eg government expenditure, tax revenue, budget deficit)
- Growth in money and credit
- Growth outlook (incl real GDP forecasts)
- Business cycle indicators (eg leading indicators, purchasing managers' index (PMI), business confidence indicators)
- Survey of inflation expectations
- Economists' forecasts of inflation
- SARB's inflation forecast

The above list underlines the importance of many of the indicators discussed in this book. For more detail on these and other related indicators, see the biannual *Monetary Policy Review* published by the SARB in May and November each year.

9.4   Some technical issues

Interest rates and discount rates

There is a difference between interest rates and discount rates. As mentioned earlier, certain securities such as Treasury bills are issued at a discount to their maturity value (ie the amount payable to the holder when the security is payable). For example, if a 12-month bill with a face value of R1 million is sold for R920 000, the discount is R80 000. The **discount rate** is then 8%:

$$\frac{80\ 000}{1\ 000\ 0000} \times \frac{100}{1} = 8\%$$

However, the actual yield or **interest rate** earned by the holder of the bill is higher, since the yield has to be calculated as a percentage of the R920 000 actually paid for the bill:

$$\frac{80\ 000}{920\ 000} \times \frac{100}{1} = 8,7\%$$

Note again that the higher the price (ie the lower the discount), the lower the yield becomes (and the lower the price, the higher the yield).

Basis points and percentage points

Participants in financial markets often refer to basis points, where 100 basis points = 1 percentage point or 1 basis point = 0,01 percentage point. For example, if the rate on a particular government bond (eg R186) changes from 8,94% to 8,88%, dealers refer to a drop of 6 basis points (or 6 points). Also note that it is wrong to refer to the above change as a drop or fall of 0,06%. The correct way of describing it is to refer to a decline of 0,06 percentage points or 6 basis points. Consider another example: a change from 12% to 14% amounts to an increase of 2 percentage points or 200 basis points. The percentage change from 12 to 14 is 16,7%:

$$\frac{14-12}{12} \times 100 = \frac{2}{12} \times 100 = 16,7\%$$

Nominal and real interest rates

The **nominal interest rate** is the actual interest rate ruling at any particular time. For example, if Joe Soap invests R1 000 in a fixed deposit for 12 months at 10%, the nominal rate is 10%. Likewise, if Ann Smith obtains a mortgage loan at 12%, the nominal rate is 12%. A **real interest rate** is equal to the nominal rate deflated by the rate of inflation. For simplicity, this may be approximated by subtracting the inflation rate from the nominal interest rate. Thus, if the ruling inflation rate is 7%, then Joe Soap is earning a real interest rate of 3% (= 10% – 7%) and Ann Smith is paying a real rate of 5% (= 12% – 7%).

When economic decisions are taken during inflationary periods real interest rates rather than nominal rates should be taken into account. The relevant inflation to be taken into account is the **expected** inflation over the period concerned (eg the period over which Joe Soap's fixed deposit will remain at the bank), rather than the historical inflation rate. However, since future inflation is unknown, the latest published inflation rate is usually taken as a proxy for expected inflation when real interest rates are calculated.

9.5   Share prices and other stock exchange concepts

The **JSE Ltd** (JSE) is the South African market for shares. The fundamental difference between shares and bonds is that shareholding represents co-ownership whereas bondholders are creditors. Apart from shares, other negotiable instruments and fixed-interest securities are also traded on the JSE. The prime function of the JSE is to provide a market where securities can be traded under regulated conditions.

Ordinary shares or **equities** (sometimes also called stocks) are shares in the issued capital of a company which are held on terms that make the holder a member of the company, entitled to vote at annual meetings, elect directors and participate in the profits of the company through dividends. A **share price** is the prevailing market price of a unit of the company's equity capital that is traded on the JSE. The latest share prices are reported regularly in the daily press. Various prices are usually indicated for each share: a price offered by potential buyers, a price quoted by potential sellers, the ruling price (usually the price at which the last transaction was concluded), the highest price during the day and the lowest price during the day. The volume of shares traded during the day concerned is also indicated, along with the movement in the share price since the previous day. Other important information provided includes earnings yield (EY), the price-earnings ratio (P/E) and yield (Y), where EY and Y are expressed as percentages (see Box 9-3).

The **earnings yield** (EY) expresses the net profits per share of the company as a percentage of the ruling market price. For example, if the earnings of Impala Platinum (Implats) is R20 per share and the share price R220, then EY is 9,1. This means that the most recently declared net profits of the company amounted to a return of 9,1% per share, given the ruling price of Implats shares.

The **price-earnings ratio** (P/E) is the inverse of the earnings yield. It is the ratio between the share price and the most recently declared annual net profits (or earnings) per share in the company. For example, if the current share price of Implats is R220 per share and the most recently declared annual net profits (earnings) were R20 per share, then the P/E is $220 \div 20 = 11,0$. The P/E can also be obtained by dividing the EY into 100. Thus, in our example, $P/E = 100 \div 9,1 = 11$. Roughly speaking, this figure represents the number of years' earnings an investor is paying for the share. Alternatively, it is the number of years at the current earnings yield that the investor will have to hold the share to recoup the purchasing price. In theory, the lower the P/E, the better. However, markets are always looking ahead. Companies with a high P/E therefore tend to be ones where investors are expecting earnings to grow rapidly (and therefore bid up the price), while companies with a low P/E might be those that are expected to show modest, if any, profits growth (and therefore have low prices). Analysts therefore distinguish between a historic P/E (the one explained above) and a forward P/E. The forward P/E is calculated by expressing the current share price as a ratio of the **expected** earnings.

The **yield** or **dividend yield** expresses the most recently declared annual dividend per share in the company as a percentage of the ruling share price. For example, if the yield on shares in Implats is 2,6% it means that the last declared annual dividend per share in Implats amounted to 2,6% of the current share price. The dividend yield depends, inter alia, on the dividend policy of the company and there is therefore no technical link (as in the case of the EY and P/E) between the dividend yield and the EY or P/E. If a share has a low dividend yield it may, for example, be that the company is currently paying out only a small proportion of its profits as dividends so that it can reinvest the bulk of the profits to achieve more rapid growth. Fast-growing companies therefore often tend to have low dividend yields. Also note that the higher the share price, the lower the dividend yield becomes, *ceteris paribus*. Sometimes shares offer a high yield because investors expect the company to cut the dividend, which causes the share price to fall.

Market capitalisation is the total market value of a company's issued share capital. It is equal to the number of fully paid shares listed on the JSE multiplied by the share price.

BOX 9-3: READING THE PUBLISHED SHARE MARKET INFORMATION

Information about the shares of all listed companies on the JSE can be obtained from the JSE's website (*www.jse.co.za*) and is also published daily in the media. The following extract from the *Business Day* of 7 July 2010 is used to explain the published data.

1 Company	2 Close (cents)	3 Day move (cents)	4 Day move (%)	5 High (cents)	6 Low (cents)	7 Volume traded (000)
Anglo	27 231	832	3,2	27 438	26 586	3 748

8 12m % move	9 12m high	10 12m low	11 Market cap Rm	12 Yield (%)	13 P/E ratio
29,8	35 002	20 600	365 693,2	0,00	13,16

The data published on 7 July show what happened on 6 July. Tuesday 7 July is the reporting day, Monday 6 July the trading day and Friday 3 July the previous trading day.

The first column shows the company name which is usually an abbreviation (eg Anglo for Anglo American Plc). The next column shows the price of the last sale of the day. In some instances the price at which buyers were prepared to buy at the end of the day (Buy) and the price at which sellers were prepared to sell (Sell) are also indicated. The next two columns show the movement in the closing price since the previous trading day, in cents and as a percentage respectively.

Columns 5 and 6 indicate the highest and the lowest price during the trading day. The daily volume in thousands of shares traded is indicated in column 7, followed by the percentage change in the share price over the past 12 months. Columns 9 and 10 indicate the highest and lowest price during this 12-month period. The next column shows the market capitalisation in millions of rand, calculated by multiplying the closing price by the number of shares in issue. Column 12 shows the yield, that is, the annualised rolling payments per share (eg dividends) as a percentage of the closing price. In this specific instance, Anglo American did not pay any dividends during the previous 12 months and the yield was therefore zero. Finally, column 13 indicates the price-earnings ratio (the closing price divided by the annualised rolling earnings per share).

The prices of individual shares may change for a variety of reasons, including changes in overall market sentiment, positive or negative reports on the performance of the company (eg by stockbrokers), rumours of takeovers, acquisitions or mergers, the appointment or departure of executives and results which beat or fall short of market expectations.

Equity (or share) markets are forward-looking and always anticipate what will happen. Expectations are built into the supply, demand and prices of individual shares. If a company's profit expectations are not met, the price of its shares will fall, *ceteris paribus*, even if the profit growth is quite high. For example, if a 50% profit growth was anticipated and a 40% increase is reported, the price of the shares will tend to fall despite the strong profit growth.

The prices of individual shares change almost continuously and may move in different directions. To obtain some benchmark of the performance of the stock exchange, various **share price indices** are constructed and updated continuously to reflect the performance of the market as a whole, as well as that of individual sectors or groups of shares. The best-known of these are the all-share index (Alsi), top 40 index, gold index, resources index, industrial index and financials index, which are reported regularly in all the news media.

A **share price index** is similar to any other price index (see Chapter 6). It has a base year, a regimen (or basket of items) and a set of weights. The **regimen** or **basket** consists of a selection of widely traded or marketable shares of large companies of sound financial standing. Market capitalisation is also taken into account. Each constituent share price is then weighted with the company's market capitalisation relative to all the shares included in the index.

Many South Africans invest in shares and other financial instruments via unit trusts. There is therefore a great deal of interest in the data on unit trusts published daily in the media. At any particular time each unit trust has a buying price (at which units can be bought) and a selling price (at which units can be sold). The buying price is usually significantly higher than the selling price since it includes commission and other costs associated with the purchase of units. The latest return on each unit trust is also shown as a percentage. The return is obtained by expressing the annual income earned on the investment (in the form of interest and dividend payments) as a percentage of the latest price. Often the total growth in investment in each unit trust over periods of one to five years is also shown. These data usually include changes in the price per unit (ie any capital gain or loss) as well as the interest and dividend yields. Always read the notes accompanying the tables since there is no uniform basis for these calculations.

9.6   Economic indicators and the financial markets

Much of the interest in economic indicators stems from their potential impact on financial markets. These markets are largely speculative markets which require news to generate movements in prices and volumes. The release of a variety of economic indicators is among the most important sources of such news. Other sources include speeches or statements by policy makers such as the Governor of the SARB, adjustments to policy variables such as interest rates, taxes and government spending, and the release of the latest financial results of major companies. In this section we briefly discuss the impact of economic indicators on financial markets, such as the equity (share), bond and foreign exchange markets. We also identify some of the main international and domestic indicators that can move these markets.

There are no simple, predictable links between particular economic indicators and particular financial markets. It is possible to postulate certain relationships on the assumption that all other factors remain the same, but in the real world everything can change at the same time and outcomes are therefore usually unpredictable. Moreover, in the highly integrated domestic economy everything tends to be related to everything else. If one adds the ever-expanding links with the global economy, it should be obvious that simple cause-effect relationships between indicators and financial markets are the exception rather than the rule. In other words, if economic indicator X (say the CPI) changes in a particular direction or at a particular rate, it is by no means certain that variable Y (say the price of a financial asset or class of assets) will always react in a predicted or anticipated manner.

The matter is complicated further by the impact of expectations. Markets tend to be forward-looking and in the financial markets the various participants' expectations tend to be incorporated in their current behaviour, and therefore in current market prices. For example, if there is a consensus in the market prior to the release of the latest inflation data that the inflation rate will increase by one percentage point (100 basis points) the expected inflation rate will tend to be priced into the market prior to the actual release of the data. When the figure becomes available, the impact on the market will depend primarily on the deviation between the actual rate and the expected rate. If the rate increased by one percentage point, as expected, the markets will probably not react, but if the actual change deviates from the expected change, the markets will tend to react. For example, if the rate increased but by less than the expected increase, the market will tend to react as if the inflation rate had fallen, because a higher rate had already been priced into the market. A higher than expected inflation rate will have the opposite effect.

Expectations about the level or rate of change in economic indicators move markets, but so do unexpected movements in these indicators. In other words, it is not whether an indicator is good or bad at the time it is released that moves markets, it is whether the indicator is above or below expectations. The more an indicator deviates from its expected value, the greater the impact that it has on the financial markets.

The impact of a particular indicator can, however, be neutralised or counteracted by other financial news, such as the release of another indicator, the release of important company news or a speech or statement by an important central bank official or cabinet minister. Thus, while market participants are forced to take note of movements in economic indicators, there are no hard and fast rules that they can apply in this regard. The speculative financial markets are characterised by risk and uncertainty.

But what are the main economic indicators that move financial markets? The single most important economic indicator in the world is the monthly employment situation report in the United States, which was introduced in Box 5-1. This report is released on the first Friday of each month and pertains to the previous month. One of the main reasons for its importance is its timeliness. It provides the first indication of where the largest economy in the world is heading, a matter of days after the end of each month. Another is its comprehensiveness. The report covers most areas of the US economy and provides a wealth of potentially useful information. The information in the report (eg on employment) is also of a type that is difficult to predict. As a result the data often catch market participants by surprise, resulting in sharp movements in market prices and volumes traded. Because the US economy is so important and because the international financial markets are so interdependent, the impact of the report is felt almost immediately in financial markets across the world, including in South Africa.

Some other important international economic indicators are listed in Table 9-1. Space does not permit a discussion of the impact of these indicators, but it should be fairly obvious why they are of interest to participants in the financial markets.

South African financial markets are very sensitive to movements in international economic indicators. As emphasised earlier, South African markets have strong links with the international markets that are influenced by these indicators. Nowadays, foreigners are also important direct participants in the South African markets and often determine the level and direction of activity in the equity, bond and currency markets. Movements in international equity markets, as reflected, for example, in the Dow-Jones industrial average in the United States or the FTSE in Great Britain, tend to have a major impact on the JSE.

Consider the following scenario: the latest employment situation report takes the US market by surprise. The employment and unemployment data are much more positive than was expected, signalling an upswing in the US economy. As a result there is a frenzy of buying on the US equity markets and the Dow-Jones index rises sharply. The optimism is also transmitted to the rest of the world. In South Africa, for example, there is an expectation that world economic growth will improve, resulting in an increase of South African exports and raising economic growth in this country as well. South African share prices therefore also increase. At the same time there may be a fear that interest rates will increase in the long run, making bonds a less attractive option in the short run. This may lead to a fall in bond prices.

Various similar and more intricate scenarios may be formulated. The basic message is that financial markets are speculative markets and as such they are influenced by expectations and changes in the news, including the release of the latest economic indicators. Apart from the important international economic indicators, various domestic indicators and events also impact on the South African financial markets. Table 9-2 contains a brief list of some of these indicators and events. Again, however, space does not permit a discussion of the possible ways in which these indicators, or the deviations from their expected values, may affect the equity, bond, currency and other financial markets.[2]

Table 9-1: Some important international economic indicators

A. United States
Employment situation report
Institute for Supply Management (ISM) report, including the purchasing managers' index (PMI)
Gross domestic product (GDP)
Consumer price index (CPI)
Producer price index (PPI)
Retail sales
Industrial production and capacity utilisation
Federal Open Market Committee (FOMC) policy announcement
Personal income and spending
Consumer confidence and sentiment indices

B. Other countries
German industrial production
German IFO business survey
German consumer price index
Japan Tankan survey (business confidence)
Japan industrial production
Eurozone and global PMIs
OECD composite leading indicators
China industrial production
India GDP and wholesale price index
Brazil industrial production

Sources: Baumohl, B. 2008. *The secrets of economic indicators*. Upper Saddle River NJ: Wharton School Publishing; Grant, J. 1999. *A handbook of economic indicators* (2nd edition). Toronto: University of Toronto Press; Jones, M and Ferris, K. 1993. *Market movers (Understanding and using economic indicators from the Big Five economies)*. London: McGraw-Hill; Rogers, RM. 2009. *The complete idiot's guide to economic indicators*. New York: Alpha Books; Yamarone, R. 2007. *The trader's guide to key economic indicators*. New York: Bloomberg Press.

---

2.   The interested reader is referred to the contribution by Mohr in Van Wyk, K, Botha, Z and Goodspeed, I (eds). 2011. *Understanding South African financial markets* (4th edition). Pretoria: Van Schaik.

Table 9-2: Some important South African economic indicators and events

Interest rate decision of the Monetary Policy Committee of the SARB

Budget speech of the Minister of Finance

Consumer price index

Gross domestic product

Retail sales

Purchasing managers' index

Employment and unemployment

Trade data (exports and imports)

Commodity prices (eg gold, platinum)

Money and credit

Consumer confidence

Business confidence

Balance of payments

To summarise: key variables in the financial markets, for example share prices, bond prices, interest rates and exchange rates, are determined by a variety of factors, including the latest economic indicators. Apart from their actual levels, the deviations of the actual values of the indicators from their expected values are key determinants of movements in the financial markets. However, because the financial markets are driven by so many variables, even a large unexpected movement in an important indicator may, on any particular day or over any period, be overshadowed by another factor or event.

Chapter 10

Fiscal indicators

Each year in February the budget of the national government generates tremendous interest among all South Africans. As the role of government in the economy grew, the interest in fiscal affairs increased among ordinary citizens as well as among economists. In this chapter we deal with some fiscal indicators (ie indicators relating to the role of government in the economy). Fiscal indicators are concerned primarily with government revenue (mainly taxes), government expenditure, the budget deficit and the public debt. They are important when analysing fiscal policy, one of the government's tools for controlling the economy. Fiscal indicators can, however, be very confusing since different statistics for the government sector are compiled and published for different purposes, for different subsets of the total government sector and for different periods.[1] The most important publications that contain data on fiscal matters are the *Budget Review*, published annually by the National Treasury, and the *SARB Quarterly Bulletin*. At the end of each month the National Treasury releases a detailed statement of the *National Revenue, Expenditure and Borrowing* until the end of the previous month. The data in these releases enable one to monitor the progress of the government's finances from month to month, against the budgeted amounts as well as compared to the previous year(s). The releases are available at *www.treasury.gov.za*.

10.1 Composition of the public sector

For analytical purposes a clear distinction must be drawn between the different elements of the **public sector**.[2] The core of the public sector is **central government**. In South

---

1. The presentation of statistics for the government sector is still evolving. For a summary of the position in South Africa in 2010, see *Website annexure W2 to the 2010 Budget Review*, available at *www.treasury.gov.za* under *Budget Review*. Consult subsequent editions of this publication to keep abreast of changes in this regard. See also De Clerck, S. 2003. A note on the revision of the Government Finance Statistics framework. *SARB Quarterly Bulletin*, September:79-88.
2. For a detailed description of the government sector, as well as of all the other sectors of the economy, see the *Institutional Sector Classification Guide for South Africa*, published from time to time by the SARB and available at the Bank's website (*www.reservebank.co.za*). At the time of writing the latest available *Guide* was dated 2005.

Africa central government includes all the different national government departments, extra-budgetary institutions such as the Financial and Fiscal Commission and the Human Sciences Research Council (HSRC), social security funds such as the Unemployment Insurance Fund (UIF) and the Road Accident Fund, and universities and universities of technology. (In the national accounts, however, universities are classified as part of the private sector, not the government sector.)

The next category of government is **general government**, which is obtained by adding the general departments and business enterprises of provincial government and local governments to the general departments and business enterprises of central government. Provincial government includes the nine provincial legislators and other provincial government units. Local governments include metropolitan councils, district councils and municipalities and other local government units.

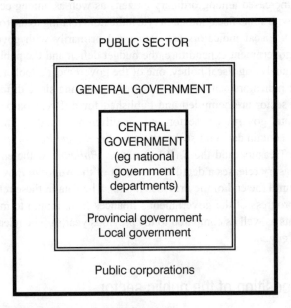

Figure 10-1: The composition of the public sector

The final category is the **public sector**, which consists of the general government plus the public corporations. **Public corporations** are firms that are controlled by government, either by the number of shares the government owns in them (often 100%) or through the appointment of members of the board of directors. Examples include Eskom, Armscor, Denel, Rand Water, the SABC, the South African Post Office and Transnet. Although public corporations form part of the public sector, their decisions are often based on the same principles as those of private business concerns.

The main categories of government are thus central government, general government and the public sector, as summarised in Figure 10-1.

10.2   Statistics on the government sector

For various reasons statistics on the government sector can be quite confusing and therefore have to be interpreted with great care.

A first possible source of confusion is that there are **different categories of government**, as set out in the previous section.

A second source of confusion is that there are **different data systems**, each with its own definitions, interpretation, aims, rules and conventions. The two basic data systems are the United Nations' *System of National Accounts* (SNA), which forms the basis of the national accounts discussed in Chapter 2, and the one set out in the International Monetary Fund's (IMF) *Manual on Government Finance Statistics (GFS)*. The focus of the SNA is on production, income and expenditure and on the avoidance of double counting. In other words, it has a macroeconomic focus. Activities in a particular period are measured on an **accrual basis** (ie regardless of whether or when payment occurs). Thus, if the purpose is, for example, to gauge the impact of government spending or taxation on total production, income and expenditure in the economy, the national accounting data based on the SNA and published in the *SARB Quarterly Bulletin* are relevant.

The primary focus of the GFS is on public finance, rather than on macroeconomic concepts. Thus, if the focus is on, for example, the financing of government expenditure and its impact on the financial sector and the public debt, then the data compiled according to the GFS are appropriate. These data are published by the National Treasury (eg in the *Budget Review*) as well as in the *SARB Quarterly Bulletin* in the section on public finance. Until the early 2000s the GFS measured transactions when payment actually occurred (ie on a **cash flow basis**). As a result, in kind transactions were included, there was no accounting for depreciation (since no cash flow was involved) and capital spending included purchases of existing assets. The SNA, however, reported on an accrual basis, included in kind transactions, provided for the depreciation of capital goods and included capital spending on new assets only.

In the 2001 edition of the GFS a number of important changes were introduced, bringing the two systems closer together, but causing some confusion. In South Africa the confusion was exacerbated by the fact that (at the time of writing) the National Treasury and the SARB had not adopted the changes to the same extent (see Box 10-1). The data published by the National Treasury are based on GFS principles but are 'adapted for South Africa's specific requirements', further adding to the confusion.

BOX 10-1: DIFFERENT WAYS OF RECORDING AND PRESENTING DATA ON GOVERNMENT TRANSACTIONS

As mentioned in the text, there were important differences between the ways in which government transactions were recorded according to the IMF's *Government Finance Statistics* (GFS) and the UN's *System of National Accounts* (SNA), respectively. In 2001, however, the IMF published a new *Government Finance Statistics Manual* (GFSM), which eliminated many of the differences between the two accounting systems. For example, both the SNA and the 2001 GFSM recommend that items should be recorded on an accrual basis. Traditionally, reporting according to the GFS was based on simple cash accounting systems, focusing on a single balancing item (the overall budget surplus or deficit) and the way in which this balance was financed. The emphasis was on liquidity considerations, with the result that no information was generated on the long-term sustainability of fiscal policies. The *GFSM 2001* attempted to eliminate some of the shortcomings of the previous GFS by (inter alia):

- switching to an accrual basis of recording flows
- focusing on the general government and encouraging the extension of the public sector (by including public financial corporations)
- valuing items at market value or as close to market value as possible
- introducing a comprehensive integrated system of reporting as well as several new or revised definitions, classifications and balancing items

The *GFSM 2001* allowed for the assessment of fiscal soundness and long-term sustainability, in addition to financial and economic performance. Both the National Treasury and the South African Reserve Bank accepted the recommendations of the *GFSM 2001,* but the former made some modifications relative to GFS recommendations 'to take into account the specific nature of the South African environment', while the latter strictly adhered to the GFS recommendations. As a result the presentation of the government accounts in the annual *Budget Review* differs from the accounts published in the *SARB Quarterly Bulletin.* Caution should thus always be exercised when using or interpreting data on government transactions. Experienced users of the data also caution against combining fiscal data published in different editions of the *Budget Review* due to changes in definition and coverage. The interested reader can consult the sources mentioned in footnote 1 of this chapter for more details in this regard.

A third possible source of confusion, related to the second and already alluded to previously, is that the SARB and the National Treasury compile data on the government sector for **different purposes**. In fact, the SARB compiles two sets of data in respect of government activity, which are both published in the *SARB Quarterly Bulletin*, one in the section on *Public finance* and the other in the section on *National accounts*. When analysing the performance of the economy in general and fiscal policy in particular, the national accounts data are usually the most appropriate. If, however, the focus is on the budget (ie on the financial aspects), including the public debt and the financing of budget deficits, it is more appropriate to consult the *Budget Review* published annually by the National Treasury to coincide with the budget speech. This publication mainly follows the public finance approach. Some similar statistics are also published by the SARB in the *Public finance section* of the *SARB Quarterly Bulletin*. However, as mentioned in Box 10-1, there may be some differences between the two sets of data.

Fourthly, national accounting data are published for **calendar years** while budget data are originally published for the **fiscal year**, which runs from 1 April to 31 March. The fiscal year also differs from the **tax year**, which runs from 1 March to 28 February.

Fifth and lastly, government spending may be **classified in several different ways**, for example:

- by **level or category of government** (see Section 10.1)
- by **department** (eg agriculture, defence, education, health) as well as by departmental programmes
- by **function** (general public services, defence, public order and safety, economic affairs, environmental affairs, housing, health, recreation and culture, education and social protection – most of these functions are served by more than one department)
- by **economic category** (current payments, transfers and subsidies, payments for capital assets and payments for financial assets)

Each classification has a particular purpose and the user should always ensure that the appropriate classification is used. Statistics on the government sector clearly have to be interpreted and used with great care.

10.3   Government expenditure

Government spending can broadly be classified into **current payments**, **transfers and subsidies**, **payments for capital assets** and **payments for financial assets**. The main categories of **current payments** are:

- **Compensation of employees** – this is the largest component of government spending (in 2009 it constituted 60,8% of final consumption expenditure by general government in South Africa)
- **Payments for goods and services** such as stationery, school books, uniforms, medicines, and so on
- **Interest and rent on land**, where interest payments depend on the size of the debt and the level of interest rates

The first two constitute **government consumption expenditure**, which forms part of expenditure on GDP. In other words, these two items form part of the national accounts (as spending on **final** goods and services). As indicated in Chapter 2, final consumption expenditure by general government is subdivided into **individual** consumption expenditure and **collective** consumption expenditure. The former pertains to government expenditure on individual consumption goods and services such as education, health and welfare, while the latter pertains to collective expenditure such as defence, law and order and public administration.

Interest payments are **transfer payments** and do not contribute to the creation of output. Such payments amount to a redistribution of income from taxpayers to the holders of government debt (eg in the form of government bonds).

Capital spending (or **investment**) by government is mainly fixed investment in infrastructure (eg construction). When interpreting investment spending (capital formation) by government it should be borne in mind that some spending is classified as current spending even though it might entail a considerable capital outlay. For example, in the case of defence spending all capital spending is classified as current spending, except the spending on capital that can be used in civilian life. Likewise, all current spending on education and training (often labelled investment in human capital), is also classified as consumption spending, although at least some of it might conceivably be regarded as investment spending.

The choice of the appropriate data on government expenditure to use in a particular analysis depends on the purpose or context of the analysis. If the focus is on total production, income and expenditure (ie on **macroeconomic** issues), the national accounting (SNA) data are appropriate. Data on consumption expenditure by general government and on government investment are included in the *National accounts section* of the *SARB Quarterly Bulletin*. There is also a separate production, distribution and accumulation account for general government (see Box 2-5).

However, if the focus is on the government's budget and the way in which budgetary expenditure is financed (ie on issues in **public finance**), the budget or GFS data are relevant. These data, which pertain to fiscal years (from 1 April to 31 March), are supplied in the *Budget Review* published by the National Treasury as well as in the *Public finance section* of the *SARB Quarterly Bulletin*.

Further details on the somewhat complicated (and often confusing) world of government spending data fall beyond the scope of this book. To conclude this section, some of the points raised earlier are illustrated by providing some examples of government spending data.

An important focus as far as government spending is concerned is on the **government spending ratio**, that is, the ratio between government spending and an aggregate amount such as GDP. However, from the preceding discussion it should be obvious that various government spending ratios can be calculated, depending on the definition of government spending used. As far as the **national accounts** are concerned, possible ratios include the ratio between consumption expenditure by general government and GDP (or GDE), and the ratio between government consumption plus investment spending and GDP (or GDE). Data on consumption expenditure by general government are provided in the *SARB Quarterly Bulletin* in the account titled *Expenditure on gross domestic product* as well as in the account titled *Production, distribution and accumulation accounts of South Africa: General government.* Data on investment spending by government are provided in the *SARB Quarterly Bulletin* in the various tables on gross fixed capital formation. Note that separate figures are provided for general government and public corporations. Which of these figures to include will depend on the category of government (eg general government, public sector) for which the ratio is to be calculated. The data for general government are also subdivided into those for general government services and those for business enterprises.

When a ratio between two values is calculated, both the numerator and the denominator must be valued using the same set of prices. Note that there is no need to convert nominal data to real data before a ratio is calculated. In fact, given the margin of error in deflating nominal variables to obtain real values, nominal comparisons are probably more appropriate than real comparisons when ratios are calculated.

Table 10-1 shows the ratio between spending by general government and GDP in South Africa for the period 2001 to 2009. The first column relates to consumption expenditure only, while the second column contains investment spending (ie capital formation) as well. The high share of final consumption expenditure by general government in GDP and the tendency for this share to increase have been major causes for concern in South Africa. In 1960, for example, the share was only 9,3%. By 1970 it had increased to 12,2% and by 1980 to 13,5%. It then tended to increase quite rapidly until the mid-1990s, after which it stabilised. Bear in mind, however, that the ratio will rise when the rate of increase in GDP (the denominator) declines, while the rate of increase in government spending remains the same. To a certain extent, therefore, the increase in the ratio during the 1980s and early 1990s was a reflection of the country's poor growth performance during this period.

Another worrying aspect of government expenditure has been the low share of capital formation, although this improved quite significantly in the new millennium due to increased spending on infrastructure.

Table 10-1: Expenditure by general government as percentage of GDP, 2001-2009

Year	Final consumption expenditure as % of GDP	Capital formation as % of GDP	Total spending as % of GDP
2001	18,3	2,3	20,6
2002	18,8	2,3	21,1
2003	19,2	2,5	21,7
2004	19,4	2,5	21,9
2005	19,5	2,5	22,0
2006	19,7	2,8	22,5
2007	19,0	3,2	22,2
2008	19,1	3,7	22,8
2009	20,8	3,5	24,3

Source: *SARB Quarterly Bulletin*, March 2010.

As far as **public finance** is concerned, current and/or capital expenditure in the budget can also be expressed as a ratio or percentage of GDP. Current expenditure in the budget includes consumption expenditure, interest payments, subsidies and transfers to households (eg pensions). Although some of these items are not relevant in a national accounting or macroeconomic context, they are relevant from a public finance perspective because the expenditure has to be financed by taxation or borrowing. The same applies as far as capital expenditure in the budget is concerned. Capital transfers and government expenditure on the acquisition of existing assets do not form part of investment spending in the macroeconomic sense, but the expenditure still has to be financed in some way or another.

In Table 10-2 budget expenditure is expressed as a percentage of GDP for the fiscal years 2003/04 to 2009/10. Note that these figures, which were obtained from the *Budget Review*, are significantly higher than those in Table 10-1. Generally speaking, however, different data on government expenditure tend to exhibit the same **trends**.

10.4 Government revenue

Government revenue consists mainly of taxation. In the 2009/10 fiscal year, for example, tax revenue constituted an estimated 98,2% of the total revenue of the national government. The ratio of tax revenue to GDP (or the tax burden) and the composition of tax revenue are important fiscal indicators.

Table 10-2: Budget expenditure as percentage of GDP, 2003/04 to 2009/10*

Fiscal year (1 April to 31 March)	Expenditure as % of GDP
2003/04	25,2
2004/05	25,4
2005/06	25,8
2006/07	25,6
2007/08	26,0
2008/09	27,4
2009/10	30,6

*   The data pertain to actual expenditure (not budgeted expenditure).

Source: National Treasury, *Budget Review 2010*.

Tax revenue is divided into two broad categories: direct taxes and indirect taxes. **Direct taxes** (also called **current taxes on income and wealth**) are levied directly on the income or property of people or companies and include taxes on personal and corporate income, donations and inheritances. **Indirect taxes** (also called **taxes on production and imports**) are levied on goods and services and include value-added tax (VAT), customs duties on imports and excise duties on home-produced goods such as cigarettes and alcoholic beverages. Separate data on direct taxes on individuals and companies respectively are also published.

Table 10-3 contains national accounting data on taxation in South Africa for the period 2002-2009. The first column shows total tax revenue as a percentage of GDP (ie the tax ratio). The tax data are the total of the figures for direct taxes (ie current taxes on income and wealth) and indirect taxes (ie taxes on production and imports) published in the *SARB Quarterly Bulletin* in the account titled *Production, distribution and accumulation accounts of South Africa: General government*. The figures in the second and third columns show the percentage contributions of direct and indirect taxes to total tax revenue. The basic data are obtained from the same source as the data in the first column. The final two columns show the percentage contributions of direct tax on individuals (mainly personal income tax) and direct tax on companies to total direct taxes. The figures for individuals are obtained from the account in the *SARB Quarterly Bulletin* titled *Production, distribution and accumulation accounts of South Africa: Households and non-profit institutions serving households*. Data on corporate taxation, however, are published in the *SARB Quarterly Bulletin* in the accounts titled *Production, distribution and accumulations accounts of South Africa: Financial Corporations* and the one for *Non-financial Corporations*.

Table 10-3: Taxation in South Africa, 2002–2009

Year	Total taxes as % of GDP	Contribution to total taxation (%)		Contribution to direct taxes (%)	
		Direct taxes	Indirect taxes	Individuals	Companies
2002	25,6	55,0	45,0	58,3	41,7
2003	25,0	53,1	46,9	58,6	41,4
2004	25,6	51,1	48,9	59,1	40,9
2005	27,5	51,7	48,3	55,8	44,2
2006	28,8	53,6	46,4	51,9	48,1
2007	28,5	54,5	45,5	50,7	49,3
2008	28,1	57,3	42,7	51,2	48,8
2009	27,0	58,1	41,9	55,8	44,2

Source of basic data: SARB Quarterly Bulletin, September 2010.

A table such as Table 10-3 contains useful information about the overall tax burden and the composition of taxation. Detailed information on individual taxes can be obtained annually from the data published by the National Treasury in the *Budget Review*. Table 10-4 serves as an example of the information that can be obtained from this source. Note, for example, the sharp increase in the contribution of personal taxes between 1980/81 and 1990/91, the spectacular decline in the contribution of tax on gold mines (even though 1980/81 was an exceptional year), the decline in the contribution of tax on companies and the significant increase in the contribution of GST (which preceded VAT) during the 1980s. By 1990/91 personal income tax and VAT together contributed 59% of total tax revenue. During the next decade the contribution of tax on companies fell further, while that of personal income tax continued to increase. However, the contribution of tax on companies subsequently rose significantly.

Table 10-4: Contributions of selected taxes to total tax revenue, selected fiscal years

Type of tax	Contribution to total tax revenue (%)			
	1980/81	1990/91	2000/01	2009/10
Personal income tax	18,7	33,6	39,2	34,5
Tax on gold mines	23,6	0,9	n.a.*	n.a.*
Tax on companies	20,4	19,7	15,2	24,8
Value-added tax/sales tax	14,1	25,4	24,7	24,8
Excise duties (including levies on fuel)	10,7	10,4	11,0	8,7

*   n.a. = not available; included in tax on companies from 1999/00 onwards.

Source of basic data: National Treasury, Budget Review, various issues.

10.5   Budget balances

One of the most important fiscal indicators is the budget balance. The **budget balance** is the difference between government revenue and government expenditure. When government revenue exceeds government expenditure, the budget is in **surplus** but when expenditure exceeds revenue it is in **deficit.** In practice, budget deficits are much more common than budget surpluses.

Economists use various definitions of the budget balance when they analyse the stance of fiscal policy:

- The conventional budget balance
- The current budget balance
- The primary budget balance
- The structural budget balance

The **conventional budget balance** is the difference between total government revenue and total government expenditure. This is the one that generally receives the most attention. Budget deficits indicate the government's borrowing requirement, which adds to the public debt. They also provide a hint of the sustainability of government expenditure. Budget balances are calculated in nominal terms, which means that they cannot be compared readily over time and between countries. To solve this problem, the budget balance is usually expressed as a ratio or percentage of nominal GDP (eg 3% of GDP).

The conventional budget balance is referred to explicitly by the Minister of Finance in his budget speech and is also regarded as an important policy target. For example, one of the main targets of the *Growth, employment and redistribution strategy* (Gear), launched in 1996, was to reduce the conventional budget deficit to 3% of GDP by 2000. This target was duly achieved in 1999.

Although a budget deficit provides an indication of the national government's borrowing requirement, it should be recognised that public corporations and other extra-budgetary institutions also borrow significant amounts (and repay their debt). By adding the **net** borrowing (ie borrowing minus repayments) by these institutions to the national government's financing requirement, the total **public sector borrowing requirement** (PSBR) is obtained. The PSBR is usually significantly larger than the conventional budget deficit.

The **current budget balance** is the difference between total *current* government revenue and total *current* government expenditure. It is important from a macroeconomic perspective. There are two broad types of government revenue and expenditure: current and capital revenue and expenditure. Capital revenue includes, for example, income from the sale of non-financial assets (ie privatisation) while capital expenditure refers to public outlays on the construction of schools, hospitals, dams, roads and so on. Both capital revenue and capital expenditure are excluded when the current balance is calculated. The latter indicates the extent of saving or dissaving by the government. If a current surplus is recorded (ie if current revenue exceeds current expenditure) it indicates that the government has saved and that such saving is available to finance capital expenditure. However, if a current deficit is recorded (ie if current expenditure exceeds current revenue) it indicates that the government has dissaved and that it had to borrow to finance current expenditure (eg wages and salaries, interest on public debt). Borrowing to finance current expenditure cannot be justified on economic grounds, since it implies that future taxpayers will have to pay for the consumption enjoyed by the current generation. As mentioned in Chapter 2, the South African government dissaved each year from 1982 to 2005 and started dissaving again in 2009.

The **primary budget balance** is the difference between total government revenue and total non-interest government expenditure, or the conventional balance plus interest payments. It indicates government's ability to service its debt (ie pay interest) out of ordinary revenue. If there is a primary surplus and the surplus is larger than the interest bill, government revenue is sufficient to pay all the interest on the public debt and redeem some of the debt. If there is a primary surplus but it is smaller than the interest bill, some of the interest is paid out of revenue (mainly taxes). The rest is paid out of borrowings and added to the public debt. Borrowing to pay interest is clearly not a sound financing practice. If there is a primary deficit (ie if total non-interest expenditure exceeds total revenue) all of the interest and some of the non-interest expenditure are financed through borrowing, thus adding to the public debt. This is regarded as a particularly unsound fiscal practice.

The **structural budget balance**, also called the cyclically-adjusted budget balance or the full-employment budget balance, is an estimate of what the budget balance would be in the absence of any cyclical influences on government revenue or expenditure. The government's fiscal position is affected by the business cycle and by the international commodity cycle. For example, when economic growth is high or when commodity prices are increasing rapidly, tax revenue tends to increase faster than usual. Conversely, if the economy is in decline, unemployment increases and government expenditure (eg unemployment insurance payments) tends to increase and tax revenue tends to fall. At the same time, nominal GDP (the denominator in the budget balance) is below the trend line and the budget deficit (expressed as a percentage of GDP) therefore tends to be higher than its trend value. Economists estimate a structural budget balance in an attempt to eliminate such cyclical influences on the conventional budget balance. They first estimate the long-run growth trend of the economy and the natural rate of unemployment and they then estimate what government revenue and expenditure, and therefore also the budget balance, would be in the absence of cyclical influences. In the 2007 *Medium Term Budget Policy Statement*, the National Treasury estimated the first structural budget balance for South Africa for the 2007/08 fiscal year. At that stage a conventional budget surplus was indicated, but a structural deficit was estimated (see *www.treasury.gov.za*).

The four different budget balances can be summarised as follows:

- Conventional balance = Total revenue – total expenditure
- Current balance = Current revenue – current expenditure
- Primary balance = Total revenue – non-interest expenditure
- Structural balance = Cyclically adjusted revenue – cyclically adjusted expenditure

10.6 Government (or public) debt

Budget deficits have to be financed. There are different ways to achieve this. One option is for the government to borrow from the central bank. This type of financing leads to an increase in the quantity of money in circulation and is potentially inflationary. Hyperinflations are inevitably characterised by large increases in government deficits being financed in this way, as illustrated again in the new millennium in Zimbabwe. Most governments therefore finance their deficits almost exclusively by borrowing in the domestic and international capital markets by issuing bonds (government stock) on which interest has to be paid. Such borrowing increases the public debt. Each budget deficit results in an equivalent addition to the government's debt.

The **public debt** is the cumulative total of all government borrowing less repayments. It is financed mainly by citizens and is often regarded as a transfer between generations. As the American president Herbert Hoover once famously remarked: 'Blessed are the young, for they shall inherit the national debt.'

The level of the public debt is usually gauged by expressing it as a percentage of GDP. Note that debt is a **stock** concept and is measured at a particular time (not over a period). South Africa's public debt increased from 30,3% of GDP on 31 March 1982 to 49,9% of GDP on 31 March 1999. The immediate implication of the rising debt was the concomitant increase in the **interest on public debt** (*ceteris paribus*), which forms part of government's current spending. As a result of the high level of the public debt and the high level of interest rates, the interest on public debt amounted to 6,1% of GDP and 20,4% of total current spending by general government in 1999. Put differently, more than 20 cents out of every rand contributed by taxpayers in 1999 was used to pay the interest on the public debt. The position subsequently improved significantly due to a relatively low level of public debt and lower interest rates. On 31 March 2010 the public debt was only 30,7% of GDP and in the 2009/10 fiscal year interest payments amounted to only about 13% of current spending by general government.

Budget deficits and the public debt are monitored closely by economists, policy makers and participants in the financial markets. Among their main concerns are the sustainability of fiscal policy, the possibility of a **debt trap** and the implications for economic and financial stability. Various rules of thumb have been developed in this regard. According to one, for example, a primary budget deficit can be maintained for some time without increasing the public debt/GDP ratio as long as the rate of real economic growth exceeds the real rate of interest. Other rules of thumb are that the conventional budget deficit should not exceed 3% of GDP and that the public debt should be kept below 60% of GDP. It is important to note, however, that there are no ideal ratios that can be applied in all countries and at all times. In the wake of the Great Recession budget deficits again reached double digits (as a percentage of GDP) in many countries (including the USA and UK), while public debts of more than 100% of GDP were not uncommon. In Japan, for example, the public debt was about 200% of GDP. At the time of writing South Africa's budget deficit and public debt were both among the lowest in the world.

10.7   Government saving (or dissaving)

Government saving (ie the saving of general government) is the difference between the current income and current spending of general government (in a national accounting context). This is shown in the *SARB Quarterly Bulletin* in the account titled *Financing of gross capital formation* as well as in the one titled *Production, distribution and accumulation accounts of South Africa: General government*. In South Africa government saving has mostly been negative (ie the government has almost consistently **dissaved**) since the early 1980s (see Section 2.11).

10.8   International comparisons

Analysts and policy makers often wish to draw international comparisons of fiscal indicators. For example, they want to ascertain how South African tax or spending ratios, deficits and debt levels compare with those of other countries. By now it should be obvious that domestic data on public finance are quite complicated. It stands to reason that international comparisons are fraught with even more problems and such comparisons are therefore best left to analysts with specialist knowledge about fiscal data. However, if comparisons have to be drawn, a standard source such as the IMF's *Government Finance Statistics*, which probably contains the most comparable set of data on the subject, should be used.

Chapter 11
Social and political indicators

Most of the indicators discussed in earlier chapters pertain to economic phenomena in the narrow sense of the word. Economics, however, is a social science and economists, particularly development economists, are often also interested in the situation in a particular social field or in society as whole. Statistics pertaining to the latter are often called **social indicators**, **development indicators** or **human development indicators**. Although there is no clear-cut distinction between social indicators and economic indicators, certain indicators (eg in respect of health and education) belong mainly to the social sphere, while others (eg production, exchange rates, prices) are mainly economic phenomena. Another possible distinction between **social** indicators and **economic** indicators is that the former are concerned with **people** while the latter deal mainly with **things**. With the shift in emphasis in recent decades from a narrow economic concept of economic (and human) development to a broader notion of human development, a lot of time and effort have been devoted to developing and improving a range of social or human development indicators. Nowadays many international organisations (eg the World Bank, United Nations and Organisation for Economic Cooperation and Development) include a wide range of social indicators in their statistical tables. In South Africa most work in this regard is undertaken or commissioned by institutions such as the HSRC, the Development Bank of Southern Africa and various government departments (including Stats SA).

Various political factors may also influence the economy, for example, via their impact on the propensity to invest or disinvest. Some political indicators may therefore also be of interest to economists.

In this chapter we identify some of the most widely used social indicators and also touch upon measures of poverty as well as some political indicators. Definitions of key indicators are provided and in certain cases the most recent position in South Africa is contrasted with those in some industrial and developing countries. It should be borne in mind, however, that the margin of error associated with some of these social indicators is probably significantly higher than in the case of economic indicators.

11.1   Examples of social indicators

In the 1970s the United Nations Research Institute for Social Development (UNRISD) studied a range of possible indicators of socioeconomic development and eventually selected the 19 core indicators listed in Table 11-1. This list gives some indication of what **development indicators** are all about. Note that some of the indicators can be classified as economic indicators (in the narrow sense).

Table 11-1: UNRISD development indicators

Field	Indicators
Health, demography	Infant mortality
	Life expectancy at birth
Nutrition	Animal protein consumption per capita per day
Education	Number of literate people as percentage of population aged 15 years and older
	Primary and secondary school enrolment among population aged 5 to 19 years
Housing, urbanisation	Percentage of population with reasonable access to water supply
Communications	Daily newspapers per 1 000 population
	Telephones per 100 000 population
	Television receivers per 100 000 population
Transport	Cars per 1 000 population
Agriculture	Agricultural production per male agricultural worker
	Adult male agricultural workers as percentage of adult male labour force
Industry	Consumption of steel per capita (kg)
	Energy consumption per capita
Foreign trade	Exports plus imports per capita (US$)
Investment	Annual investment per economically active person (US$)
GDP	GDP per capita
Employment	Wage/salary earners as percentage of economically active population
	Professional/technical workers as percentage of economically active population

Source: RV Horn, 1993, *Statistical indicators for the economic and social sciences*, Cambridge: Cambridge University Press:77.

A further indication of what **social indicators** (in the narrower sense) constitute is provided in Table 11-2, which contains a list of social concerns and social indicators compiled by the Organisation for Economic Cooperation and Development (OECD) in 1982.

Table 11-2: OECD list of social concerns and social indicators

Social concern	Indicators
Health	
Length of life	Life expectancy, perinatal mortality rate
Healthfulness of life	Short- and long-term disability
Education and learning	
Use of educational facilities	Regular and adult education experience
Employment and quality of life	
Availability of employment	Unemployment
Quality of working life	Work hours, travel to work, leave, earnings, injuries, environmental nuisance
Time and leisure	
Use of time	Free time, free-time activities
Command of goods and services	
Income	Distribution, low income, deprivation
Wealth	Distribution
Physical environment	
Housing conditions	Indoor and access to outdoor space, amenities
Services accessibility	Proximity of selected services
Environmental nuisance	Exposure to air pollution and noise
Social environment	Social attachment, suicide rate
Personal safety	
Exposure to risk	Fatal and serious injuries
Perceived threat	Fear for personal safety

Source: RV Horn, 1993, *Statistical indicators for the economic and social sciences.* Cambridge: Cambridge University Press:153.

11.2   Definitions

This section contains some definitions of commonly used social indicators. Many indicators (eg newspapers per 1 000 people, population per physician, cars per 1 000 population) require no further explanation. Definitions are therefore provided only where the meaning of the indicator is not immediately obvious. In most cases the definitions are those used by the World Bank and the UN in compiling the annual *World Development Indicators* and *Human Development Report* respectively.

Demography and fertility

The **crude birth rate** is the annual number of live births per 1 000 population.

The **crude death rate** is the annual number of deaths per 1 000 population.

The **age-specific fertility rate** is the ratio of the number of children born live to women of a specific age to the number of women in that age group (ie the probability of bearing a child at a specific age).

The **total fertility rate** is the average number of children that would be born alive to a woman if she were to live to the end of her childbearing years and bear children at each age in accordance with prevailing age-specific fertility rates.

Life expectancy at birth is the number of years a newborn infant would live if prevailing patterns of mortality at the time of its birth were to stay the same throughout the child's life.

Health and nutrition

The **infant mortality rate** is the number of infants who die before reaching one year of age per thousand live births in a given year. It is thus the probability of dying between birth and exactly one year of age multiplied by 1 000.

The **under-five mortality rate** is the annual number of deaths of children under the age of five per thousand live births averaged over the previous five years. It thus indicates the probability that a newborn baby will die before reaching age five.

Access to health care is the share of the population for whom treatment of common diseases and injuries is available within an hour's walk or travel.

Access to safe water is the percentage of the population with reasonable access to adequate amounts of safe water (including treated surface waters or untreated but uncontaminated water from sources such as springs, sanitary wells, and protected boreholes).

Access to sanitation is the percentage of the population with at least adequate excreta disposal facilities that can effectively prevent human, animal and insect contact with excreta.

Education

The **primary school enrolment ratio** (gross) is the ratio of children of all ages enrolled in primary school to the population of primary school age children (usually 6 to 11 years).

The **secondary school enrolment ratio** (gross) is the ratio of children of all ages enrolled in secondary school to the population of secondary school age children (usually 12 to 17 years).

The **tertiary school enrolment ratio** (gross) is the ratio of the number of learners enrolled in all post-secondary schools and universities to the population in the 20 to 24 year age group.

Net enrolment is the percentage of school-age children who are enrolled in school (the net figure is obtained by adjusting the gross figure to eliminate over- or under-age children).

Adult illiteracy is the proportion of the population over the age of 15 who cannot, with understanding, read and write a short simple statement about their everyday life.

11.3   Some international comparisons

In this section the South African situation in respect of certain social indicators is compared with the position in selected other countries. As mentioned earlier, the estimates of these indicators are subject to a significant degree of error. The comparison therefore provides only a very broad indication of the position in South Africa relative to other countries. It is generally accepted, however, that South African social indicators are weak in comparison with the country's economic indicators (eg GDP per capita). In other words, the country's social indicators generally compare unfavourably with those of other countries with roughly similar levels of GDP per capita.

For the purposes of the comparison three countries were selected from each of the four categories of countries identified in the 2010 edition of the World Bank's *World Development Indicators*. The World Bank distinguishes between low-income, lower-middle-income, upper-middle-income and high-income economies on the basis of GDP per capita (in US dollars). On the basis of 2008 data South Africa was classified as an upper-middle-income economy in the 2010 edition.

The data in Table 11-3 confirm the general conclusion that South African social indicators are weak in comparison to the country's level of per capita income. South Africa's social indicators were more in line with the low-income countries in Table 11-3 than with any other group and consistently weaker than those of the other middle-income countries included in the table.

11.4   Human development index

In 1990 the United Nations Development Programme (UNDP) published its first annual *Human Development Report*. To obtain a quantitative indication of the level of human development in member countries, these countries were ranked according to a **human development index** (HDI). The HDI can be regarded as a measure of people's ability to live a long and healthy life, to communicate, to participate in the community and to have sufficient means to be able to afford a decent living. The index has three basic components: **longevity** (a long and healthy life), **knowledge** and **income** (a decent standard of living).

Table 11-3: Some social indicators in selected countries, 2008

Category/ Country	Life expectancy at birth (years)	Crude birth rate	Crude death rate	Under-5 mortality rate (per 1 000 live births)	Total fertility rate
Low-income					
Tanzania	56	42	11	104	5,6
Uganda	53	26	13	135	6,3
Zimbabwe	44	30	16	96	3,4
Lower-middle income					
China	73	12	7	21	1,8
Thailand	69	15	9	14	1,8
Turkey	72	18	6	22	2,1
Upper-middle-income					
Argentina	75	17	8	16	2,2
Chile	79	15	5	9	1,9
Malaysia	74	20	4	6	2,6
High-income					
Australia	81	14	7	6	2,0
Japan	83	9	9	4	1,3
United States	78	14	8	8	2,1
South Africa	**51**	**22**	**15**	**67**	**2,5**

Sources: World Bank, World Development Indicators, 2010.

The only indicator of longevity used is **life expectancy at birth**. Knowledge is measured by two educational variables: **adult literacy** (ie the proportion of persons 15 years and older who can read and write) and the **combined primary, secondary and tertiary gross enrolment ratio.** The measure of knowledge (the education index) is then obtained by assigning a weight of two thirds to literacy and one third to the combined gross enrolment. Income (or standard of living) is measured by using **GDP per capita converted to purchasing power US dollars (PPP$)** (see Section 7.5). The conversion, based on the results of the United Nations International Comparison Project (ICP), is an attempt to solve the currency problem encountered in international comparisons of value data (see Chapter 12).

Each of these components of the HDI is first normalised to a scale between 0 and 1 before the index is calculated, where 0 corresponds with the minimum value of the relevant indicator and 1 with the maximum value. Since 1994 fixed minimum and maximum values have been used. As far as longevity is concerned, 25 years is taken as the minimum and 85 years as the maximum. The minimum literacy rate is set at 0% and the maximum at 100%, while the minimum and maximum gross enrolment ratios are also set at 0% and 100% respectively. The minimum level of per capita income (in PPP$) is taken as $100 and the maximum as $40 000, but the logarithm of income is used.

The HDI is subsequently calculated as the arithmetic average of the normalised values of the three indicators (ie equal weights are accorded to the indicators). Countries are then divided into four categories: those with **very high human development** (HDI above 0,9); those with **high human development** (HDI between 0,8 and 0,9); those with **medium human development** (HDI between 0,5 and 0,8); and those with **low human development** (HDI below 0,5).

At the time of writing the latest available report was the 2009 report in which 182 countries were ranked from 1 (highest level of human development) to 182 (lowest level of human development) on the basis of data for 2007. According to the criteria set out above, the countries were classified into the four groups: very high human development (1 to 38), high human development (39 to 83); medium human development (84 to 158) and low human development (159 to 182). Table 11-4 shows figures for four countries in each group.

The first three columns show the basic information used to calculate the index in the fourth column and the last column shows the country's rank. By comparing the levels of the different indicators for a particular country over time, a statistical indication of the development process in that country can be obtained (see *www.undp.org*).

For South Africa, for example, the following HDIs were estimated over time: 0,658 (1980), 0,680 (1985), 0,698 (1990), 0,717 (1995), 0,688 (2000), 0,678 (2005) and 0,683 (2007). These figures indicate little progress over time. One of the major drawbacks was the impact of the high incidence of HIV/Aids on the average life expectancy in the country.

11.5   Poverty indicators

Poverty is yet another example of a phenomenon that is easy to recognise but difficult to measure. Poverty has traditionally been measured in money terms and for this purpose a distinction is drawn between **absolute poverty** and **relative poverty**. Absolute poverty occurs when people cannot afford a basket of goods and services that is regarded as essential for survival or a minimum standard of living. Relative poverty, on the other hand, draws the line between poor and non-poor by considering a person or household's income relative to the distribution of income or to a median or average value.

While relative poverty may vary from country to country, absolute poverty is supposed to be objective and universal. The most familiar measure of absolute poverty is the PPP-adjusted US$1 per day determined by the World Bank in 1990 with a view to counting the total number of poor people in the world. The $1 was later adjusted to $1,25 and $2 is sometimes also used. Some countries also developed their own national poverty lines (see Table 11-5).

Table 11-4: Human development in selected countries, 2007

Group/ Country	Life expectancy at birth (years)	Education index	Real GDP per capita (PPP$)	Human development index	Rank
Very high human development					
Norway	80,5	0,989	53 433	0,971	1
Australia	81,4	0,993	34 923	0,970	2
United States	79,1	0,968	45 592	0,956	13
United Kingdom	79,3	0,957	35 130	0,947	21
High human development					
Poland	75,5	0,952	15 987	0,880	41
Chile	78,5	0,919	13 880	0,878	44
Argentina	75,2	0,946	13 238	0,866	49
Brazil	72,2	0,891	9 567	0,813	75
Medium human development					
China	.72,9	0,851	5 383	0,772	92
South Africa	51,5	0,843	9 757	0,683	129
India	63,4	0,643	2 753	0,612	134
Kenya	53,6	0,690	1 542	0,541	147
Low human development					
Malawi	52,4	0,685	761	0,493	160
Zambia	44,5	0,682	1 358	0,481	164
Mozambique	47,8	0,478	802	0,402	172
Niger	50,8	0,282	627	0,340	182

Source: United National Development Programme, *Human Development Report*, 2009.

Many observers contend, however, that poverty should be assessed on a much wider basis than income. The UNDP, for example, developed a human poverty index for developing countries (HPI). Like the HDI, this index had three dimensions: a long and healthy life, knowledge and a decent standard of living. The following indicators were used: the probability at birth of not surviving to age 40 (a long and healthy life), the adult illiteracy rate (knowledge) and a combination of (i) the percentage of the population without sustainable access to an improved water source and (ii) the percentage of children underweight for age (a decent standard of living). The higher the value of the HPI, the greater the degree of poverty was in the country concerned (see Table 11-5).

In 2010, however, the human poverty index was replaced by a new **multidimensional poverty index** (MPI), developed by the Oxford Poverty and Human Development

Initiative (OPHI) at the University of Oxford. For the 2010 edition of the UNDP's *Human Development Report* the OPHI estimated MPIs for 104 developing countries, including South Africa.

Table 11-5: Various poverty indicators, selected countries*

Country	Percentage of population			Human poverty index (%)
	PPP $1,25 a day (2000–2007)*	PPP $2,00 a day (2000–2007)*	National poverty line (2000–2006)*	
Argentina	4,5	11,3	n.a.**	3,7
Bolivia	19,6	30,3	65,2	11,6
Brazil	5,2	12,7	21,5	8,6
Colombia	16,0	27,9	64,0	7,6
China	15,9	36,3	2,8	7,7
India	41,6	75,6	28,6	28,0
Thailand	<2	11,5	13,6	8,5
Vietnam	21,5	48,4	28,9	12,4
Kenya	35,8	57,4	37,5	29,5
Mozambique	74,7	90,0	54,1	46,8
Tanzania	88,5	96,6	35,7	30,0
Zambia	64,3	81,5	68,0	35,5
South Africa	**26,2**	**42,9**	**n.a.**	**25,4**

*   Data pertain to most recent year in the period.
**   n.a. = not available

Source: UNDP, *Human Development Report 2009 (www.undp.org)*.

The MPI has three dimensions: education, health and living standard. Ten indicators are used: schooling and child enrolment (education), child mortality and nutrition (health) and electricity, sanitation, drinking water, floor, cooking fuel and assets (living standard). Note, in particular, that income is not one of the indicators.

The MPI estimates poverty by estimating the fraction or percentage of households who lack certain basic things. A household is counted as poor if it is deprived in at least 30% of the ten indicators used. This information is then used to estimate the fraction or percentage of people in each country who are 'multidimensionally poor'.

The MPI reflects both the incidence of poverty (H), that is, the proportion of the population that is multidimensionally poor, and the average intensity of their deprivation (A), that is, the average proportion of indicators in which the poor are deprived. The MPI is then calculated by multiplying the incidence of poverty by the average intensity across the poor. Table 11-6 shows the MPI for each of the countries included in Table 11-5. The second column shows the year of the survey on which the MPI was based. The third column shows the percentage of the population classified as poor (ie deprived in at least three of the ten indicators) and the fourth column shows the average deprivation percentage for the poor. In Argentina's case, for example, the 37,7 indicates that although only 3,0% of Argentinian households were classified as poor, the latter were (on average) deprived in 3,77 (or 37,7%) of the ten indicators of poverty. The last column shows the result of multiplying the third column by the fourth and dividing by 100. This therefore shows the percentage of households that were multidimensionally poor. In the original studies these data are shown as fractions instead of percentages, but percentages correspond to the third and fourth columns and are easier to interpret.

Table 11-6: Multidimensional poverty index, selected countries

Country	Year	Incidence of poverty (%) (H)	Average intensity of poverty (%) (A)	Multidimensional poverty index (MPI) = (H x A/100)
Argentina	2005	3,0	37,7	1,1
Bolivia	2003	36,3	48,3	17,5
Brazil	2003	8,5	46,0	3,9
Colombia	2005	9,2	44,1	4,1
China	2003	12,5	44,9	5,6
India	2005	55,4	53,5	29,6
Thailand	2005	1,6	38,5	0,6
Vietnam	2002	14,3	52,5	7,5
Kenya	2003	60,3	50,0	30,2
Mozambique	2003	79,8	60,2	48,1
Tanzania	2008	65,3	56,3	36,7
Zambia	2007	63,7	51,0	32,5
South Africa	**2003**	**3,1**	**46,7**	**1,4**

Source: Oxford Poverty and Human Development Initiative (OPHI), obtainable at *www.ophi.org.uk.*

Although there is merit in estimating an MPI, the data in Table 11-6, particularly the low figure for South Africa, clearly indicate the shortcomings of this measure. It was realised from the outset that the more developed a country is, the less meaningful the MPI becomes as a measure of poverty. Also note the differences between the measures in Table 11-5 and those in Table 11-6.

11.6 Domestic comparisons

Social or development indicators can, of course, also be used to compare the quality of life or level of human development between different groups, areas or regions within a country. With the adoption of the *Reconstruction and Development Programme* (RDP) by the new South African government in 1994, attention was focused on development indicators and in May 1995 Stats SA (in conjunction with the HSRC) published *Statistical release P0015* entitled *Human development index (HDI) for the RSA: 1980 and 1991*. In this publication the methods adopted by the UNDP were used to calculate HDIs for the different provinces, genders and population groups for the two census years. In 2001 HDIs for 1996 were published.

In 2003 the UNDP published a separate *Human Development Report for South Africa*, which contained HDIs for each province for each year from 1990 to 2003.

Table 11-7 shows the HDIs for the different provinces in four years. The indices for the first three are from Stats SA and those for the last from the UNDP. These data, particularly the earlier ones, clearly indicate the margin of error associated with such exercises.

In 2002 Stats SA also started conducting an annual *General Household Survey* (GHS) to obtain data on social and economic development for the different provinces, population groups and age groups and for the country as a whole. The purpose of the surveys is to determine the level of development in the country and changes therein. In this way, for example, the performance of development programmes can be assessed or monitored on a regular basis. The GHS covers six broad areas: education, health, social development, housing, household access to services and facilities, and food security and agriculture. It contains data on scores of indicators in these and related fields and potentially provides a wealth of information for analysis.

Since 2009 separate publications containing in-depth analyses of the GHS data have been produced by Stats SA. The first, published in July 2009, contained an analysis of social grants in 2003 and 2007 (*Statistical release P0318.1*). This was followed in May 2010 by *Statistical release P0318.2*, entitled *Selected development indicators 2009 as sourced from the General Household Survey, 2009* This document contains scores of indicators for each province as well as for the country as a whole. The broad topics (with the number of indicators in brackets) are: agriculture (8), education (13), the environment (8), health (5), housing (8), social development (20), transport (4) and water and sanitation (17).

11.7 Some political indicators

This final section touches on a few regularly published political indicators that may impact on the economy. More politico-economic indicators are introduced in Section 12.6 in the next chapter.

Political freedom

Freedom House, an American watchdog organisation based in Washington, DC, publishes an annual report, *Freedom in the World*, which provides a comparative assessment of global political rights and civil liberties (available at *www.freedomhouse.org*). In the report

**Table 11-7: Human development indices for the different provinces:
1980, 1991, 1996, 2003**

Province	Human development index			
	1980	1991	1996	2003
Gauteng	0,634	0,818	0,771	0,735
Western Cape	0,643	0,826	0,762	0,771
Northern Cape	0,545	0,698	0,679	0,686
Free State	0,556	0,657	0,671	0,672
KwaZulu-Natal	0,491	0,602	0,658	0,631
Mpumalanga	0,513	0,694	0,657	0,649
Eastern Cape	0,416	0,507	0,643	0,618
Limpopo	0,367	0,470	0,629	0,594
North-West	0,483	0,543	0,608	0,606

Source: Statistics South Africa. 2001, *Human development index 1996 (Statistical release P0015, 25 June)* UNDP. 2003. *South Africa: Human Development Report 2003.* Oxford: Oxford University Press (for the UNDP).

countries are ranked, on the basis of a variety of criteria pertaining to political rights and civil liberties, on a scale that ranges from 1 (highest degree of freedom) to 7 (lowest degree of freedom). Countries with an index value of 1,0 to 2,5 are classified as 'free', those with a value from 3,0 to 5,0 as 'partly free' and those from 5,5 to 7,0 as 'not free'. In 2009, 194 countries were ranked: 89 free, 58 partly free and 47 not free. South Africa (2,0) was free, while Zimbabwe (6,0) and China (6,5) were not free.

State fragility

The Centre for Systemic Peace and the Centre for Global Policy at George Mason University in the United States annually publish a *State Fragility Index* in *Global Report: Conflict, Governance, and State Fragility* (available at *www.systemicpeace.org*). The index ranges from 0 (no fragility) to 25 (extreme fragility). For many industrial countries the index value for 2009 was 0, for the USA it was 2, for South Africa 9 and for Somalia 25.

Corruption

Transparency International, a global civil society organisation based in Berlin, annually compiles a Corruption Perceptions Index for 180 countries (available at *www.transparency.org*). The index ranges from 1,0 (completely corrupt) to 10,0 (totally uncorrupt). In 2009 New Zealand (9,4) was at the top, with South Africa (4,7) in the 55th position and Somalia (1,1) at the bottom.

Failed states

Since 2005, the Fund for Peace, a US think tank, in collaboration with the magazine *Foreign Policy*, compiles and publishes a Failed States Index. In 2010, 177 countries were ranked according to a combination of four social indicators, two economic indicators and six political indicators. The higher the value of the index (out of a maximum of 120), the greater the degree of failure. In 2010 Somalia (114,3) was ranked first, with Zimbabwe (110,2) in fourth place and South Africa (67,0) in 115th position. Other notable results were: China (83,0; 62nd), India (79,2; 79th), Russia (79,0; 80th), Brazil (67,4; 119th), USA (35,3; 158th) and Norway (18,7; 177th). Full details are available at *www.fundforpeace.org*.

Chapter 12

International comparisons

There is a large and growing need for international comparisons of economic data. For example, politicians want to know how conditions in their countries compare with those in other countries. They are naturally particularly interested in comparisons that can be turned to their political advantage. Policy makers want to compare the levels of critical policy variables between countries. Development economists want to compare the levels or stages of economic development in different countries. People with internationally marketable skills or qualifications want to know how local remuneration packages, tax rates and the cost of living compare with those overseas. Business people require information about economic conditions in other countries for planning purposes.

International comparisons of economic data, however, are subject to even more possible errors than domestic comparisons and should therefore be handled and interpreted extremely carefully. The following statement by the renowned American economist Oskar Morgenstern is as valid today as it was when it was made in 1963:

> Figures giving international comparisons of national incomes are among the most uncertain and unreliable statistics with which the public is confronted. The area is full of complicated and unresolved problems, despite great efforts to overcome them. This is a field where politics reigns supreme and where lack of critical economic appraisal is particularly detrimental. (O Morgenstern, 1963, *Qui numerare incipit errare incipit, Fortune* 68 (October):173.)

Politicians and their advisors often issue statements containing absurd international comparisons of economic data. For example, when announcing a price increase, a cabinet minister will assure the South African public that the good or service is still cheaper in South Africa than in any of the major industrial countries. The more the rand depreciates against the major currencies, the more commonplace such statements tend to become, and when the rand appreciates, the comparisons lose their attractiveness (or usefulness)!

12.1   Sources of error

At various places in this book we have referred to problems encountered when economic indicators are compared across national boundaries. Apart from all the problems associated with domestic comparisons, international comparisons are subject to two important additional sources of error:

• differences in definitions, methods of calculation, and the coverage and quality of data between countries

• errors in converting valuations in national currencies to a common unit of valuation by, for example, using the prevailing exchange rate

In most cases (eg comparisons of GDP data) both sources of error are encountered. There are, however, instances in which comparisons can be conducted in national currencies, thereby avoiding the second type of error. These include comparisons of **ratios** (eg productivity, the share of government expenditure in total expenditure, tax ratios, saving rates) and comparisons of **rates of change** (eg inflation rates, growth rates).

Most international comparisons involve at least one of the possible sources of error. For some of the problems, such as definition problems, there are no satisfactory solutions. Others, such as the currency problem, can sometimes be avoided, or at least be handled more satisfactorily, by making certain adjustments. The following general guidelines are proposed for dealing with the problems associated with international comparisons:

• Note possible causes of errors.

• Avoid the errors as far as possible.

• Try to compensate for unavoidable errors in some way.

• Always qualify findings and conclusions.

• Discard the comparison if the margin of error appears to be unacceptably large.

12.2   Differences in definitions, methods of calculation and coverage of data

As mentioned above, one of the basic problems associated with international comparisons is variations in the definition, method of calculation and coverage of data. Various attempts have been made by agencies such as the UN, IMF and ILO to standardise economic data, but many problems still remain. For example, in some countries comprehensive estimates of the value of informal sector production are included in estimates of GDP, but in other countries this practice is not followed (as was the case in South Africa prior to 1994). The CPI is another example. In South Africa the CPI is a comprehensive measure which covers different income groups, all the different geographic areas and a wide range of consumer goods and services. In some countries, however, the CPI covers only a specific income group in a single urban area. In addition, spending patterns (ie the basket of goods and services) may also vary considerably between countries. Similar types of difference are encountered in most economic data. Moreover, the quality of the data also varies considerably from country to country. The implication is clear: if domestic data have to be handled carefully, then international comparisons have to be approached very carefully indeed.

12.3   The currency problem

The fact that most economic data are expressed in national currencies is probably the most important obstacle to the international comparison of such data. As mentioned earlier, this problem can sometimes be avoided by working with **ratios** and **growth rates** instead of the absolute levels of the relevant variables. For example, if the defence expenditure of several countries has to be compared, it would be much more significant to express the expenditure in each country as a percentage of GDE or GDP and to compare these ratios, rather than to convert the absolute expenditure figure for each country to a single currency by means of the prevailing exchange rates. Similarly, comparing the rates of economic growth in different countries is beset by fewer difficulties than a comparison of the absolute levels of GDP. On the other hand, mere comparisons of growth rates without any reference to the levels of the variables might create a distorted picture since it is always easier to grow off a low base than off a high base. Another procedure that could be used to avoid the currency problem is to use **indicators that are not measured in value terms**. For example, comparisons of production, consumption or living standards could be conducted using indicators such as the volume of electricity production, food consumption per capita (in physical units), the number of motorcars produced, per capita ownership of television sets, radios or telephones, literacy, mortality rates and other social indicators.

In many instances, however, the currency problem cannot be avoided and some solution has to be sought. Under a system of fixed exchange rates and with relatively small international variations in inflation rates, as was the case in the 1950s and 1960s, conversions based on prevailing exchange rates do not necessarily yield absurd results. But since the advent of floating exchange rates in the 1970s and the subsequent large variations in exchange rates and inflation rates, such conversions tend to produce arbitrary and meaningless results. For example, in Table 12-1 South Africa's annual real GDP at constant (2005) prices between 2000 and 2009 is converted from rand to US dollar, using the average rand/ dollar exchange rate for each year. The absurdity of the results is clearly indicated by the annual real growth rates in the two series as shown in the last two columns of the table. When the rand depreciates sharply, the dollar growth rate is significantly negative, while an appreciation of the rand has the opposite effect.

Table 12-1: South African real GDP (at 2005 prices) in rand and US dollars and the corresponding growth rates, 2000-2009

Year	Real GDP (Rm)	Average R/$ exchange rate	Real GDP ($m)	Annual growth rate (%) R	Annual growth rate (%) $
2000	1 301 773	6,9353	187 702	–	–
2001	1 337 382	8,6031	155 454	2,7	–17,2
2002	1 386 435	10,5165	131 834	3,7	–15,2
2003	1 427 322	7,5647	188 682	2,9	43,1
2004	1 492 330	6,4499	231 373	4,6	22,6
2005	1 571 082	6,3623	246 936	5,3	6,7
2006	1 659 121	6,7672	245 171	5,6	–0,7
2007	1 750 139	7,0544	248 092	5,5	1,2
2008	1 814 521	8,2517	219 897	3,7	–11,4
2009	1 782 061	8,4372	211 215	–1,8	–3,9

Source of basic data: SARB Quarterly Bulletin, March 2010.

Erroneous conversions and comparisons often appear in the media. On occasion, for example, a newspaper carried a full-page article comparing the tax structure and levels of taxation in South Africa with those in the United Kingdom. In the comparison the British figures were converted to rand values by simply applying the prevailing exchange rate. Apart from the question whether it is at all meaningful to compare the tax system in a highly developed industrial country with that of a developing country such as South Africa, the use of prevailing nominal exchange rates is inappropriate in such a comparison. Exchange rates are affected by a wide range of economic and political factors and therefore do not necessarily reflect purchasing power parity. In other words, if the exchange rate between the dollar and the rand is $1 = R8,00 (or R1 = $0,125), it does not necessarily follow that a 'basket of goods' which costs $100 in the United States will cost R800 in South Africa. An author of a well-known textbook on economic data stated this problem as follows:

> To begin with, since the range of goods and services entering into international trade is quite limited in most countries, there is no reason to expect that overall purchasing-power relationships should be given by exchange rates. Even for traded goods, exchange rates may give a misleading impression of relative price levels, for exchange rates are not free to vary with market conditions but are pegged by governments and defended by various devices that restrict free trade. Where exchange rates do come close to being free equilibrium rates, the fact that they have to balance not only exports and imports but capital movements means that they are not really appropriate measures of the relative prices of goods and services alone. (W I Abraham, 1969, *National income and economic accounting*, Englewood Cliffs: Prentice Hall:128.)

Nevertheless, international economic comparisons have to be made from time to time, which is why international organisations such as the UN, the IMF, the World Bank and the OECD have gone to great lengths to try to cope with the currency problem. The methods used are complex, however, and cannot always be applied directly for the purpose of drawing international comparisons. Another drawback is that South Africa is sometimes excluded from the calculations, which means that even the published results are not always useful for South African analysts.

Various methods of effecting meaningful international comparisons of values expressed in national currencies are adopted in practice. Although these methods are less comprehensive and sophisticated than those of the OECD, the World Bank and so on, they nevertheless yield more meaningful comparisons than those based purely on prevailing nominal exchange rates.

12.4   Possible ways of dealing with the currency problem

One method of drawing international comparisons of the purchasing power of particular amounts is to express the amounts concerned in terms of the prices of certain consumer goods. For example, the annual salary of a university lecturer in South Africa can be expressed as a multiple (or fraction!) of the number of motorcars (of a particular make and model) that can be bought with the salary. The lecturer's salary can then be compared with that (expressed in the same terms) of a counterpart in another country. Note that this type of comparison is essentially the same as comparisons in terms of the Big Mac Index, which was explained in Section 7.5. Alternatively, the period for which the lecturer would have to work in each of the countries concerned to afford a motorcar of the chosen description can be calculated (if we assume that the lecturer's entire salary is spent on acquiring the vehicle). The advantage of such comparisons is that they require relatively little information; however, they are also clearly of limited use.

In principle it is preferable to use the prices of a representative basket of goods and services (instead of a single product) but such data are not readily available internationally. Fortunately, some institutions do periodically conduct international surveys of prices that incorporate South African data. Possibly the best known of these is the survey on *Prices and earnings (a comparison of purchasing power around the globe)* conducted every three years in a number of cities by the Economic Research Department of UBS. At the time of writing the latest available edition was the 2009 edition, pertaining to the first quarter of 2009. One can use the changes in the consumer price indices of the countries concerned to update the comparisons between surveys. As in all the previous editions, the data for South Africa were collected in Johannesburg.

The main advantage of the UBS surveys is that the cost of a basket of 154 different items (weighted according to Western European habits) is estimated in each city in the domestic currency. As with the Big Mac Index, the appropriate (purchasing power parity) exchange rate between two currencies is then indicated by the ratio of the cost of the basket in the different currencies. The only difference with the Big Mac Index, of course, is that instead of using the price of a hamburger, the cost of a wide range of goods and services is used. The 'purchasing power parity' exchange rates can then be used in international comparisons. Note that these are **absolute** PPPs, not relative PPPs (see Section 7.5).

Consider the following example. On 15 August 2010 Deakin University in Australia advertised a Professorship in Economics in the *Sunday Times* (in South Africa). The salary offered was AUD156 936 per annum. At that stage the exchange rate between the South African rand (ZAR) and the Australian dollar (AUD) was about ZAR6,60 to the AUD. On the face of it, therefore, it seemed as though the professor in Australia was being offered a salary of ZAR1 035 777 (156 936 × 6,60), which was considerably more than the salary earned by professors at South African universities at that stage. But, as repeatedly stressed in this chapter, the prevailing nominal exchange rates cannot be used for such comparisons. To obtain a better indication of the living standard or purchasing power of the Australian professor in South African terms, it is preferable to use the cost of a basket of goods and services, for example, as published by UBS.

According to the UBS survey, the cost of a basket in March 2009 was AUD3 048 in Sydney (the only Australian city in the survey) and ZAR14 297 in Johannesburg. Using the CPIs of the two countries to update the data yields a cost of approximately AUD3 136 in Sydney and ZAR15 169 in Johannesburg. These figures imply a 'true' or 'purchasing power parity' exchange rate of AUD1,00 = ZAR15 169/3136 = 4,84, whereas the exchange rate prevailing at the time was AUD1,00 = ZAR6,60.

This information can now be used in two ways to calculate the approximate rand-equivalent of the Australian professor's salary. The first method is to calculate the number of baskets of goods and services his or her salary can purchase and to multiply the result by the rand price of a basket:

$$\text{Number of baskets} = \frac{156\ 936}{3\ 136} \approx 50 \text{ baskets}$$

Rand value of 50 baskets = 50 × R15 169 = R758 450

Alternatively, the exchange rate implied by the respective values of the basket (ie AUD1,00 = ZAR4,84) can be applied directly to the AUD156 936 to calculate the rand value of the Australian professor's salary. The answer is 156 936 × 4,84 = R759 570. The difference between the two answers is the result of rounding. A sensible conclusion would therefore be that the Australian professor was offered a salary approximately equal to R759 000 (which was much closer to the remuneration of his or her South African counterpart than the R1 035 777 obtained by using the prevailing exchange rate). The calculations are summarised in Table 12-2.

Table 12-2: Estimating the South African equivalent of an Australian salary

	Australia ($)	South Africa (R)
(a) Salary of Australian professor in August 2010	156 936	
(b) Cost of basket of goods and services in August 2010	3 136	15 169
(c) Number of baskets that could be purchased with salary in (a)	50	
(d) Rand equivalent of salary in (a) (50 x 15 169)		758 450
(e) True exchange rate reflected by relative cost of basket in (b) $1 = R4,84		

Sources of basic data: Sunday Times 15 August 2010 (salary); UBS, 2009, *Prices and earnings, www.ubs.com* (prices).

Another possible solution to the currency problem is to use purchasing power parity **indices** or real exchange rates which were explained in Section 7.5. These are indices or exchange rates that have been adjusted for international differences in price levels as measured by price **indices**. The problem with such an approach is that the figures obtained in this way are all expressed in terms of a base-year figure (instead of in actual amounts). They can therefore only be used for comparisons over time and not for cross-sectional comparisons between countries at any point in time or during any period. Moreover, these figures are based on the implicit assumption that the base-year figure is in some way 'normal' or 'correct'.

12.5   Comparing South Africa with other countries

When South African economic indicators are compared with indicators in other countries, the first question is which countries or groups of countries to select. In some instances the focus might be on a comparison with one or more specific countries but quite often a choice has to be made.

Various regional and economic groups of countries are distinguished by the IMF, World Bank and UN and data are often collected, both individually and collectively, for the members of international organisations. Various other formal and less formal groupings have also emerged in recent years. The following are some of the best-known categories or groups of countries (the members being those at the time of writing).

G-7, G-8, G-10 and G-20

Canada, France, Germany, Italy, Japan, the United Kingdom and the United States form the Group of Seven (G-7). Russia joins the G-7 to form the G-8. Belgium, the Netherlands, Sweden and Switzerland join the G-7 to form the G-10 (which consists of 11 countries). Argentina, Australia, Brazil, Canada, China, France, Germany, Ireland, Indonesia, Italy, Japan, Mexico, Russia, Saudi Arabia, South Africa, the Republic of Korea, Turkey, the

United Kingdom and the United States form the Group of Twenty (G-20), which consists of 19 countries!

European Union (EU)

Austria, Belgium, Bulgaria, Cyprus, the Czech Republic, Denmark, Estonia, Finland, France, Germany, Greece, Hungary, Ireland, Italy, Latvia, Lithuania, Luxembourg, Malta, the Netherlands, Poland, Portugal, Romania, Slovakia, Slovenia, Spain, Sweden and the United Kingdom form the EU.

Industrial countries

Australia, Austria, Belgium, Canada, Denmark, Finland, France, Germany, Greece, Iceland, Ireland, Italy, Japan, Luxembourg, Netherlands, New Zealand, Norway, Portugal, Spain, Sweden, Switzerland, the United Kingdom and the United States are the industrial countries.

Organisation for Economic Cooperation and Development (OECD)

In December 2010 this organisation was formed of the industrial countries plus Chile, the Czech Republic, Hungary, Israel, Korea, Mexico, Poland, Slovakia, Slovenia, and Turkey.

Sub-Saharan Africa

These are all the African countries (including South Africa) without a Mediterranean coastline.

Southern African Development Community (SADC)

Angola, Botswana, the Democratic Republic of Congo (DRC), Lesotho, Malawi, Mauritius, Mozambique, Namibia, South Africa, Swaziland, Tanzania, Zambia, Zimbabwe form the SADC.

Organisation of Petroleum Exporting Countries (OPEC)

Algeria, Gabon, Ecuador, Indonesia, Iran, Iraq, Kuwait, Libya, Nigeria, Oman, Qatar, Saudi Arabia, the United Arab Emirates and Venezuela form the OPEC.

Emerging markets

Since the 1990s there has been a growing interest in the more promising developing countries, which were labelled as countries with emerging market economies or simply as emerging markets. *The Economist*, for example, classifies the following 25 countries (including South Africa) as emerging markets: Argentina, Brazil, Chile, China, Colombia, the Czech Republic, Egypt, Hong Kong, Hungary, India, Indonesia, Israel, Malaysia, Mexico, Peru, the Philippines, Poland, Russia, Singapore, South Africa, South Korea, Taiwan, Thailand, Turkey and Venezuela. Note that South Africa is the only emerging market economy on the African continent. At the time of writing a great deal of attention was focused on four large and comparatively successful emerging market countries, the so-called Bric countries (Brazil, Russia, India and China). In January 2011 South Africa was invited to join this group, which subsequently became the Brics countries.

Other categories

The World Bank distinguishes between **low-income** economies, **lower-middle-income** economies, **upper-middle-income** economies and **high-income** economies. Separate data are also published for various regions such as sub-Saharan Africa, Latin America and the Caribbean, the Middle East and North Africa, as well as for the world at large. The UNDP distinguishes between countries with **very high human development**, **high human development**, **medium human development** and **low human development** and also publishes separate data for **high**, **middle** and **low-income** countries, **all developing countries**, **least developed countries**, **developing countries** in various regions (eg sub-Saharan Africa) and the **world at large**. The IMF distinguishes between **industrial countries** and **developing countries** (the rest). The developing countries are divided into five groups: Africa, Asia, Europe, the Middle East and the Western Hemisphere. The countries listed include IMF member countries only and total figures are provided for each group as well as for the world as a whole.

This list is by no means exhaustive, but it gives some indication of the categories of data that are available for the purposes of international comparison. A major problem often encountered in international comparisons, however, is that recent data might not always be available for all the countries one wishes to select.

When comparing South Africa with other countries, a choice usually has to be made between using data for individual countries or using those for a category or group of countries. If individual countries are chosen, there is always the possibility that the wrong countries might be selected. Averages for groups of countries are sometimes probably safer to use, but these averages might conceal important differences between the countries which make up the group. The most sensible approach, therefore, is to select individual countries from different groups of countries. In this way one can ensure that the comparison is fairly universal while differences between specific countries and groups of countries are also highlighted.

South African indicators may be compared, for example, to those in a selection of other countries. A sensible approach is to select (say) five groups of three countries each: three highly developed industrial countries, three industrial countries that were formerly all British dominions (like South Africa), three Asian developing countries that have developed rapidly since the early 1970s, three Latin American developing countries that share a number of features with South Africa, and three other African countries that were all formerly British colonies. In making such a selection, care should be taken, for example, to avoid very small countries (in terms of population or area) such as the city states of Hong Kong and Singapore, oil-rich countries such as Kuwait and the United Arab Emirates, and small African economies such as those of Botswana, Lesotho and Namibia.

12.6   Politico-economic indicators

A number of politico-economic and related indicators have been developed over the years to compare the different countries of the world. Some of these indicators (eg the *Index of Economic Freedom*) are estimated and published regularly, while others were or are the result of once-off or sporadic investigations. Examples of the latter include indicators of central bank independence, fiscal reform, tax policy reform, fiscal freedom, openness to trade, trade restrictiveness and capital controls. This section introduces some of those indicators or comparisons that are compiled and published regularly.[1]

International competitiveness

Two comprehensive surveys of international competitiveness are conducted and published annually, in the *World Competitiveness Yearbook* and the *Global Competitiveness Report* respectively.

Since 1989 the Institute for Management Development (IMD), a top-ranked international business school based in Switzerland, annually publishes a *World Competitiveness Yearbook* in which a number of countries are ranked on the basis of a wide range of criteria. Four main competitive factors are distinguished: economic performance, government efficiency, business efficiency and infrastructure.

In 2010, 58 countries were compared on the basis of 327 criteria, of which two-thirds were hard statistical data and one-third survey data. South Africa was ranked in 44th position overall and as follows as far as the four broad factors were concerned: economic performance (56), government efficiency (21), business efficiency (31) and infrastructure (51). Some of the notable overall country rankings were: Singapore (1), the United States (3), China (18), India (31), Brazil (38) and Russia (51). Details are available at *www.imd. org*, but the full report is not available electronically free of charge.

Although the *World Competitiveness Yearbook* contains a host of detail and the results regularly receive a lot of media attention and are probably taken quite seriously by

---

1.   For information on a variety of other politico-economic indicators, see Banaian, K and B Roberts (eds). 2008. *The design and use of political economy indicators*. New York: Palgrave Macmillan.

politicians, business people and other decision-makers, their significance and reliability are open to question. Some analysts query the usefulness of the notion of country competitiveness, while others question the techniques applied and the quality of some of the data used. As far as the latter are concerned, the IMD uses partner institutes in the different countries. In South Africa's case, this is Productivity SA.

The Centre for Global Competitiveness and Performance of the World Economic Forum publishes a variety of reports on international competitiveness, including global reports, separate regional reports (eg for Africa) and periodic country studies. The main publication is *The Global Competitiveness Report*, an annual report that dates back to 1979. Other global reports are *The Global Enabling Trade Report*, *The Global Gender Gap Report*, *The Global Information Technology Report* and *The Travel and Tourism Competitiveness Report* (see *www.weforum.org*).

In the 2010/11 edition of *The Global Competitiveness Report* more than 100 indicators were used to rank 139 countries from 1 (most competitive) to 139 (least competitive) for 2009/10. Switzerland was ranked first, the United States fourth, China 27th, India 51st, South Africa 54th, Brazil 58th and Russia 63rd.

The indicators are grouped into three main categories (basic requirements, efficiency enhancers, and innovation and sophistication factors) and each of these is divided into a number of 'pillars of competition' (12 in total). In the 2010/11 report South Africa was ranked as follows in the different categories:

- *Basic requirements* (79): institutions (47), infrastructure (63), macroeconomic environment (43), health and primary education (129)
- *Efficiency enhancers* (42): higher education and training (75), goods market efficiency (40), labour market efficiency (97), financial market efficiency (9), technological readiness (76), market size (25)
- *Innovation and sophistication factors* (43): business sophistication (38), innovation (44)

The Centre also has partner institutes in the various countries and in South Africa's case these are Business Leadership South Africa and Business Unity South Africa.

Economic freedom

Two annual international surveys on economic freedom regularly make the headlines when they are published. The first is the *Index of Economic Freedom*, compiled by the Heritage Foundation, a US think tank based in Washington, DC, since 1995. Ten components of economic freedom are identified (trade freedom, business freedom, investment freedom, fiscal freedom, property rights, monetary freedom, financial freedom, labour freedom, government spending and freedom from corruption) and for each a score is awarded on a scale of 0 to 100, with the latter representing maximum freedom. The ten component scores are then averaged to obtain an overall economic freedom score for each country (see *www.heritage.org/index/*).

In the 2010 edition 183 countries were examined but four could not be ranked because of a lack of sufficient information. Among the notable results were the following, with the ranking and score of each country in brackets: Hong Kong (1; 89,7), Singapore (2; 86,1), United States (8; 78,0), South Africa (72; 62,8), Brazil (113; 55,6), India (124; 53,8), China (140; 51,0), Russia (143; 50,3), Zimbabwe (178; 21,4) and North Korea (179; 1,0).

South Africa's score placed it in the category of 'moderately free' countries. The country's scores in respect of the various components were as follows: business (73,0), trade (76,0), fiscal (69,1), government spending (76,8), monetary (70,2), investment (45,0), financial (60,0), property rights (50,0), freedom from corruption (49,0) and labour (59,0).

The second annual international survey on economic freedom, *Economic Freedom of the World* (available at *www.fraserinstitute.org*), is published by The Fraser Institute, a free-market oriented Canadian research institute. The report contains an index that measures the degree to which the policies and institutions of countries are supportive of economic freedom. The cornerstones of economic freedom are regarded to be personal choice, voluntary exchange, freedom to compete and security of privately owned property. Forty-two data points are used to construct a summary index and to measure the degree of freedom in five broad areas: size of government (expenditure, taxes and enterprises), legal structure and security of property rights, access to sound money, freedom to trade internationally, and regulation of credit, labour and business.

In the *2010 Report* (which pertained to 2008 data) 141 countries were ranked. Some of the significant rankings were as follows (with the ratings in brackets): 1. Hong Kong (9,05 out of a possible 10); 2. Singapore (8,70), 6. the United States (7,96); 82 (tied). South Africa and China (6,65); 84. Russia (6,62); 87. India (6,51); 102. Brazil (6,18) and 141. Zimbabwe (3,57). South Africa's rank and rating in respect of each of the five main areas were as follows: size of government (112; 5,33), legal structure and security of property rights (48; 6,33), access to sound money (87; 7,60), freedom to trade internationally (74; 6,76) and regulation of credit, labour and business (52; 7,25). Data are available for individual criteria and data series go back to 1970.

Globalisation

The Swiss Institute for Business Cycle Research (KOF), which forms part of the Swiss Federal Institute of Technology Zurich (ETH), annually compiles and publishes the KOF index of globalisation. Three main dimensions of globalisation (economic, social and political) are measured separately and then combined into an overall index. A number of subindices are also published and annual data are available from 1970 onwards. In the 2010 report 208 countries were ranked from 1 (most globalised) to 208 (least globalised). In the overall index Belgium was the top-ranked country, with South Africa at 54; Singapore was economically the most globalised (South Africa 53rd); socially Switzerland was first (South Africa 107th); and politically France came out on top (South Africa 36th). Full details are available at *http://globalization.kof.ethz.ch*.

Innovation

INSEAD (The Business School for the World) and the Confederation of Indian Industry regularly compile and publish a *Global Innovation Index* (available at *www. globalinnovationindex.org*). In the 2009-2010 edition,132 countries were compared. The report contains masses of information and dozens of indices. In the overall rankings, Iceland was placed first, followed by Sweden and Hong Kong. Other rankings included the United States (11), Germany (16), China (43), South Africa (51) and Zimbabwe (131). As far as innovation input is concerned Sweden was ranked first, with South Africa 35th. On the output side Hong Kong was first, with South Africa 99th. Areas in which South Africa fared particularly badly included the quality of the educational system (118), availability of scientists and engineers (122) and innovation efficiency (129).

Some useful websites

International economic organisations

International Labour Organisation	www.ilo.org
International Monetary Fund	www.imf.org
Organisation for Economic Cooperation and Development	www.oecd.org
United Nations	www.un.org
United Nations Development Programme	www.undp.org
World Bank	www.worldbank.org

South African websites

Bureau for Economic Research (Stellenbosch)	www.ber.sun.ac.za
Bureau of Market Research (Unisa)	www.unisa.ac.za/dept/bmr
Business South Africa	www.bsa.org.za
Chamber of Mines of South Africa	www.bullion.org.za
Cosatu (trade union federation)	www.cosatu.org.za
Department of Labour	www.labour.gov.za
Department of Minerals and Energy	www.dme.gov.za
Department of Trade and Industry	www.dti.gov.za
Economic Society of South Africa	www.essa.org.za
Human Sciences Research Council	www.hsrc.ac.za
National Treasury	www.treasury.gov.za
South African Government	www.gov.za
South African Reserve Bank	www.reservebank.co.za
South African Revenue Service	www.sars.gov.za
Statistics South Africa	www.statssa.gov.za

Index